THE MOC... ... TOAST

A Year in the Life of a Cricket Statistician

Andrew Samson

TSL Publications

First published in Great Britain in 2016
By TSL Publications, Rickmansworth

ISBN / 978-1-911070-18-4

For

Carolien, Charlotte and Hailey

INTRODUCTION

Numbers. Radio. Cricket. Computer programming. Travel. These are a few of my favourite things. So now you know, Mary Poppins. I therefore consider myself extremely fortunate to be in an environment that allows me to combine all those into one job — cricket statistician. In order to do the job I maintain a comprehensive database, which I program myself, that allows me to look up cricket numbers whenever and wherever I and my laptop find ourselves. (There, I managed to cover all those five favourite things in one sentence).

'Synergy' is one of those words common in business speak. The Oxford English Dictionary defines synergy as 'The interaction or cooperation of two or more organizations, substances, or other agents to produce a combined effect greater than the sum of their separate effects'. If I was to compile a dictionary, under Synergy I would just put 'Cricket and radio'. I certainly don't know of any better examples of synergy than cricket and radio. The rhythms and tempos of cricket make it ideal for the medium of radio with the time taken between play allowing plenty scope for discussion of what is happening in the match and, indeed, of things not happening in the match and quite possibly not at all relevant to the match. So, radio makes cricket better and cricket makes radio better.

In recent years I have had a few people ask me when am I going to write a book. Well, here it is. After some consideration I decided to do a diary in the hope that you, dear reader, will find something of interest in how a year in the life of a cricket statistician pans out. There is an entry for each day of the year of 2015, covering how my year went.

One of the prerequisites for a book on cricket statistics is to have an 'As at' date — the cutoff date when the stats are calculated to. Sometimes this is given 'Correct as at', but I will not use that expression. After all there are inevitably one or two errors that creep into virtually every book. So, to be correct it is best not to write 'Correct as at'. In this day and age of incessant cricket any book recording it is inevitably out of date by the time the author presses the send button on the email. The 'as at' date for this book is a bit different. All stats in this book are as at the date they are noted and not necessarily as at any other date. Many of the records will be broken over time. While I hope they are at least 99.9% correct, anything that isn't is entirely my fault. Already my brief mention of the highest score ever recorded in cricket (628* by AEJ Collins in 1899) is out of date. Just five days into 2016, 15-year-old Pranav Dhanawade made an unthinkable 1009* in a schools game in India.

Coming up with a title for a book is more challenging than you might think. The one I have decided on has, of course, no cricketing relevance at all, but refers to one of my favourite comments of the year. I am not going to let you know what it is. You will have to read the book to find out. As a clue I can let you know it is not on January 1. You are going to have to read a bit to find it. And I must, of course, apologise to all those readers who have inadvertently happened upon this book in either the astronomy or cooking sections.

I hope you enjoy the read.
ANDREW SAMSON
JANUARY 2016

January 1

Cape Town. It's the place to be at this time of the year. The mountain, the sea, the wine farms are spectacular as ever. But, for all that, the real reason to be here now is the New Year's Test. The West Indies are the visitors this time and it will be the 16th time in the past 23 years since South Africa returned to international cricket that I will be fortunate enough to be at the New Year's Test at Newlands. For four of the other seven New Years I have been in Sydney and for the remaining three I have been at home watching South Africa play the Sydney Test on TV. If all goes according to plan, I will be at a total of 15 Test matches this year. My record for one year, in case you are interested, is 16 which I did in 2001, much of which was spent in Bulawayo and Harare.

January 2

D'Artangan. That's who Neil Manthorp compared the flourish of my scoring style to while he was commentating on SABC's Radio 2000. It's not often that musketeers, even the most famous fourth one, and cricket statisticians get mentioned in the same sentence.

Simon Harmer makes his Test debut for South Africa, which means that South Africa have had a debutante in each of their past four Test matches following Temba Bavuma, Stiaan van Zyl and Dane Piedt. The last time that South Africa had debutantes in four or more consecutive Tests was between 1958 and 1960.

A lot of cricket stats get researched without seeing the light of day, or indeed the light of Twitter. There was an example of this today. Harmer took three wickets in the day, so I looked up most wickets taken by a bowler on his first day of Test cricket. If he had got to four it would have been interesting as only three South Africans: Richard Snell, Marchant de Lange and Dane Piedt had taken this many on debut since 1992. Apart from Piedt you have to go back to 12 March 1889, South Africa's inaugural Test cricket day, to find the only other spinner to take four or more wickets on their first day of Test cricket for South Africa. Bertie Rose-Innes took five on that auspicious day.

Dale Steyn took two wickets and now has 391 in total in Test cricket, passing Makhaya Ntini's 390 and making him South Africa's second and the world's 12th highest wicket-taker. Passing Shaun Pollock's 421 seems as inevitable as it has since the day Pollock retired.

January 3

At the Basin Reserve in Wellington, Kumar Sangakkara becomes the fifth batsman to reach 12 000 Test runs. He averages over 58. They don't come much better than that. At Newlands Alviro Petersen falls for 42. He has now gone 26 Test innings without a century. His ability to get in and get out is unsurpassed in Test cricket history. Of the 59 times he has been dismissed in Test cricket he has 28 scores between 20 and 49. His 47.45% is the highest of anyone who has played 50 or more Test innings. Consistency is a good thing in an opening batsman, but it is big scores that really boost the old average.

Along with Aslam Khota and Hussain Manack, I use Radio 2000 as a platform to campaign for the Boxing Day Test to be played in Johannesburg. Sure, most of Johannesburg goes away at this time of the year. But there must still be a few million left behind who have nothing much to do on Boxing Day. They would come to the cricket. The good folk of Durban and Port Elizabeth and their northerly visitors have other distractions, e.g. the beach, so are never likely to match the crowds that could be achieved at The Wanderers. And why wouldn't you play on the biggest day of the Test match year at the biggest ground in the country?

January 4

Some people say that Twitter is 'not about the numbers'. I tweet that Kraigg Brathwaite is the first player to get off the mark in a Test innings with a scoring shot worth seven which becomes my second century on Twitter as I get 103 re-tweets and my following jumps to 6 589. Of course it's about the numbers. What isn't? Last year I did a Sobers when my first century on Twitter turned into a triple-century (Garry Sobers' first Test century was the then world record 365*) with 364 re-tweets of 'Sharma's 264 is 18 runs more than the average total by teams batting first in ODIs this decade.' It is a bit of a process to confirm that Brathwaite is the first to get off the mark with a seven. I need to search through ball-by-ball data of Test matches and extract cases of scoring shots of seven or eight. I find nine sevens and four eights in total. Then I need to check each case individually to ascertain what score the batsman was on when he hit the seven (or eight) and was pleased to find none of the others was on nought when making the seven. Incidentally the most recent seven was made a year ago to the day. On 4 January 2014 Chris Rogers scored one against England at Sydney.

There was an interesting start to the day when I woke up in time to see that Sri Lanka, having been 78-5 overnight in Wellington, were all out for 356 mostly thanks to an astonishing 203 from Kumar Sangakkara. This is his 11th Test 200 and puts him one behind Sir Donald Bradman's world record of 12. He is contemplating Test retirement. Don't go, Kumar!

January 5

It's not supposed to rain much in Cape Town in summer. But the amount of rain in the morning led to the question of when last was a full day's Test match play lost at the ground. Fortunately we got under way at 3pm, leaving 1 January 1936 as the only day's play without a ball bowled in 52 Test matches at Newlands.

January 6

Early finish today, just before lunch. Back-to-back Tests (we have had three in the past 21 days) are hard work for everyone, so it is good to be able to spend a lazy afternoon with old friends in suburban Cape Town.

Alviro Petersen announces his retirement. He joins Billy Griffith, John Hampshire, Sourav Ganguly and Thilan Samaraweera as the only players to have made a century in their first Test innings and a duck in their last. Petersen and Jacques Rudolph are the only players to have scored a century on debut and taken a wicket in their first over in Tests. Ironically, Sulieman Benn, who was Petersen's only Test wicket, ended his career when he bowled him last night.

A significant world record always causes a frisson of excitement in statistically-minded circles, and I woke to the news that the world record sixth wicket partnership had been broken. Kane Williamson and BJ Watling added 365* against Sri Lanka at the Basin Reserve. What makes this one truly remarkable is the fact that the record they broke was set by BJ Watling himself with Brendon McCullum in the previous Test match played at the same ground against India in February 2014.

January 7

Jo'burg. It's the place to be on 7 January. It's good-bye to Cape Town and back home for my first night's sleep in my own bed for the year. New Zealand complete a remarkable win having been just 24 runs ahead in the third innings of the match when their fifth wicket fell. Only six teams in Test match history have gone on to win from a worse position at that stage of a match.

I already have a standard query in the database for chronological highest score and chronological best bowling figures, and BJ Watling's feats inspire me to write a little program to do chronological partnership records as well. A bit of playing with the new toy reveals that Jack Hobbs and Wilfred Rhodes are the only pair to break their own world partnership record for a particular wicket in Tests. They collected the first wicket record in 1910 when they added 221 against South Africa at Cape Town and surpassed it in 1912 with 323 against Australia at Melbourne.

In Sydney, Steve Smith continues his sublime form and becomes just the second player to score a century in each of his first three Tests as captain with 117 against India. He has a couple of games to go to catch Alastair Cook who scored a century in each of his first five Tests as England captain. But, if Michael Clarke returns from injury, Smith may have to wait a bit for his next turn at the helm.

January 8

Virat Kohli trumps Steve Smith by scoring a century in each of his first three *innings* as captain, becoming the first player to do this.

Afghanistan beat Scotland in the opener of the Associates Tri-Series in Dubai. I am mildly perplexed when a glance at the scorecard fails to reveal the name of Hashmatullah Shaidi in the Afghanistan team. It turns out that he is merely a stand-by player for the squad. Afghanistan played a four-day domestic competition for the first time in October and November last year. The matches were not first-class as ICC Associate members cannot decide on status of matches for themselves. Playing for Amo Region in that competition, Hashmatullah Shaidi registered scores of 261

& 50*, 52 & 74 and 208 and 100*. A small matter of 745 runs in three matches at an average of 186.25. Not many people have done that at any level of the game. But, apparently, it is not quite good enough.

January 9

Having been selected to play for South Africa A against England Lions Andrew Puttick is missing a first-class game for the Cape Cobras for the first time in the franchise's history. Fortunately, in their previous game, he had become the first player to appear in 100 consecutive first-class games for any team in South African domestic cricket history.

January 10

Australia and India draw the fourth Test at Sydney and we now face 92 days without Test cricket until England take on West Indies in Antigua on 13 April. Half of that time will, of course, be occupied by the World Cup. I am notified of my first mistake of the year. I have omitted Dwayne Bravo from the West Indies T20 squad in the stats pack that I send out to the media before each game. Oh well, at least I have something in common with the West Indies selectors who have omitted him from the ODI and, presumably, World Cup squad.

I have been working on 'upgrading' old scorecards from official scorebooks where possible. Modern day electronically generated scorecards contain much information that was simply not published in newspapers and annuals in the pre-historic days of paper. For instance, innings timings and boundaries, which batsman was dismissed at the fall of each wicket, and no-balls and wides bowled by individual bowlers. Much of this information was recorded in scorebooks, and can be captured if you can find the old scorebooks. So today, in between watching various episodes of *Ice Age* with my daughters, I manage to capture some details from Natal B scorecards of the 1978/79 season. And now I know for instance (not that it matters much in the greater scheme of things) that Ian Tayfield scored his 70 against Rhodesia B at Pinetown in 1979 in 58 minutes with 7 fours and 3 sixes.

January 11

It rains sixes and records at The Bidvest Wanderers Stadium as West Indies make 236 to achieve the highest total to win batting second in not just a T20 International, but any T20 match. Of All Time. Ever. Although 'Ever' and 'All Time' tend to seem a tad less impressive when you realise the T20 game is less than 12 years old. On days like this the sense that all cricket fans really want to see is the ball being pinged incessantly all over, and, preferably, out of the park, is overwhelming and it is not hard therefore to wonder whether there is any point in Test cricket. Certainly you get the feeling, given that the commitment differential between the two formats appears to be unnecessarily excessive, that this sentiment is highly prevalent in the West Indies. In a world slightly more ideal than that currently inhabited by cricket governance, countries that actually want to play Test cricket, as Afghanistan and Ireland appear to do, would be encouraged and promoted, if necessary at the expense of countries that don't. The demise of West Indies' Test cricket in the 21st century is undoubtedly one of the saddest things in the game.

January 12

It's a quiet day in Cricketville. Mondays often are. South Africa A begin a four-day match against England Lions (the Team Formerly Known As England A) at Paarl. I have never understood how these matches are referred to as 'Unofficial Tests' by many sources. They are of course not official Tests, but they are entirely official. My preference is to call them 'A-Tests', in much the same way, for example, as a multi-day match between Under-19 teams representing two countries is known as an 'Under-19 Test'. Theunis de Bruyn, who made a century on first-class debut 11 months ago, scores 202* to become the second player after Pakistan's Munir-ul-Haq, in 1989, to make a double-century on A-Test debut. De Bruyn was playing for South Africa, not England, in case you were wondering.

January 13

It's a feel-good day today as Jonathan Trott scores 176* at Paarl, while captaining England Lions against South Africa A in his first international match since he left the Ashes tour in November 2013 with a stress-related condition.

Bedtime reading for the kids is a book called *The Cricket in Times Square*. I am disappointed, but not terribly surprised, to discover that it is about an insect.

January 14

Jonathan Trott goes on to reach 211* as the A-Test ends in a high-scoring draw.

In Abu Dhabi Scotland's Josh Davey becomes the first Associate player to score a 50 and take six wickets in an innings in an ODI with 53* and 6-28 against Afghanistan. He is the fifth player overall to do this after Lance Klusener, Scott Stryris, Paul Collingwood and Shahid Afridi.

My youngest daughter is 2 000 days old today. One of the downsides of being the offspring of a numerically inclined father is that you end up as one of the very few kids who get to know their age milestones in days and other units of measurement. To save you reaching for a calculator, 2 000 days is about five and a half in years.

Ali Bacher requests some stats on the famous glorious partnership between Barry Richards and Graeme Pollock against Australia at Durban in 1970. It is well-known that they added 103 runs in the hour after lunch which was taken at the fall of Bacher's wicket. Stats were nowhere near as pervasive in those days as they are now, but were the match played today the TV graphics would have looked something like this:

Richards and Pollock third Wicket Partnership
103 off 103 balls in 61 minutes with 17 fours
Contributions:
Richards 46 off 52 balls with 7 fours
Pollock 53 off 51 balls with 10 fours.

January 15

The news this morning is that Morne van Wyk set a world record last night by facing the most balls in a T20 International innings. He made 114* off 70 balls against West Indies in Durban. That's a lot of balls out of an innings which lasts for only 120 of them. The superheroes of Twenty20 are naturally the brutal ball-bashers, but I reckon the ability to keep the strike is an altogether more admirable skill, providing of course that you pay due care and attention to the old strike-rate.

As part of their build-up to the World Cup the BBC has requested members of the Test Match Special team to select their all-time World ODI XIs. I went for: Sachin Tendulkar, Hashim Amla, Viv Richards, Ricky Ponting, Zaheer Abbas, MS Dhoni (wk), Imran Khan (capt), Wasim Akram, Dennis Lillee, Joel Garner and Muttiah Muralitharan. Jonty Rhodes seemed the obvious 12th man. Viv Richards was the first name I wrote down and, naturally I have gone for the ones with the better stats when there is a close call, e.g. Ponting v Lara and Muralitharan v Warne. It is hard to imagine anyone ever bettering Joel Garner's record: 146 wickets in 98 matches at 18.84 with an economy rate of 3.09.

Brett Lee retires from Twenty20s. One of the great joys of being a multi-format sport with numerous different competitions at various levels is that, if you manage it well, you get to retire many times. Someday a statistician will no doubt let us know who has the record for most retirements.

At the other end of the career spectrum, Emmanuel Sebareme makes his first-class debut for Western Province, having played for the South African Schools team in December. Apparently, his family walked from Rwanda to Cape Town when he was very young.

January 16

With the World Cup looming the ODI bandwagon is stirring into action. The Tri-Series in Australia and the West Indies series in South Africa get underway today, joining the ongoing New Zealand v Sri Lanka series and the Associates Tri-Series in the United Arab Emirates. In Durban, Hashim Amla reaches 5 000 runs in his 101st innings comfortably beating the record of 114 held by Viv Richards and Virat Kohli. Amla now has the set of fastest to reach 2 000, 3 000, 4 000 and 5 000. He can play a bit.

Imran Tahir takes 3-30 in Durban to reach 50 ODI wickets in his 28th game. This is the second quickest for South Africa behind Lonwabo Tsotsobe's 27. The contrast between Tahir's Test and ODI records is about as glaring as it gets: Tests: 43 wickets at 46.39, RPO 3.56; ODIs: 50 wickets at 20.50, RPO 4.34. I decide to see where he rates in ODI RPO to Test RPO ratio and am a bit disappointed to discover that there are five players with a lower ratio (amongst those with at least 200 overs in each format). Fellow leggie Graeme Cremer has the lowest ratio with 1.155 (ODI 4.69, Tests 4.06) while Tahir comes in at 1.219.

Meanwhile the Premier Championship begins in Sri Lanka. With six games in that competition, eight Ranji Trophy games going into their final day and seven matches in South Africa there are 21 first-class matches going on today. I suspect that this is not a record, but I decide to have a look anyway. To make it a bit easier, I just check matches that started on the same day and it turns out that the most first-class matches that started on one day is 26 on 10 November 2010, featuring 11 Quaid-e-Azam Trophy matches in Pakistan, 13 Ranji Trophy matches in India and two Sheffield Shield matches in Australia.

January 17

While capturing the recently completed Ranji Trophy matches into my database, I notice that Aditya Shrivastava has scored 91 and 108* on his first-class debut playing for Madhya Pradesh against Karnataka. Scoring a century and a 90 on first-class debut is likely to be quite rare, so I am pleasantly surprised to see that he is actually the first to do this. Paul Gibb of England and Gordon Greenidge both did it on Test debut.

World Cricket League Division Two begins in the Namibian capital, Windhoek, today between the teams effectively ranked seventh to 12th amongst the Associates. Netherlands beat Canada, the hosts beat Kenya and Uganda surprise Nepal. Matches at this level are often a lot more closely contested and less predictable than much of the play between the ICC's Full Members and there is usually a lot at stake. The top two teams in this Division will get to play in the ICC Intercontinental Cup. This will result in a regular schedule of four-day and one-day matches over the next three years as well as increased funding that goes with it. So, there really is a lot at stake for these teams.

January 18

Like many players, I am managing my workload, so I am not at The Wanderers today. But, my plans for a quiet Sunday are ruined when more records are plundered on what must currently be the best pitch to bat on in the world. AB de Villiers smashes 149 off 44 balls. Hashim Amla (153*) and Rilee Rossouw (128) get the 'thanks for coming' award as South Africa pile on 439-2. De Villiers reaches his 100 off 31 balls, easily the quickest, not just in ODIs but all List A matches, breaking the previous record of 36. He is out within one run of virtually halving the record for the quickest ODI 150 which remains 83 balls by Shane Watson for Australia v Bangladesh at Mirpur in 2011.

The limited overs game is, in essence, a race: Score as many runs as you can in the overs allotted. As a consequence, speed records are the primary ones in this game and whenever a record is broken it merely redefines what is mundane. So for example, when AB de Villiers scores 149 off 44 balls the superlatives come gushing out. However, the next time someone makes, say 129 off 44 balls it will just be 'quite good' as the 149 has already trumped that.

One of the world records that I look forward to being beaten one day is that for the highest winning 10th wicket partnership in the fourth innings of a first-class game. It is a special record as you are down to your last wicket. One ball and the game could be lost. This particular record has stood since 1936 when Tom Leather and Ron Oxenham added 77 to win the game for Australia against Madras at Madras in 1936. Today Cape Cobras needed 85 for the last wicket against Warriors in Port Elizabeth, so I follow the Internet ball-by-ball commentary intently as Justin Kemp and Dane Paterson threaten the record. But hopes are crushed again when Paterson gets out with the partnership on 68.

January 19

The average annual rainfall in Edinburgh is 704 mm. In Glasgow it is 1 245 mm. Dublin has 714 mm a year on average while Belfast gets about 930 mm. So, it is fair to expect that cricket games between Ireland and Scotland are likely to be interrupted by the rain. The average annual rainfall in Dubai is 94 mm. That is where Ireland and Scotland were scheduled to play against each other today. Not a ball was bowled. The match was rained out. Irritatingly, the rain relented long enough for a toss. I say 'irritatingly' as according to ICC regulations this means that the match counts as game played. It is not a regulation that I agree with. Surely for it to count as a match played there should be some actual play?

January 20

I spend rather more of the morning than I would have liked sorting out the Sarabjit Singhs in my database. There are three players with this name who have played in India recently, including one who is also stored as Sarabjit Singh Ladda in the database, and I have managed to allocate the wrong one to a number of matches and it takes a bit of fixing.

In the afternoon I fly to East London, which is effectively ranked seventh on the table of South Africa's venues and does not get to see many international matches these days. Tomorrow's ODI is just the third international here since 2006. No wonder I can't remember when I last visited.

January 21

While it is quite pleasant to be beside the seaside, the game in East London is truly dire, as West Indies are thrashed having made just 122. Sulieman Benn briefly threatens to make the top score batting at number 11. Alas, this did not happen, leaving the game devoid of the consolation, albeit minor, of even a statistically redeeming feature. At least we are done and dusted before 7pm. I am not a fan of night games that drag on after my bedtime, so an early finish is generally a relief. The good folk of East London, for whom this was a big day, can't have been amused, however.

On Radio 2000 I ask the question whether there is any point in powerplay overs. In the match at The Wanderers South Africa had scored 80 runs in 15 powerplay overs at 5.33 runs per over and 359 runs in 35 non-powerplay overs at 10.25 runs per over. Teams are now so wary of losing wickets in powerplay overs that their original purpose of encouraging big shots, with most fielders forced inside the circle, seems to have been lost.

January 22

The cricketing family is remarkably diverse culturally considering how few countries actually play the game at a high level. The number of people involved in different roles within the game also covers a wide spectrum. Amongst the 20 or so (note to self: more statistical accuracy, please) passengers on the 50-seater plane from East London to Johannesburg this morning are Cricket South Africa's commercial manager, Marc Jury, and security consultant, Rory Steyn. Rory's claim to fame was being Nelson Mandela's chief of security and today he is heading home for his son's 21st birthday party before going back to Port Elizabeth for the next ODI. It occurs to me that his son would have been born three months before South Africa's landmark election in 1994, so that must have been a particularly hectic time for Rory. For those of us who were adults during South Africa's transition period in the early 1990s it is quite remarkable to think that the 'born-frees' are turning 21 this year.

January 23

The ODIs today seem to support my view of redefining what is ordinary in cricket. England make 303-8 in Hobart and Australia chase this down with one ball and three wickets to spare. The same game played twenty years ago would have had observers waxing lyrical, but in the modern era where teams can chase 438, the superlatives for today's game are generally from the B-List. Ian Bell becomes the second Englishman to reach 5 000 ODI runs and also passes Paul Collingwood to become England's leading ODI run-scorer. There are 68 players from other countries who have scored 5 000 ODI runs, so England are well behind.

Across the Tasman, Luke Ronchi plays an extraordinary innings of 170* off 99 balls batting at number seven for New Zealand against Sri Lanka at Dunedin as he and Grant Elliott add the ODI world sixth wicket record to the Test sixth wicket record in New Zealand's statistical trophy cabinet. Ronchi's is the highest score by a number seven not just in ODIs but all List A limited overs matches. MS Dhoni (139* Asia v Africa at Chennai in 2007) and Yusuf Pathan (148 for India A v New Zealand at Chennai in 2008) used to hold those records, respectively. Again had that innings been played 20 years ago it would have immediately been hailed as one of the best ever. In an era where batsmen are scoring 149 off 44 balls, or 175 off 66 balls, 170 off 99 is merely very good.

Mind you, there are few better settings in the international cricket circuit than the Bellerive Oval in Hobart (now known, somewhat less romantically, as the Blundstone Arena) and the University Oval in Dunedin.

Meanwhile, in Windhoek, Netherlands engineer a great escape in World Cricket League Division Two. Starting the day with a net run-rate of -0.197 they bowl Uganda out for 79 and reach their target in 6.3 overs, turning around their net run-rate to +0.641. Kenya then beat Nepal, causing Nepal's net run-rate to drop below Netherlands. This means that Netherlands finish second behind Namibia in the league and thus qualify, crucially, for the ICC Intercontinental Cup and World Cricket League Championship of 2015-2017.

I manage to get a rare opportunity to play some bridge this evening (of the very social variety). Apart from three consecutive hands where I can open one no trump, I get my usual dismal array of cards. I have always been convinced that my bridge hands are significantly below average. However, as a statistician, I suspect that if I had actually kept a record of all of them they almost certainly would turn out to be almost exactly average. Perception is not always supported by numerical reality.

January 24

In common, I suspect, with many fields of human interest, cricket statisticians are always looking for new angles. In their provincial three-day match against North West at Potchefstroom this weekend South Western Districts had six ducks in their first innings. This is a lot of ducks, but not a greatly notable record: The South African record in first-class cricket is seven and the world record is eight. So, we need to look for a new angle. South Western Districts made a total of 177 in that innings. This, it turns out, is the highest first-class total in South Africa to include six or more ducks. The world record is 295 (with six ducks) by Canterbury against MCC at Christchurch in 1922.

January 25

I am not in Port Elizabeth where West Indies sneak a one wicket win to end a sequence of 16 ODIs against South Africa without a win (15 losses and one tie). Instead, I am with family celebrating my mother's birthday. My career means that I am not always in town for family events, and on my mother's actual birthday on the 28th I will be at the ODI in Centurion.

January 26

Apart from all the 'glamour' matches, I also keep statistics on various amateur leagues in my role as Cricket South Africa's statistician. The Rural League has finished this past weekend and I have to capture the final round of seven matches and send out the logs as soon as possible. Fortunately the various scoresheets all arrive in my email inbox in time, making the task a lot easier.

Meanwhile two of cricket's major countries are celebrating national days: So 'Happy Australia Day' and 'Happy Republic Day' in India.

January 27

Today, I add only five matches to my database. I capture all first-class, List A and T20 matches into the database as well as various other matches (see yesterday's entry for example). This amounts to roughly 3 000 matches per year. So, only five in one day makes it a reasonably quiet one.

World Cup preparation starts today when I begin capturing the squads for each team into my database.

January 28

I am in the fortunate position that I rarely have to attend meetings, which are undoubtedly the bane of many other people's working lives. Today is an exception. The Cricket South Africa Awards committee has their first meeting of the year at Centurion in the morning before the ODI. As statistics form a significant part of judging the awards, I provide the stats for the various categories as well as sitting in on all the meetings.

After rain threatens to wash the game out the weather clears up in time for another slugfest. And this one does go past my bedtime. I arrive home about 14 hours after I left. South Africa plunder 361-5 from their 42 overs, with 198 coming in the last 13 at 16 runs per over. Sometimes I wonder if I am the only person in the world who actually likes bowlers. Hashim Amla and Rilee Rossouw add the South African third wicket record to their collection. Having put on a first wicket record 247 at The Wanderers 10 days ago, they add, er, 247 again today.

On Radio 2000 Peter Kirsten lets on that he preferred making scores in even numbers to odd ones. So, I couldn't resist checking his career and reveal to the listeners that of Kirsten's 509 dismissals in first-class cricket 266 were for even numbers and 243 for odd numbers.

January 29

There are many publications documenting scorecards of historical cricket matches and one of the best is Ray Webster's two volume work on Australian first-class cricket up to 1976/77. The word 'meticulous' must hold the world record for being the adjective most used to describe cricket statisticians. But it is highly appropriate in this case as Webster was certainly meticulous in his research of each game in that period. Particularly useful are his notes for each match which contain innings timings and boundaries for most major innings (mainly scores of 50 or more). I mention this, because today I finally complete the long term project of capturing these additional details into my database when I key in the details for the first ever first-class match in Australia: Tasmania v Victoria in Launceston in 1851.

Tomorrow I have to go to hospital for an operation for Cubital Tunnel Syndrome. Basically my ulnar nerves have been trapped in my elbows and need to be released. There are a few hand-related symptoms with the main one, in my case, being loss of grip. My measurements on the Grip-O-Meter (I am sure it must have a proper medical name) were 12 in my right hand and 20 in my left. They are supposed to be around 50. Anyway it has been caused by 30 years sitting at a computer keyboard with my elbows bent more than they should be. If I had stuck to the ICC's regulatory 15 degrees, I may have been alright. Baseball pitchers often have something known as Tommy John surgery, named after the man it was first performed on successfully. I hope future generations of cricket statisticians don't end up having 'Andrew Samson' surgery. Straighten those elbows, people!

I am having the right elbow done tomorrow and the left one will be later in the year. So, having to type left-handed, I suspect that the next few days' diary entries will be quite short.

January 30

Typing left-handed. Slowly. Operation, or 'minor procedure' to be slightly more medically accurate, seems to have gone off well.

The day, however, is not entirely devoid of cricket statistics as planned. South Africa A have added three players to their squad for tomorrow's game against England Lions. So, I have to redo the stats pack to include these players. Left-handed.

January 31

I wake up to see that Sanju Samson has done the family name proud by scoring 207 for Kerala v Services in the Ranji Trophy. He is easily the best of the three Samsons to have played first-class cricket. Oswald Samson played 49 first-class matches, mostly for Somerset, between 1900 and 1913 and averaged 18 with the bat and took five wickets, while Quinton Samson played 17 first-class matches for Free State in the South African provincial competition between 2004 and 2007, taking 35 wickets at an average of 44. Sanju, on the other hand, has already played for India Under-19s, collected two first-class 200s and is on his way to becoming an IPL superstar while still short of his 21st birthday.

Samson's 207 was not, however, the highlight of yesterday's Ranji Trophy action. KL Rahul, who had made a horribly skittish Test debut last month in the Boxing Day match at Melbourne and followed it with a fine century in the Sydney Test, scored 337 for Karnataka against Uttar Pradesh. It is Karnataka's first 300 and the eighth highest score in Ranji Trophy history.

In Bulawayo, Luke Jongwe becomes the first Zimbabwean teenager to score a century and take five wickets in an innings in a first-class match. One to watch, perhaps?

When she heard of the death of Calvin Coolidge, one of America's least interesting presidents and known as 'Silent Cal' because he very rarely spoke, the great wit Dorothy Parker remarked 'How can they tell?' This thought comes to mind when I hear that Dwayne Bravo has retired from Test cricket. It is over four years since his last one and for someone who should have comfortably made 5 000 runs and taken 200 wickets in Tests his final figures of 2 200 and 86 are disappointing.

Bad weather scuppers plans to head down to The Wanderers Club for the Gauteng v Namibia game, so instead I watch the live streaming of a playoff game between Perth Heat and Sydney Blue Sox in the Australian Baseball League, which the Heat win 9-2 to advance to the Championship Series against Adelaide Bite. I adopted the Heat as my ABL team when I watched one of their games at Barbagallo Park during the Ashes tour in 2010. Major League Baseball are a significant funder of the Australian Baseball League, which suggests a much more outward-looking, expansionist view than that which the current cricket authorities seem to have.

February 1

The day is dominated by painkiller-induced drowsiness. Fortunately there is not a lot of excitement in the cricket world, unless you count Karnataka not bothering to enforce the follow-on against Uttar Pradesh in the Ranji Trophy despite having a first innings advantage of 499. This is the fifth highest first innings' lead in the history of first-class cricket for a team that declined to enforce the follow-on.

Meanwhile the Auckland team that played Central Districts in the final of New Zealand's limited overs competition had seven South African-born players in their XI as well as one born in Harare. It does not help much, as they lose by 78 runs.

February 2

I am not really interested in the NFL, or any other oval-shaped ball game for that matter. But I generally watch the Superbowl each year. Because it is there, I suppose. It seems a good excuse to sit on the couch for recuperation purposes this time. I recorded the game, as a 01:30 start time in South Africa is a bit early in the morning for me to wake up. The New England Patriots beat the Seattle Seahawks to win their fourth title since 2002. With three World Series, a Stanley Cup and an NBA title so far this century, Boston can lay claim to being North America's leading sporting city.

Back at the cricket, Ben Stokes becomes the sixth player to hit 15 or more sixes in a List A innings while scoring 151* off 86 balls for England Lions v South Africa A in the first List A game to be played at the Mamelodi Oval. Gerrie Snyman holds the world record for most sixes in a List A innings with 17 for Namibia v United Arab Emirates at Windhoek in 2007. It is not a record that has much of a sense of permanency at the moment.

February 3

Many people have an image of cricket as a conservative game that changes slowly and reluctantly. This is a strange view as it is hard to imagine that there is any other game that has changed as much in the last 50 years, and seems to revel in innovating as often as possible, as cricket. The Inter-varsity T20 tournament starts in South Africa today with Power Play Plus Overs where runs are doubled in a nominated over (although wickets in these overs cost five runs) and you can score a 10 if you hit one of the strategically placed targets at the side of the field. Oh, and good luck to the scorers of these games. What cricket will look like 50 years from now is simply unimaginable.

In the final official ODI before the World Cup starts, Kane Williamson continues his prime form for New Zealand as he scores 112 against Pakistan in Napier. He has reached 50 in 12 of his last 16 ODI innings and is the first player to have done this. Javed Miandad and Dean Jones both had sequences of 11 fifty-plus scores in the space of 16 innings.

February 4

I was alerted to an extraordinary schools game by Julia Scully, who shares Radio 2000 scoring duties with me. It was an Under-14C game (which is the level I would have played at school, if we had had a 'C' team. But we only had a 'B' team, so I played for that) between St Andrew's and Selborne in the Eastern Cape. St Andrew's made 46 with a top-score of two, one other player scoring one, nine noughts and 43 extras. They then bowled Selborne out for 26 to win, having scored just three runs off the bat. There are, of course, no extensive records kept of games at that level so it is pretty much impossible to find where this would fall in cricketing records, but it certainly is a cracking game.

February 5

It is a very rare day as there are no games to be added to the database today. The only major game yesterday was the ODI between New Zealand and Pakistan which finished early enough South African time for me to process it yesterday.

We are load-shedded for the first time in the year, as South Africa's electricity crisis continues. I suppose we shouldn't complain too much as it has taken until 5 February for our suburb to have its turn. So, with no computer from 2pm to 6:30pm it is a quiet afternoon reading, which is actually a relief as my right arm is still in a sling. The reading material is tennis player Gordon Forbes' wonderful book *Too soon to panic.*

February 6

I am never normally particularly concerned with who wins or loses games of cricket. Of course, I have teams that I support, but in general I find the narrative of the game far more interesting than minor details such as who wins. But there is one situation that creates an exception for me. As Cricket South Africa's statistician I am the guy who needs to work out all the permutations of which teams can finish in which position in the logs in the final round of league games in the various competitions. As such, in the later rounds I fervently support those teams that can get the results which make those permutations as simple as possible. Tonight is one of those nights. It is the penultimate round of the Momentum One-day Cup and I will be hoping that the Cape Cobras beat the Dolphins and the Titans beat the Warriors. If this happens it will guarantee first place to the Cape Cobras, second place to the Titans, eliminate the Knights and Warriors, and leave just third place to be resolved between the Lions and Dolphins in Sunday's final round of games. And this resolution will be pretty simple as there is only a small likelihood of these teams finishing equal on points and the final log positions between them will be able to be resolved without resorting to net run-rate calculations. Come on you Cobras, Come on you Titans!

February 7

The Cobras lose. The Titans lose. No great surprise then. It was looking good at half-time, however. At Cape Town, Dolphins made 249-9 in their 50 overs and you would think that a quality team like the Cobras should be able to chase that down, but they slump to 19-4 and go on to lose by 25 runs. At Centurion the Titans rattle up 353-5. Now, 350 plus scores are becoming a lot more common these days, and this is the 13th such score this year already in the 198 List A matches to date. And, over 95% of targets over 350 have been successfully defended in limited overs history. The Warriors barely raise a sweat, knocking off the target with 14 balls to spare. So, I have to bring out the net run-rate calculator and figure out all the scenarios. It's not actually as complicated as it can be in these situations and I need only 12 lines in the spreadsheet to explain all the possible outcomes.

The return of the Sheffield Shield after a few months of Big Bash gives me something to listen to while doing all these calculations: Perth Sports Radio does ball-by-ball commentary on all Western Australia's games and I listen to the live-streaming whenever I get the chance.

Srikar Bharat scores 308 for Andhra against Goa in the Ranji Trophy to become just the fifth wicket-keeper to score a triple-century in first-class cricket after Billy Murdoch, Clyde Walcott, Imtiaz Ahmed and Kushal Perera. Thinking that it must be closing in on 200, I decide to check how many first-class 300s have been scored. It turns out that Bharat's is number 199. So, I will be watching closely for number 200. This diary will be the first to know. Well, the first after Twittersphere, that is.

February 8

I spend much of the afternoon following the Momentum One-day Cup matches with the net run-rate spreadsheet open. Although the Warriors win with a bonus point and the Titans lose, the required turnaround for the Warriors of around 190 runs inevitably turns out to be too much.

In one of the 31 first-class matches taking place in seven different countries today, Chris Lynn is 250* overnight for Queensland v Victoria in the Sheffield Shield. Could he be the 200th 300? The first thing I will do when I wake up tomorrow, or at least when the computer wakes up, will be to check that scorecard.

When I was growing up cricket was an 11-a-side game and Rugby Union 15-a-side. Now, if you want to play in the Olympics at least, Rugby Union is seven-a-side, while cricket, for warm-up games anyway, appears to have become a 15-a-side game. This will certainly be the case for the World Cup warm-up games which started today. With the general lack of interest in, and therefore lack of quantity of, warm-up games on tours the evolution to 15-a-side for such matches was fairly inevitable. With so few matches the only way to get game time, however minimal, for all squad members is to play them all in the same game. Call me old-fashioned, but I still prefer cricket as an 11-a-side game.

The Perth Heat wins the Championship Series of the Australian Baseball League against the Adelaide Bite. The competition has only being going for five years in its current incarnation and this is the Heat's fourth title.

February 9

Alas, Chris Lynn did not add to his overnight score, so we are going to have to wait for the 200th 300. Lynn's consolation prize (and I suspect that this will really make his day) is that his 250 is the highest score ever made in first-class cricket by a batsman who was dismissed on his overnight score.

My best friend of the past 10 days got binned this morning. The sling has served its purpose and was removed along with bandages and dressings on my follow-up visit to the surgeon. Tomorrow I need to start exercises that will help my ulnar nerve get used to its new home in the deep, dark recesses of my elbow.

It is to the deep, dark recesses of cyberspace that I need to resort in an attempt to establish whether the D Joon who made his debut for Wellington over the weekend is the same player who appeared for Haryana in India between 2004 and 2007. It is relatively easy to confirm that in each case it is Deepak Joon, but it takes a 2010 article in an Indian newspaper (found on page three of the Google search) about the Haryana player saying that if he does not get any more chances in Haryana he will move to New Zealand to confirm that it is the same player. It is one of the challenges of cricket statistics to make sure that the correct player is credited with the correct matches and there are occasions when career records need to be merged, or separated for that matter. One famous example of this is the case of EAC Hunte. Known as Errol, he played three Tests for the West Indies in 1930. A typist managed to mishear 'Errol' as 'RL' in one of his Tests and as a result he had two separate career records for a while.

Apart from a few members of the Indian touring party who played as guests in the Plunket Shield in 2008/09, Joon is just the third player to appear in both the Ranji Trophy in India and the Plunket Shield in New Zealand. The others are Dhiru Patel who played for Gujarat between 1966 and 1970 and for Northern Districts in 1971/72, and Albert Wensley, who, apart from playing 373 first-class matches for Sussex between 1922 and 1936, also managed to find time to turn out for Auckland and Nawangar. This is a good effort, considering this was the era before jet travel became ubiquitous. He must have spent a fair portion of his life on a ship.

February 10

I have my first session at the hand therapist as rehab begins in earnest. I have a new best friend: Tubigrip has replaced the sling in that role. And, I am given a set of exercises to do regularly.

In Bangladesh, Rony Talukdar has scored 201 for Dhaka Division v Chittagong Division. This is his third score over 150 in consecutive first-class innings following 227 and 163. He is the 16th player to make three consecutive scores over 150. Can he get another one in his next innings and equal the world record of four held by Vijay Merchant and Greg Blewett?

February 11

Sometimes when I am away and phone or Skype home my seven-year-old daughter will tell me that she has nothing to tell me and says goodbye. It is one of those days for this diary. I use the quiet time to start preparing stats packs for the World Cup. There is nothing else to tell you. Goodbye.

February 12

In the Twenty20 era there is a lot of angst about the longer versions of the game. Inevitably the 50 over game itself will be under scrutiny in this World Cup again. Expanding from a two-format game to a three-format game in 2003 has resulted in an exponential increase in the diversity of views of the game itself. There are some happy people who genuinely enjoy each format equally, but as is natural in human behaviour most followers of the game will have preferences to varying degrees. One view, for example, is that Test cricket remains the 'real' game and T20 is now the entertainment format. In this view, the 50-over game is the Piggy-In-The-Middle, no longer has any real relevance and should probably be binned. Another view is that Test cricket is too long and slow, Twenty20 too short and frenetic, and Fifty50 is just right, and I call this, as you may have guessed by this point in the sentence, the Goldilocks option. Me? Well, I like cricket *because* it is a long, slow and contemplative game. The traditional two innings, multi-day game provides far more variety in terms of the challenges it gives to players, the situations it creates, and the opportunities it gives for epic individual and team performances than the shorter limited overs game. From that point of view, if the game has to be played as an overs game (and the overwhelming majority of cricket games at all levels these days are played as overs games) then the more overs there are the better. Fifty-over games retain more of the essence of cricket than Twenty20.

February 13

It is Friday the 13th, but I get out of bed anyway and it is the proverbial calm before the storm as the World Cup nears. The World Cup will occupy the next 44 days. That is about the normal length of the tournament these days, but I have yet to meet anyone who thinks that it is too short or says 'Gee, I wish it was longer'. But a six to seven week tournament is what we are stuck with, and it ain't going to change anytime soon.

I will be doing a number of games for Radio 2000 in the SABC studios, as well as helping the BBC website guys with some stats. The starting times of matches are not ideal for South Africa, ranging from midnight to 05:30 apart from the few 08:30 starts in night games at Perth, which may be the highlight of the tournament for me. Sleep is going to be an interesting challenge.

I am fortunate to be on the ICC's mailing list and today I receive an email announcing Mondelēz International as their Official Confectionery Partner for the ICC Cricket World Cup 2015. I am surprised, but delighted, to discover that the ICC has (or even needs) an Official Confectionery Partner.

February 14

WC Day 1. And so, it starts. New Zealand beat Sri Lanka easily and Australia beat England even more easily. Steve Finn takes England's first World Cup hat-trick, or, more accurately, is given England's first hat-trick as Australia throw away wickets slogging at the last three balls of the innings. Finn's 5-71 is the second most expensive five-for in ODI history. Only Scotland's Gordon Goudie, with 5-73 v Australia at Edinburgh in 2009 has conceded more runs while taking an ODI five-for.

There is a fascinating conversation on Radio 2000 during the Australia v England game with Lawrence Mahatlane. Lawrence has many years of coaching experience within the provincial and franchise structures in South Africa and is currently the national Under-19 coach. (The previous SA Under-19 coach, Ray Jennings, led the team to a World Cup win last year. So, no pressure there, Lawrence). As a statistician, I have obviously noticed the increasing rate of ODI scoring in recent times with the change from five fielders allowed outside the circle to four, but Lawrence explains it from a coaching point of view. With only four fielders outside the circle, the bowler has virtually no option in terms of what type of ball he can bowl given his field. The batsman, of course, knows this and it makes big hitting in the late overs very easy. Lawrence demonstrates this by checking the field before each ball and predicting with virtual 100% accuracy what type of ball will be bowled. As the camera pans the field he says, 'This one will be full and wide outside off-stump'. They cut back to the bowler running in and the batsman is already standing outside off-stump waiting for it. Predictability in the game will eventually filter down from players and coaches to the average fan.

It is Valentine's Day, so we have a party. Not for Valentine mind you, but the family has a joint celebration of mine and my brother's birthdays. His is on the 12th and mine the 17th, so we often share the party.

200th-300-Watch comes to an abrupt end as Kithuruwan Vithanage belts 351 off 283 balls with 37 fours and 14 sixes for Tamil Union Cricket and Athletic Club v Sri Lanka Air Force Sports Club. Sri Lanka is an unexpected source for the 200th 300 as most of the first-class cricket there is of three days' duration and Vithanage's is just the third triple-century in Sri Lankan domestic first-class cricket history.

February 15

WC Day 2. South Africa recover from a potentially embarrassing 83-4 against Zimbabwe with the help of a world ODI record partnership for the fifth wicket of 256* between David Miller and JP Duminy. In their last five ODIs, South Africa have broken their own first, third and fifth wicket records. To great delight and excitement (except amongst Zimbabweans), the last 10 overs see 146 runs plundered. It is, however, only the joint second most in the last 10 overs in South Africa's last five ODIs, following 163 at Johannesburg and 146 at Centurion against West Indies.

The big game of the day, and it is as big as it gets, is India v Pakistan at Adelaide. It turns out to be a bit disappointing as India amble to 300 and Pakistan are never in the game. The only note of much statistical interest is that India manage to maintain their 100% record in World Cup matches against Pakistan (six out of six).

Trying not to stress my arm too much, I have resorted to a very minimalistic scoring method (e.g. using only initials for players instead of full names, not bothering with timings, and just scribbling the number of runs for each ball instead of the usual details I put in) and as a result, my scorebook is even messier than usual.

February 16

WC Day 3. And a top of the morning it is, as Ireland beat West Indies in Nelson. Clobber them, actually. It is the fifth successful chase of a target of 300 or more in a World Cup match and three of these have been by Ireland. As a general rule when there are upsets in cricket it is invariably because the better team has batted badly. They have either batted first and made a low score, or failed to chase a low target. For the unfavoured team to win chasing a big target, as Ireland did against England in 2011 and again today, is really impressive. I suspect Ireland's win does not get much attention in India, however, as it is IPL Auction Day. Yuvraj Singh will probably earn more from this year's IPL than Ireland and Afghanistan's cricket boards earn combined in a year.

Meanwhile in Sri Lanka, WLR Perera has affected three run outs as a substitute fielder in a first-class match, playing for — or actually, not playing for — Badureliya Sports Club against Ragama, including dismissing DET Rathnayake in both innings.

February 17

WC Day 4. Happy Birthday to me. I think it is the first time that I have ever been awake at midnight for the start of my birthday, as that is the starting time in South Africa for the New Zealand v Scotland game and I am working on it. Scotland become the second team, after Bangladesh v Sri Lanka at Pietermaritzburg in the 2003 World Cup, to have three first-ball ducks amongst the top five batsmen in any ODI. The Bangladesh case was the famous one where Chaminda Vaas took a hat-trick with the first three balls of the match. Scotland add another first-baller to their collection later in the innings and become the third team to have four first-ball ducks in one innings in all ODIs.

I keep an eye on the Dhaka Division v Sylhet Division match in Fatullah, but sadly Rony Talukdar is out for five and his run of 150-plus scores comes to an end, which is good news for Vijay Merchant and Greg Blewett.

At the lovely Pukekura Park in New Plymouth (is there a prettier ground in world cricket?) Dean Brownlie provides first-class 300 number 201. His 334 for Northern Districts v Central Districts is the highest score in New Zealand since the heyday of Bert Sutcliffe in the early 1950s.

February 18

WC Day 5. Afghanistan become the 20th team to appear in a World Cup match and, quite probably, the last. The next World Cup will only be 10 teams as the ICC appears determined to shrink the game. If there is a 21st team to play in the World Cup it won't be for a very long time. After a promising start Afghanistan allow Bangladesh to get to 267 and then collapse to 3-3 and don't get close.

I am asked on air on Radio 2000 to work out how many centuries were scored for South Africa in their first 50 ODIs. When I produce the answer (three) a minute or two later, Colin Bryden asks how I manage to do it so quickly. My database works on the basis that you first select the matches that you want to analyse and then run the appropriate query. In this case I selected all South Africa's ODIs and then listed the matches to find out the date of the fiftieth ODI. I then returned to the Match Selector and selected all South Africa's matches up to that date and then ran the query to list all the centuries. So, it is fairly simple really. To me, anyway.

The Tournament Sixes Counter makes its first appearance on TV coverage today (or at least it is the first time I have noticed it). We have had 62 already. The most sixes hit in a World Cup tournament is 373 in 2007, so there will be great excitement when the counter ticks, inevitably, over to 374 at some stage in this one. As someone who thinks bowlers are people too, I would love to see a Maiden Over Counter. It wouldn't appear very often, but it would be something really impressive to acknowledge when it did.

February 19

WC Day 6. United Arab Emirates, regarded as the most rank of the outsiders, put up an impressive display in their first World Cup game in 19 years. Zimbabwe choose to bowl for the 18th time of the last 19 that they won the toss (must be some sort of record, but I couldn't be bothered to check), but UAE score 285-7 and push Zimbabwe all the way. UAE provide the third and seventh oldest players in World Cup history. Khurram Khan is 43 years, 243 days and captain, Mohammad Tauqir is 43 years, 36 days. I still suspect that the record of Netherlands' Nolan Clarke is safe at 47 years, 257 days.

February 20

WC Day 7. The New Zealand v England game produces the most impressive display of this World Cup to date: Tim Southee bowls brilliantly to take 7-33 in nine overs. He is the first New Zealander to take seven wickets in an ODI and his figures are the third best in World Cups and sixth best in all ODIs. The only disappointment is when the last wicket falls as Joe Root holes out to Adam Milne, depriving Southee of the chance to take eight wickets in the innings. Only Chaminda Vaas has done that in ODIs. Southee bowls four of his victims and joins Joel Garner (West Indies v England in the 1979 final) and Lasith Malinga (Sri Lanka v Kenya in 2011) as the only bowlers to have done this in a World Cup match.

Having bowled England out for 123, normal ball-bashing service returns as New Zealand look after their net run-rate. Brendon McCullum smashes 77 off 25 balls. He reaches 50 off 18 balls, which beats his own World Cup record of 20 balls against Canada in 2007. His 8 fours and 7 sixes represent 96.10% of his runs in boundaries and this is the highest boundary percentage of any ODI innings over 70. At 24.50 runs per over, Steve Finn's 2-0-49-0 are the most expensive in ODI history of anyone bowling two or more overs.

When England have bowled 12.2 overs, with New Zealand on 119-2, I inform the Radio 2000 listeners that at least they have avoided their worst ever defeat (Australia beat them in 12.2 overs at Sydney in 2003). I had overlooked the possibility of the game-ending five wides, which Stuart Broad duly produces to ensure that the record is equalled.

February 21

WC Day 8. Mark Twain comes to mind today. Clearly, reports of the death of West Indies cricket have been greatly exaggerated. After making 310-6 they reduce Pakistan to 1-4 (Yes, that is one run and four wickets) and win comfortably. Pakistan's one is the lowest score at the fall of a fourth wicket in ODI history beating Canada's four against Zimbabwe at Port-of-Spain in 2006. Andre Russell hits 42* off 13 balls and so, along with AB de Villiers' 149 and Brendon McCullum's 77, the three fastest innings over 40 in ODIs have all been played in the last five weeks.

The ICC is on record as justifying a 10 team competition for future World Cups by saying that matches need to be 'between teams that are evenly matched and competitive'. Of the 10 matches so far in this one, the six involving two Full Members have been completely one-sided while the four involving Associates have been largely competitive. No doubt there will be some close contests between Full Members and some thrashings for Associates as the tournament progresses. But, right now, the ICC is looking pretty silly. At least to those of us who think that the game is actually worth spreading beyond its Test-playing base. In fairness, it is a bit lazy to knock the ICC as an organisation for their apparent reluctance to spread the game. The ICC currently has 105 members. Of these 10 are Full Members and 95 are either Associate or Affiliate Members. I suspect that these 95 are unanimously in favour of globalisation of the game, but they are effectively outnumbered by those with the money and the votes.

In Brisbane, Cyclone Marcia forces the abandonment of the Australia v Bangladesh match. Surprisingly, this is just the second World Cup match to be rained out without a ball bowled after the Sri Lanka v West Indies match at The Oval in 1979. Whatever the ICC may do wrong, they are pretty good at controlling the weather for World Cups.

There is good news for bowlers as left-arm spinner Bernard Scholtz takes 13-182 (8-116 & 5-66) for Namibia against Boland at Paarl in the Sunfoil Provincial Three-day Cup to record Namibia's best first-class match figures. Boland escape, however, to get the draw with nine wickets down in the fourth innings of the match.

February 22

WC Day 9. As a mere statistician, my literary repertoire is being challenged by the need for variety in the verbs used to describe the regular one-sided World Cup games. I am going to use 'thump' this time. I considered 'clout', but that seems more appropriate for an individual rather than a team, so I am going to save it for the next time someone scores a ridiculous amount of runs off not many balls, which will inevitably happen in the next few days. India thump South Africa by 130 runs at the MCG in front of 86 876 spectators in a match of limited statistical interest.

Meanwhile, 2 711 spectators turn up at the University Oval in Dunedin where Afghanistan push Sri Lanka all the way. Sri Lanka collapse to 51-4 chasing 233 to win before a century by Mahela Jayawardene helps them to a four wicket win with 10 balls to spare. Sri Lanka's Lahiru Thirimanne and Tillakaratne Dilshan provide only the second instance in ODIs of both openers being dismissed for first-ball ducks, matching Zimbabwe's Pete Rinke and Terrence Duffin who managed this against West Indies at Georgetown in 2006. Yet again it is the match between two Full Members that is one-sided and the one involving an Associate that is more competitive. The trend won't continue, of course. But it is tremendous fun while it does.

If Afghanistan had won that game it would have provided the excitement for the day, but instead the most exciting thing in cricket today, especially if you are South African, was Kagiso Rabada taking 9-33 for Lions in the Sunfoil Series match against Dolphins in Johannesburg to give him match figures of 14-105. At 19 years, 273 days he is the youngest to take 13 or more wickets in a first-class match in South Africa. Sadly, he took more wickets than there were spectators at the game.

And, there is another nine-down draw in South Africa as the Sunfoil Series match in Kimberley between Knights and Cape Cobras produces a similar finish to the Provincial match in Paarl yesterday.

February 23

WC Day 10. It has taken until Day 10 and Match 14, but there is finally something for the Ten Team World Cup Fan Club to cheer about as England beat Scotland by 119 runs in Christchurch. It is a stroll in the park, really. Hagley Park, to be precise. It probably won't go down as one of the great wins in the annals of English cricket, but it is their biggest run margin in a World Cup match since they beat East Africa by 196 runs in 1975. Perhaps the highlight of the day was the tweet by a Scottish fan 'You may take our wickets, but you'll never take our freedom.'

February 24

WC Day 11. For the first 10 days of the World Cup my wake-up call has ranged from midnight to 4am, with a clear tendency to favour the earlier of that time range. My average wake-up time has been about 01:53 and 38 seconds (No, I didn't actually work that out. I just estimated it while typing the sentence). Today it is 5:30. It is like having a lie-in, and by the end of the day I feel almost normal.

Mark Twain may be dead, but West Indies cricket seems truly alive, as Chris Gayle clouts (told you I would use 'clouts' soon) Zimbabwe for 215 in Canberra. It is the first double-century in a World Cup game and the fifth overall in ODIs. It is not a good day for South Africa: Gary Kirsten's World Cup record score of 188* set 19 years ago against UAE in 1996 falls, as does David Miller's World Cup record of 9 sixes in an innings, set nine days ago against Zimbabwe. Gayle clears the boundary 16 times to equal the overall ODI record. He then picks up 2-35 and a catch in Zimbabwe's innings to become the first player to do the double of 150 and two wickets in a match twice in ODIs, and also the first to do the triple of 150 runs, two wickets and one catch in a match.

Of even more esoteric statistical interest Sean Williams makes 76. He has now reached 70 eight times in ODIs, but his best is 78*. It is easily the longest run of scores over 70 without getting to 80 in ODIs as nobody else has done more than five.

February 25

WC Day 12. Another 'lie-in' to 05:30, and I even get to take the kids to school for the first time in the World Cup. It is funny how everyday duties become simple pleasures when they aren't happening every day.

Today's match in Brisbane is the best of the tournament so far, and certainly meets the ICC desire for games that are 'between teams that are evenly matched and competitive'. It is, of course, between two Associates. Chasing 279 to win, Ireland beat UAE by two wickets with four balls to spare and they now have four of the top 10 successful World Cup run-chases to their credit. I am going to try to stop banging on about the 10-team 2019 World Cup, but it is almost impossible to watch a game like today's without being saddened by the thought that the chances of either of these teams appearing in England in four years' time is slim and the chances of both being there can only be measured by resorting to a large number of noughts in the decimal columns.

Reports today suggest that the ICC's premier event may shrink even further than expected in 2019 as there are proposals within the England and Wales Cricket Board to reduce ODIs to 40-overs. England is the only country in the world that has had regular 40-over games at domestic level. All of the current administrators there would have grown up watching the 40-over Sunday League games on TV and they have clearly maintained a strong sentimental attachment to that. It is hard to see any good reason to slice 10 overs off the one-day game, especially if you want to keep it differentiated from Twenty20.

For most of the history of Indian cricket, Mumbai has been the powerhouse. Imelda Marcos would have been satisfied to have had as many pairs of shoes as Mumbai has Ranji Trophy titles. Famously, they won all 15 editions between 1958/59 and 1972/73. In today's semi-final against Karnataka (the team that ended that sequence by winning in 1973/74) Mumbai were bowled out for 44.

I collect a new first-class cricket ground today: Traegar Park in Alice Springs. I am not actually there, of course. But, with the World Cup hogging all the major grounds in Australia, the state teams have had to find new homes for their Sheffield Shield fixtures. Victoria are using Traegar Park for a few of their games and so today the ground makes its first-class debut. I 'collect' grounds where first-class cricket has been played by trying to visit them when I can on my travels, and on the last Ashes tour in 2013/14 England played a two-day (not first-class) warm-up game there, which I and Mrs S popped into while on a drive from Darwin to Adelaide (it took nine days). Alice Springs is venue number 214 in my spreadsheet. Of these I have actually watched first-class cricket at 87.

February 26

WC Day 13. The Associates outdo the Full Members again. Don't bang on, don't bang on! It is a cracking game in Dunedin, as Afghanistan overcome a collapse from 85-2 to 97-7 to reach 211-9 and produce the fifth one-wicket win in World Cup history against Scotland. The match sees ninth wicket partnerships over 60 in both innings for the first time in any ODI. Afghanistan add 114 after the fall of the seventh wicket to win the game, which is the third most that any team has added after the fall of the seventh wicket to win an ODI batting second. I like that kind of stat as it helps to put the effort into perspective showing the degree of difficulty they overcome and therefore the rarity of the performance.

Meanwhile at the MCG two teams that will be at the 2019 World Cup produce another dull one-sided game as Sri Lanka don't even bother to lose more than one wicket while dispatching Bangladesh. The main point of statistical interest is that Bangladesh lose a wicket in the first over of their innings, which they have now done in all three World Cup games that they have played against Sri Lanka following the famous day in Pietermaritzburg in 2003 when they lost four in the first over and then one in the match at Port-of-Spain in 2007. In the tournament to date Dunedin's Entertainment Value to Number of Spectators Ratio is astronomical compared to Melbourne's.

I manage to sneak out of World Cup duties for a little while to accompany my five-year-old daughter to Market Day at school. Efforts to persuade her to buy anything with a sugar content below 95% are in vain.

February 27

WC Day 14. There is another assault on the records, the senses and the ball. Having missed out on smashing Shane Watson's fastest ODI 150 off 83 balls on 18 January, AB de Villiers makes amends by reaching this milestone off 64 balls today. A comprehensive search through available thesauruses fails to deliver any new superlatives to describe his innings.

He was only on 95 at the start of the 48th over, but scored 67 more in the last three. His partnership of 80 with Farhaan Behardien came off 3.2 overs at 24.00 runs per over, the quickest ODI partnership over 50. (Behardien kindly contributed 10). On the way de Villiers reached 3 000 runs in just 60 innings as ODI captain, 10 fewer than the previous record-holder MS Dhoni.

Having begun with a spell of 5-2-9-1, Jason Holder finishes with 10-2-104-1, conceding 34 and 30 off his last two overs. It is the most expensive 10-over spell in World Cup matches, although Martin Snedden still holds the record for most runs conceded (12-1-105-2 for New Zealand v England at The Oval) in a World Cup match, having been allotted two extra overs back in the dim and distant days of 60-over matches in 1983.

If you have no computer programming expertise or interest, I recommend you skip the next paragraph and jump to the following one.

Holder's two 30-plus overs creates an interesting problem for me in the database. I have a table for most runs off an over and when I created it I indexed it with a primary key of match, innings, bowler. It had not occurred to me that a bowler would have an over whacked for so many runs more than once in an innings. So, I need to remove 'bowler' from the index before I can enter Holder's second case from today's match.

There is not much doubt that AB de Villiers is the best batsman in the world today and one of the great talents in the history of the game. But, some of the reaction to his recent innings in which he has made big scores faster than anyone suggests that context is a diminishing commodity in cricket. Surely really great innings are played when facing a high degree of difficulty: a great bowling attack, a tricky pitch, a hopeless match situation, a combination of all of that and more. Plundering runs on flat pitches against equally flat bowling attacks from advantageous match situations with playing conditions that are designed to help them (e.g. only four out-fielders and two balls in an innings) doesn't strike me as particularly challenging for the modern batsman, especially given the quality of the bats they now use.

In Durban, Divan van Wyk scores 171 and Morne van Wyk 103* for Dolphins against Knights in a Sunfoil Series match. Surprisingly, this turns out to be only the second time in South African domestic first-class cricket that two brothers have both scored centuries in the same innings following Gary and Peter Kirsten who managed it for Western Province v Eastern Province at Port Elizabeth in the Currie Cup final in 1990.

In between all of this, I manage to capture a number of Women's Provincial League matches from last weekend and send out the logs and averages for that competition as well as taking the kids for their weekly swimming lesson.

It's been a busy day. And, I have a 01:30 wake-up call for tomorrow.

February 28

WC Day 15. There is a proper game in Auckland. New Zealand knock Australia over for 151, including their worst ever eight wicket collapse in ODIs of 26 runs (80-1 to 106-9), and then nearly lose. Trent Boult has one of the great spells in World Cup history taking 5-1 in 17 balls at one stage on his way to final figures 10-3-27-5. Then Mitchell Starc takes 6-28 as New Zealand scrape home by one wicket. Starc records the third best figures by anyone finishing on the losing team in an ODI. (Imran Khan 6-14 for Pakistan v India at Sharjah in 1985 and Shane Bond 6-23 for New Zealand v Australia at Port Elizabeth in 2003 are the top two). The game was really a mini-Test match as opposed to the Maxi-T20s that most of the World Cup has seen so far and features the most aggressive field settings and bowling changes I have ever seen in an ODI. Cricket fans who fall into the 'Never watch a Test match — too boring' category probably needed to learn the names of a few fielding positions they had never seen before, e.g. short leg, third slip, fourth slip etc. Cricket may have become primarily a runs and overs game despite its original design as a runs and wickets game, but it is, and always will be, a better game when wickets are falling than when they are not.

The choice as to what stat to use is not always clear-cut. Boult and Starc's heroics have statisticians scrambling for their keyboards looking for left-armers taking wickets in the same game. Some statisticians go with 12 wickets by left-arm seamers (Corey Anderson also took one) being the most in any ODI. I choose to tweet that 14 wickets by any left-arm bowlers (Daniel Vettori added the other two) is the second most by any left-arm bowlers in an ODI behind the 16 between India and Australia at Mumbai in 2007.

New Zealand score 11 off the first ball of their innings from Mitchell Johnson: Four off a no ball and then six off the free hit. So, I have to see if I can find more than that off the first ball of an ODI innings. And I do. Coincidentally, it is in a match between the same teams at the same venue 10 years ago. Daryl Tuffey managed to concede 14 off the first official ball of that match with the help of four no balls, two wides and 2 fours (one of which was off a no ball).

Thanks to my recent surgery and recovery process, I am able to help the

Radio 2000 commentators out when they are looking for the name of the compression band thingy that Brendon McCullum gets on his arm after he is hit by a ball from Mitchell Johnson. 'It's called Tubigrip,' I say, with my arm up in the air. I still have it on.

In Perth (five time zones behind Auckland) the UAE make 102 and India win by nine wickets. So, overall the day is a lot shorter than it could have been.

March 1

WC Day 16. At the Westpac Stadium in Wellington (colloquially known as the Cake Tin, because it, er, looks like a cake tin) England are quite pleased to make 309 against Sri Lanka with Joe Root becoming their youngest World Cup centurion. However, Sri Lanka again don't bother to lose more than one wicket, or much sweat, knocking off the target with Lahiru Thirimanne matching Root to become Sri Lanka's youngest World Cup centurion and Kumar Sangakkara joining countryman Sanath Jayasuriya as the only players with sub 75-ball centuries in consecutive ODIs. Sri Lanka are the second team after India (362-1 v Australia at Jaipur in 2013) to successfully reach a target over 300 for the loss of just one wicket in ODIs. England are the first team to lose nine ODIs after making 300 batting first and their percentage in this department is 31.03, well worse than any other Test playing country.

There is a bit of excitement amongst lovers of arcane cricket statistics when I tweet that Pakistan have lost their last 26 ODI wickets to catches. The sequence, which began after Umar Akmal was bowled by Grant Elliott in their last match before the World Cup ends at 28 when Umar Akmal (again) is bowled by Zimbabwe's Sean Williams at the Gabba. This is over 50% more than the previous longest such sequence in ODIs of 18. Proportionally therefore, this, I suppose, makes a case for it to be regarded as the Bradman of arcane cricket statistics.

March 2

WC Day 17. Yipee! There are no World Cup games today. It is a brief break, the only day off between 14 February and 15 March. No doubt many fans will be disappointed that all they have on the cricket channel on their TV are matches that have already been played, but overwhelmingly those working in the game will welcome the day off. When I wake up today at 06:30, I have been asleep for 13 of the previous 16 hours including my afternoon nap yesterday.

The whole family goes to the dentist in the afternoon for check-ups and I think I set a personal record by not needing a single filling. Mrs S, on the other hand, needs the first ones of her life.

March 3

WC Day 18. South Africa score 411-4 against Ireland, swatting 131 in the last 10 overs, to no great acclaim. After all, 131 is just South Africa's fourth highest last 10 over total in their previous eight games. All very ho-hum. South Africa become the first team to reach 400 in consecutive ODIs and the second team, after Australia (v Scotland and Netherlands in 2007), to win consecutive ODIs by more than 200 runs. Hashim Amla scores 159 off 128 balls to become the first South African to make three scores over 150 in ODIs. It is his 20th century in just his 108th innings, making him easily the quickest to this milestone, leaving Virat Kohli's 133 innings barely visible in his rear view mirror. Amla and Faf du Plessis add 247 for the second wicket and South Africa have now broken their ODI records for the first, second, third and fifth wickets in the past eight games. The records for each of the first three wickets are now all 247 and all involve Amla. Is this a weakness for the opposition to exploit, perhaps? They are likely to lose a wicket when the partnership reaches 247.

I am always amazed how many people will happily pick Chris Gayle ahead of Amla for current or All-time ODI XIs. Gayle is without doubt the mega-hero of cricket's micro-format, but his average in the middling format of ODIs is currently 37.30 compared to Amla's 56.72. Presumably Gayle is regarded as being more destructive, but his ODI strike-rate is 84.81. Amla's strike-rate? 89.85. I am picking the guy who is going to score 20 runs an innings more, and score them faster. Who are you going for?

I manage to dash across town from the studios to get to the school in time for my seven-year-old daughter's first competitive sporting contest: A tee-ball game. Tee-ball is basically baseball/softball without a pitcher — you hit the ball off a tee instead. This is a concept that I suspect will have huge appeal to many cricket fans. Imagine the game without bowlers, they could easily score 1 000 in 50 overs. How good would that be? Just don't mention it to the ICC.

March 4

WC Day 19. There are different types of draws in Test cricket. Sometimes they are rain-affected, sometimes they are very exciting with one or both teams in with a chance of winning right until the end, and occasionally (and it really is very occasionally these days) you get the 'bore-draw' where there are so many runs and so few wickets there is never a prospect of an outright result. Today Pakistan get a 'bore-win' over United Arab Emirates. They stroll to 339-6 and then fail to bowl UAE out, allowing them 210 runs but only taking eight wickets in the 50 overs. The end of the Pakistan innings represents the halfway point of this World Cup. We have now had 24 and a half of the 49 matches. I prefer to count down in small units, so am pleased to see that by the end of the match we now have fewer than 600 hours left before the end of the tournament. Sure it is fun while it lasts, but I am looking forward to the break (and some sleep!) at the end.

Australia break the World Cup record with a total of 417-6 against Afghanistan. David Warner threatens not just Chris Gayle's freshly minted World Cup record 215 but also Rohit Sharma's ODI record of 264 and Ali Brown's List A record of 268 for that matter, but gets himself out for 178 made in 37.3 overs. This is the most anyone has made at that stage of an ODI innings for a team batting first. Sharma, by comparison had 'only' 146 at that stage of the innings when he made his 264 against Sri Lanka in Kolkata. Glenn Maxwell, who replaces Warner at the crease belts (have I used 'belts' before?) 88 off 39 balls and is out 9.5 overs later. If Warner had made those 88 runs he would have been 266* with 16 balls remaining in the innings. Dawlat Zadran (10-1-101-2) joins Martin Snedden and Jason Holder as the only bowlers to concede 100 runs in a World Cup match. Remarkably, all three have included at least one maiden in their spells. Australia then bowl Afghanistan out for 142 to add the World Cup record victory margin (275 runs) to their collection.

There are fires raging around Cape Town and long-time colleague Neil Manthorp's family have to evacuate their house. Neil, of course, is 11 765 km away in Auckland on World Cup duties. For those of us who travel quite a lot on the cricket circuit the idea that you will not be at home when your family needs you most always lurks at the back of your mind. Fortunately, the Manthorps' house survives although some in the near vicinity are not so lucky.

March 5

WC Day 20. Scotland and Bangladesh combine for the 18th and 19th scores over 300 in the tournament to date. The previous most in a World Cup is 17 in 2011. And we are only just over halfway through the event. Bangladesh pass Scotland's 318 quite easily to post their highest winning ODI total chasing and the second highest ever in World Cup games. And they do so without the help of an individual century (Tamim Iqbal top-scores with 95). No team has played more than their 29 World Cup games without anyone making a 100, although Sri Lanka had to wait 28 for their first and Kenya are yet to get one in 29 matches.

The fundamental change that computers brought to cricket statistics is that they moved from being list based to database query based. What I mean by this is that in the old days statisticians would keep lists of notable events (highest totals, best scores, best bowling figures, etc.) and update these whenever necessary, whereas today statisticians don't store the lists, but rather store all the scorecards in a database and then run a query (a small computer program) to generate the records from those scorecards. This certainly allows us to interrogate the data in far greater depth than was ever possible without the current technology. But it does occasionally throw up some interesting things. There was an example today. Kyle Coetzer scored 156 for Scotland, which is the highest World Cup score made for an Associate team. Checking their database-generated list of highest scores and searching for Associate teams leads some statisticians to claim that he beat Klaus-Jan van Noortwijk's 134* for Netherlands v Namibia in Bloemfontein in 2003. However, the record was actually held by Dave Houghton who scored 142 for Zimbabwe v New Zealand at Hyderabad in 1987 when Zimbabwe were still an Associate team.

There are some stirrings amongst twitterati and commenterati on the Internet to the effect that maybe the degree to which the bat is dominating the ball in ODIs these days might not be The End Of Tedium As We Know It after all. So, it is possible I might not be all alone in the world. There seem to be a few others who also think that maybe, just maybe, the game would be better if the bowlers had more of a chance.

March 6

WC Day 21. I suspect that Dolly Parton never worked from *9 to 5* in her life, but she did claim some fame by singing about it. Today I work from 9 to 5 as the only World Cup game is in Perth. Actually it is more like 8:30 to 4:30, but that does not have quite the same musical lilt to it as *9 to 5*. The reason I am mentioning all of this is because there was virtually nothing of interest in the cricket. India bowl West Indies out for 182 and although they wobble a bit at 107-5 they win quite easily. Jason Holder provides the statistical excitement by making 57 to become the first player to make a 50 in consecutive ODIs batting at number nine each time following his 56 against South Africa.

Someone tweets that Umesh Yadav has now bowled nine balls to Denesh Ramdin and dismissed him five times in ODIs. I am a bit peeved with myself, as that is a great stat and I should have been on to it.

Peter Siddle is merely a Test-match specialist, so is watching most of the World Cup from his sofa. When he isn't playing for Victoria, that is. Today he takes 8-54 against South Australia at the Gliderol Stadium in Adelaide. Eight-fors are increasingly rare in modern first-class cricket and Siddle's figures are the best in a Sheffield Shield match in four and a half years. South Australia's first 393 Sheffield Shield games were all played at the same venue: Adelaide Oval, before the Gliderol made its debut in 2013. But, with the World Cup taking priority, the Gliderol has become South Australia's home for the past few weeks. I must collect it next time I am in Adelaide.

March 7

WC Day 22. It is Oliver Twist who comes to mind today. 'Please sir, may we have some more?' The 2007 World Cup encounter between Ireland and Zimbabwe resulted in a tie and today they produce another classic as fortune shifts one way then the other before Ireland prevail by five runs. Here is the thing though: These two teams, who probably fit the description '... that are evenly matched and competitive' better than any other head-to-head in world cricket, have played the grand total of four ODIs against each other in the eight intervening years between their World Cup meetings. Surely the interests of both these teams and the game as a whole would be best served by finding a way to ensure that they meet each other more often. Sean Williams finally gets out of the 70s and his innings of 96 is ended by a match-deciding close call for a catch on the boundary rope by John Mooney. It is called a catch so he is out, but if it had been a six Zimbabwe would most likely have won the game. Just a millimetre or two ...

Ireland have now won five World Cup matches against Test playing countries, the most by an Associate against Full Members in World Cups, passing Kenya's four. Here is a list of the last three countries to obtain Full Member status with their number of wins against Test teams in World Cup matches before being granted Test status: Sri Lanka (1), Zimbabwe (2), Bangladesh (1). Ireland have five (that is more than those three teams combined, for those who need a bit of arithmetical assistance) and yet Test status seems to remain a distant dream.

In the earlier game today, South Africa are set a target of 232 in 47 overs by a combination of Pakistan and Messrs Duckworth and Lewis. They collapse to 102-6 on a pitch with a bit of life in it and against a bowling attack with a lot of life (and left-handedness) in it. AB de Villiers makes a bold bid to win the game single-handedly with 77 off 58 balls but South Africa fall 29 runs short. Had De Villiers won the game for his team it would have been easily his best innings of the year, notwithstanding the 149 off 44 and 162 off 66. He does, however, have the consolation of passing Ricky Ponting's record of 31 World Cup career sixes. For the second time in a week nine of the wickets taken by Pakistan fall to left-arm seam bowlers. These are the only two such instances in all ODI history.

March 8

WC Day 23. Glenn Maxwell clobbers Australia's fastest ODI century off 51 balls and just misses Kevin O'Brien's World Cup fastest of 50 balls as actual cricket continues its relentless pursuit of merging with the Playstation version of the game. Australia make 376-9 against Sri Lanka at Sydney. Sri Lanka fall short despite Kumar Sangakkara becoming the first player to make centuries in three consecutive World Cup games. The great man is playing as well as ever, but is determined to retire before the year is done. Don't go, Kumar!

In the early game New Zealand dispatch Afghanistan easily with Daniel Vettori taking 4-18 in 10 overs. In the 50-over era he is just the second bowler to take four or more wickets while conceding less than 20 runs in a full 10 overs in a World Cup game, after Andrew Hall's 10-2-18-5 for

South Africa v England at Bridgetown in 2007. More interesting, however, is that the match is Afghanistan's 50th ODI and Mohammad Nabi has played all 50 of them making him the first player to appear in each of his country's first 50 ODIs.

The Canadian five dollar bill has a picture of Sir Wilfrid Laurier on it. Laurier has more than a passing resemblance to Star Trek's Mr Spock. Following the death of Leonard Nimoy some naughty Canadians have taken to adding more Vulcan features to Sir Wilfrid on their bills. The authorities (quite rightly) make disapproving noises, but the story no doubt provides a bit of upward curvature to the lips of those perusing it. This, of course, has nothing to do with cricket. Sadly, for a country with a notable cricketing history (everyone knows that Canada played the first international match v America in 1844), not much in Canada does. The country boasts a significant number of immigrants from cricket-playing nations and yet their team has slipped from appearing in the World Cup four years ago to Division Three now. As the effectively 21st ranked team in the world, perhaps the good folk of Toronto, Vancouver and Saskatoon will be cheering Sachin Tendulkar's recent call for a 25-team World Cup.

March 9

WC Day 24. There is merriment and mayhem in Mirpur and despair in Downing St and Doncaster as Bangladesh beat England to qualify for the quarter-finals and knock the 2019 hosts out. Bangladesh finally get a World Cup century in their 30th match as Mahmudullah makes 103. And, yet again a sub-300 total produces a closer game than the 300-plus efforts, as England get within 15 of Bangladesh's 275. This is the 16th game of this World Cup in Australia and now 13 of them have been won by the team batting first. By contrast 10 of the 16 in New Zealand have been won by the team batting second. Did I mention that England chose to bowl after winning the toss today in Adelaide?

There is some amusement in England when a graphic is produced showing that Ireland's winning percentage against Full Members in World Cup games since 1996 (29%) is higher than England's (27%). After England's first game of the tournament there were a lot of jokes that their Irish-born captain Eoin Morgan would not get into the Irish team. On current form (44 runs in four innings in the tournament to date and four ducks in his last eight innings), the Irish selectors would probably agree with the comedians.

Futurist Ray Kurzweil has predicted that the Singularity will occur around the year 2045. In my, admittedly limited, understanding the Singularity is the point at which all artificial intelligence on earth will outnumber all human intelligence. Wallowing in my angst-ridden view that cricket is on the verge of becoming a 'Batsman Only' zone, it occurs to me that cricket's Singularity — the final triumph of bat over ball — will take place when there are more sixes per match than wickets. So, I have to do the calculation. The average number of wickets per ODI is fairly static at around 14.5 per game. The number of sixes per game, however has been steadily rising from about five per game 10 years ago to 8.7 this year so far. Using a standard linear regression on the numbers I calculate that cricket's Singularity will occur in 2037. Other, more sophisticated, statistical techniques are available. But, I don't bother to use them. This is, after all, not really a serious problem. Especially not when set against, for example, the possibility of machines wiping out humankind. Perhaps the ICC's first cyborg President will be bored enough with every second ball being bashed out of the park that he (she? it?) will decide to reinvent bowlers.

March 10

WC Day 25. After a good start (206-3 after 38.5 overs) Ireland collapse to 259 all out and India beat them easily. The difference in bowling performances between overs 41 and 50 in the tournament thus far by the top four teams (Australia, India, New Zealand and South Africa) combined and the other 10 teams is stark. (Starc?) My tweet 'Bowling in overs 41-50 in WC: Aus/Ind/NZ/SA combined: RPO 5.28, RPW 9.60. Other 10 teams combined: RPO 9.35, RPW 31.52', however, is met with general indifference. It is tweets about masses of runs and sixes that are more likely to get cricket fans flicking the mouse over the retweet button.

I have been contemplating trying to put some statistical perspective to modern batting by comparing, say, Viv Richards to AB de Villiers, the preeminent batsmen of their eras. Richards had a strike-rate of 90 in ODIs compared to de Villiers' 98 and an average of 47 compared to De Villiers' 52. But the overall average runs per over in the matches that Richards played in was 4.29. For de Villiers it is 5.25. Fortunately, S Rajesh on ESPNCricInfo saves me the trouble of having to do the actual calculations. It turns out that Richards' Era-Adjusted Average Times Strike-Rate Ratio is the best of all-time at 2.19. (Or, in plain language, he was 2.19 times better than average). Despite having a higher average and strike-rate than Richards, De Villiers is at 2.05, although this does put him second on the list.

Meanwhile in Port-of-Spain the headlines probably read 'Keiron Pollard Plays First-class Match'. The Twenty20 superstar scored 45 and took 5-36 for Trinidad and Tobago against Windward Islands in the wonderfully named West Indies Cricket Board Professional Cricket League Regional Four Day Tournament. Pollard is on record as saying he wants to play Test cricket and a few performances in first-class cricket wouldn't do him any harm in that regard (assuming he is really serious). His controversial omission from the West Indies World Cup squad gives him a chance to play the long game for a change and this is just his seventh first-class game in the last six years. He has played 250 T20 games in that time. The mothballs must have been having fun with his whites.

In other news, Bette Midler has been putting Kim Kardashian's tweets to music and singing them to grand piano accompaniment. So, all is well with the world.

March 11

WC Day 26. Karun Nair makes 328 for Karnataka v Tamil Nadu to beat Gul Mohammad's 319 for Baroda v Holkar in 1947 as the highest score in a Ranji Trophy final. After bowling Tamil Nadu out for 134, Karnataka had slumped to 84-5 before Nair came to the rescue. Karanataka are finally bowled out for 762. I suspect Karnataka's first innings' lead of 628 might just prove to be enough. Their 678 runs after the fall of the fifth wicket are the most in any innings in first-class cricket. Those of their opponents in this match who might be interested in such things will be a bit miffed to hear that this record was previously held by Tamil Nadu themselves when they added 652 after the fall of the fifth wicket at 260 to finish on 912-6 against Goa in 1989.

At the World Cup Kumar Sangakkara becomes the first player to score four consecutive 100s in ODIs with 124 against Scotland. And he becomes the first to reach 500 dismissals in ODIs. And he breaks Adam Gilchrist's record for most World Cup dismissals. Don't go, Kumar!

March 12

WC Day 786. Enthusiasm levels are declining rapidly. The World Cup is too long. And, it is back to a 01:30 alarm after a few 5:00 ones. When I am feeling a bit more rational I may change my current view that today's match between South Africa and UAE is the most boring in the history of the game. Or, I may not.

Karnataka's 628 run first innings lead does prove to be enough as they win by an innings and 217 runs. The various domestic seasons around the world are starting to wind down.

March 13

WC Day 28. If I was a prolific hash-tagger I would probably have included '#busses' in one today. The old joke about busses is that you wait for hours for one to come along and then two arrive at the same time. In Bangladesh's last game Mahmudullah scored a century. It was his 114th ODI. Today he adds 128 against New Zealand to become the second Bangladeshi after Shahriar Nafees to score consecutive ODI 100s. He also becomes the first player to score his first two centuries in consecutive matches having waited over 100 ODIs for his maiden one.

One of the primary reasons cited for England's demise in this World Cup is their perceived over-reliance on data analysis. The topic of data analytics in sport is a very interesting one, having been made sexy by Michael Lewis's book *Moneyball* and even sexier by Brad Pitt's film of the book, but proper discussion of it is beyond the scope of a mere diary entry. Since the start of 2014 Brendon McCullum has a strike-rate of 157.14 and average of 45.83 against seamers and a strike-rate of 93.10 and average of 16.20 against spinners in ODIs. Today Bangladesh open the bowling with two spinners. It is just the second time that this has happened in a World Cup game after New Zealand did it against South Africa at Mirpur in 2011. Shakib Al Hasan duly dismisses McCullum for eight. Somebody in the Bangladesh camp has been having a proper look at the data.

The wire is well and truly in sight by the time New Zealand sneak home in the match, chasing Bangladesh's 288. So far in the World Cup 20 teams have scored 300 batting first and just two of those games have produced a close finish. On the other hand, the 16 games where the team batting first failed to reach 300 have seen nine close finishes. (Technical note: I have defined close finishes as 'Margin <=20 runs or <=3 wickets or <=2 overs remaining'). World Cups often define prototypes. Think 1987 reverse sweeps, 1992 Greatbatch and Patel opening (batting and bowling, respectively), 1996 Jayasuriya and Kaluwitharana pinch-hitting, etc. If this World Cup gives us a prototype for future ODIs that is: Team batting first smashes/bashes/clobbers/insert breathless verb of choice to 380 and team batting second then muddles/fiddles/slogs/insert desperate verb of choice to 250, then I won't be the only one yawning by the time 2019 rolls into view.

In a damp Sydney, Afghanistan and England (and possibly Duckworth and Lewis), end their World Cup campaigns. There have been a few periods of good play and hope, some individuals who have impressed, and a win over Scotland. But, overall it has been a bit of a disappointing tournament. For Afghanistan, that is. England have had a win over Scotland.

March 14

WC Day 29. It is International Pi Day today. That's the Pi that is the Duckworth to R-squared's Lewis of circle measurements. March the 14th (3-14, geddit?). Sadly, no bowler concedes even an approximation to 3.1415926... runs per over at the World Cup. In fact, only Mitchell Starc concedes less than that with his 4-14 in 4.4 overs against Scotland including his ninth and tenth bowled victims of the tournament. In just five outings he has already dismissed the most batsmen bowled in one tournament, bettering the nine by Wasim Akram in 1992. Mrs S makes shoo fly pi(e) for dessert in honour of the famous number. Ah, the joys of living in a numerically-inclined household.

Brendan Taylor scores 138 off 110 balls for Zimbabwe in what is probably his last innings for Zimbabwe, having signed a Kolpak contract with Nottinghamshire. If his retirement does prove to be final, he will be the only player to have scored centuries in his last two ODIs.

There is great excitement when MS Dhoni smashes Tawanda Mupariwa over long on for six to provide the 374th six of the tournament beating the previous record for one World Cup tournament. Or is there? The Tournament Six Counter ticks tiredly over to 371 on the TV coverage. This means that the program providing the six-count is only including the game that is being scored for the purposes of the graphic (India v Zimbabwe), and not the other game that is going on at the same time.

51

There had already been 3 sixes in the simultaneous Australia v Scotland match when Dhoni launched that ball into the Auckland night sky. It could be that the excitement was reserved for the other channel: David Warner hit the first ball after a long rain delay for six in that game, at roughly the same time as Dhoni's clout. Whether his or Dhoni's was the 374th may be a matter of conjecture. Or maybe it really doesn't matter that much after all.

March 15

WC Day 30. The Irish will be back home on St Patrick's Day. They lose fairly comfortably to Pakistan, despite Will Porterfield becoming the first Associate team captain to score a World Cup century. You would have thought that somewhere in World Cup history a wicket-keeper would have made more for Pakistan than Moin Khan's 63 against South Africa at Nottingham in 1999. But they hadn't, until today anyway, when Sarfraz Ahmed makes amends with 101*.

Keiron Pollard's return to the long game proves to be, well, short. After just one game he is now taking an 'indefinite break' from first-class cricket. Which seems like a long way to say something short like 'retire'. But there is hope in West Indies cricket. The 21-year-old Shai Hope makes 211 for Barbados against the Windward Islands. And, in taking 452 balls to make that score he suggests that he may, just possibly, be more suited to Test cricket than the IPL.

More hope for West Indies is that they beat UAE comfortably to qualify for the quarter-finals, despite a seventh wicket partnership of 107 between Amjad Javed and Nasir Aziz, which equalled the World Cup record set by the UAE themselves earlier in the tournament when Shaiman Anwar and Amjad Javed added that many against Ireland. In all, the UAE added 331 runs for the seventh wicket in the tournament at 55.16, the highest aggregate for any team for the seventh wicket in a World Cup. Not bad for an Associate team.

But that isn't even the best seventh wicket partnership for the day. At Centurion, the Dolphins collapse to 58-6 in their Sunfoil Series match against Titans chasing just 177 to win. But they get home thanks to a seventh wicket partnership of 116 between Morne van Wyk and Calvin Savage. In domestic first-class competition in South Africa there has been only one higher seventh wicket partnership in the fourth innings for a winning team: Dave Emslie and Pierre Tullis hold that obscure record with 138* for Eastern Province B v Western Province B at Uitenhage in 1985.

March 16

WC Day 31. There are two days off between the group stages and knockouts in the World Cup. And they are most welcome. The day is not as quiet as I would like it to be as the weekend's Sunfoil Series matches and Women's League matches need to be processed and the various logs and stats for these competitions need to be distributed. Not to mention dealing with numerous emails that I have not got around to replying to in the busyness of the World Cup. But, I am going to take it easy on the diary today. Although it is worth noting that KwaZulu-Natal Inland (45) and Mpumalanga (72) combined to bowl 117 wides in their 50-over Women's League game.

March 17

WC Day 32. It is St Patrick's Day, so it seems a good time to consider Ireland. Alert readers who have got this far in the diary will probably have noticed that I am in favour of their promotion to Test cricket (along with Afghanistan). Let me start with a stat: Over the past three World Cups combined Ireland have five wins over Full Members. Compare that to the four by England and Bangladesh and zero by Zimbabwe. It is also only one behind the West Indies' six. In short, Ireland have done all that they could have done to prove their ability in World Cups.

Statisticians like to have decent sample sizes that are without bias in order to make inferences, but with so few countries actually playing Test cricket out of the ICC's 105 members it is difficult to come to statistically based conclusions about the effects of Test cricket on a country. But, academics also like to look at case studies. And cricket has a very good case study in this regard. In 1997 Kenya and Bangladesh as the leading Associate members of the time were effectively ranked 10th and 11th in world cricket, respectively. That year, ICC awarded these two countries One-day International and first-class status (they were a bit more outward looking in the 20th century). Fast forward to 2015 and where are those two teams? Bangladesh are the ninth best team in the world and are playing in the World Cup quarter-finals this year. Kenya are languishing in the lower regions of World Cricket League Division Two, effectively the 19th best team around. Here is the difference: In 2000 Bangladesh got Test status, Kenya didn't. Test status allowed Bangladesh to play more matches across all formats and has irrefutably been beneficial to their cricket even though they have not, as yet, actually won many Tests. Surely this would be the same for other countries allowed into the exclusive fold. My view is that Ireland and Afghanistan should get Test status with regular matches against teams like Bangladesh and Zimbabwe, teams that they are clearly evenly matched and competitive with. It can only be beneficial to these countries, and the game as a whole, for there to be regular matches between these teams. It is hard to imagine that many people have ever been encouraged by being shut out, so why not make an attempt to be more inclusive? And the last point of this rant: It is surely undeniable that no team or individual in any sport has ever improved by *not* playing.

The day off also gives the CSA Awards Committee a chance to meet again, so it is off to the office I go for that one.

March 18

WC Day 33. Before every major game there is always speculation by those of all shades of expertise. And the bigger the game the more predictions float about. The quarter-finals start today with South Africa against Sri Lanka at Sydney and 'they' are all wrong. 'We' are all wrong. Sri Lanka score 133 and South Africa win with nine wickets and 32 overs to spare. It is the shortest successful run-chase in a World Cup knockout match, bettering the 20.1 overs Australia took to beat Pakistan in the 1999 final at Lord's.

The quarter-finals are an Associate-free zone, so we should have matches that are 'between teams that are evenly matched and competitive'. Wrong.

South Africa have not won a World Cup knockout game, or for that matter any of their last eight knockout games in ICC events stretching back to 2000. Therefore, they will 'ch ...' again. Wrong.

Sri Lanka are the only team apart from Australia with a positive win-loss record against South Africa. They should win. Wrong.

It will be another slugfest. After all there have been 25 totals over 300 in the tournament to date. Wrong.

Sixes, sixes everywhere like the rest of the tournament. Wrong. It is the first of the 42 games played in the tournament to date without a single ball flying over the ropes.

South Africa are in trouble if they bat second. They have won 25 and lost eight ODIs batting first since 1 January 2013, and won nine and lost 14 batting second in that time. Teams batting second in matches in Australia in this World Cup have won just six out of 20 matches. Wrong.

It is South Africa's seamers v Sri Lanka's batsmen. Wrong. For just the fourth time in their ODI history South Africa's spinners (Imran Tahir four, JP Duminy three) take seven wickets between them.

South Africa have had an uncharacteristic shortage of all-rounders lately so there is a constant debate between whether to choose seven batsmen or five bowlers. Perhaps they should go with five bowlers in such a big match. Wrong. The seventh batsman/fifth bowler, JP Duminy, takes South Africa's second ODI hat-trick (Charl Langeveldt v West Indies at Bridgetown in 2005 is the other) on his way to figures of 9-1-29-3.

They must drop Quinton de Kock who is having a terrible time at the tournament with just 53 runs in six innings. Rather get De Villiers to keep wicket. Wrong. De Kock starts proceedings with a great catch to dismiss Kushal Perera early on, and finishes them off with a sublime 78* off 57 balls.

All wonderfully, gloriously wrong. If you are South African, that is. It is not so wonderful and glorious for one of the great partnerships in world cricket history: The match is the final ODI for both Kumar Sangakkara and Mahela Jayawardene. They have played 376 ODIs together, easily the most by any pair (second are Sanath Jayasuriya and Muttiah Muralitharan on 307). But, it is not a happy ending for them.

By the way, De Kock wasn't even born on 22 March 1992, the day when South Africa's wretched relationship with World Cup knockouts began with the famous '22 off one ball' match at Sydney. He was born on 17 December 1992 and I did notice at least one wag, clearly an expert in birds and bees and subtraction, suggest that therefore 22 March may have been the day he was conceived.

It is interesting how the role of media statistician has changed in the 27 years that I have been doing it. In the old days when I started, the radio or TV statistician at the match was pretty much the sole source of statistics. In the modern world of pervasive media, stats are being generated all over the place. So, it is important for the statistician to be aware of all the stats floating around on the day and not just their 'own'. Thus, I tend to keep Twitter as well as ball-by-ball commentary open on the laptop, in order to be in touch with whatever other stats commentators may be aware of. Today I was caught out a bit when Mluleki Ntsabo mentions on Radio 2000 that Sri Lanka's Tharindu Kaushal is the second player to make his

ODI debut in a World Cup knockout game. He has either spotted that on TV or Twitter and having not thought of that, I have no idea who the other one is. A quick query on the database reveals it to be England's Wayne Larkins in 1979.

March 19

WC Day 34. India beat Bangladesh in the second quarter-final in a match of limited statistical interest. India have bowled the opposition out in all seven games in the tournament so far. They are the first team to dismiss all their opponents in seven consecutive World Cup matches. South Africa held that record with six consecutive games in the 2011 World Cup. MS Dhoni collects his 100th win as captain in ODIs joining Ricky Ponting (165) and Allan Border (107).

I have a bit of fun on Radio 2000 reading out a report saying that the World Cup in 2019 will have 20 teams and they are looking to expand this in 2023, before revealing that the World Cup referred to is in Japan in 2019 and is Rugby Union's. Still it is good to know that some sports administrators believe that their game is good enough that it should be possible to get people in non-traditional markets to play it.

March 20

WC Day 35. Pakistan lose all 10 wickets to catches for the third time in this World Cup as they limp to 213 against Australia. In the previous 10 World Cups there had been a grand total of two such cases. There have been four now in this World Cup including Pakistan's three. Australia win fairly comfortably despite an electrifying spell by Wahab Riaz. It is mildly disturbing however that two consecutive World Cup quarter-finals have produced so little to excite the world's stattos.

Playing for Dolphins v Lions in Durban, Daryn Smit collects his 100th first-class wicket, which is not a bad effort for a wicket-keeper. He also has 13 stumpings. This makes him the 17th player to have taken over 100 wickets and 10 stumpings in a first-class career. However this is a really ancient type of performance, as 14 of the other 16 all finished their careers by 1909. The remarkable George Brown managed to find time in between taking his 626 first-class wickets to whip the bails off with the batsman outside his crease 79 times. He also scored 25 649 runs in 612 matches between 1908 and 1933. The other multi-tasker of note since 1909 was Alan Smith who famously removed the gloves while captaining Warwickshire against Essex at Clacton-on-Sea in 1965 and became the only nominated wicket-keeper to take a first-class hat-trick.

March 21

WC Day 36. It is one of the most important days of the year. The Association of Cricket Statisticians and Historians is having their AGM in Derby. It is a wonderful organisation, and I have been a member since 1980. I have only managed to get to the AGM twice in that time, as the commute from Johannesburg to England is quite far. The Committee report notes that ACS has 1 076 members as at 30 November 2014, although disappointingly only 139 of these are from outside the UK. Declining sales of actual books made with real paper is an issue, as it is with most publishers these days. But, the ACS is joining the digital world: One item on the Agenda is to amend the rules to allow for 'attendance' at committee meetings to include Skype and telephone conference calls, and the project to digitise the remarkable publication *Cricket: A Weekly Record of the Game* is to go ahead. This journal ran from 1882 to 1913. And if that isn't enough to entice members, a lunch menu of Poached Salmon starter, Roast Leg of Pork with a Cider Apple Jus and Bakewell Tart for dessert should do the trick.

Oh, and there is also another World Cup quarter-final. It is a whackathon of note, even by this World Cup's standards. The unbelievable becomes ever more believable as Chris Gayle's highest ever World Cup score of 215 turns out to not even be the highest World Cup score of 2015. Martin Guptill scores 237* for New Zealand against West Indies at Wellington. It is the second highest ODI score and the fourth highest in all List A limited overs matches. There are 643 runs in the match off 80.3 overs at 7.98 runs per over, the third highest of all ODIs in which at least 50 overs were bowled. Having had the day off during the South Africa v Sri Lanka the Tournament Six Counter is back in business today and is busier than ever, as the 31 sixes is the joint second most in an ODI and smashes the previous World Cup record of 22. The West Indies reply to New Zealand's 393-6 with an even quicker run-rate, but their wicket-rate is predictably also much faster and they lose easily despite Chris Gayle becoming the first player to include 7 sixes in his first 50 runs in an ODI.

March 22

WC Day 37. There were only three days off in the first 36 of the tournament, but five of the remaining eight days have no play scheduled unless it rains. Today is the first day of the English season and there is definitely no rain on the opening game. It is a glorious 28 degrees centigrade as the first ball of the season is bowled. The game, of course, is taking place in Abu Dhabi. This is the sixth season that the traditional opening fixture between the champion county (Yorkshire, this time) and the MCC is being played under lights in Abu Dhabi. The main reason for this, apart from missing the usual cold April start at Lord's, is to experiment with a pink ball with a view to the possibility of playing Test cricket under lights. There is a dramatic start to the season as Ryan Sidebottom dismisses MCC captain Nick Compton with the first ball of the day. For me it is mainly the first chance of the year to listen to the dulcet (and not so dulcet) tones of the county commentators on the online streaming of the BBC radio commentary coverage of county cricket.

In Hobart, Victoria's leg-spinner Fawad Ahmed produces the best ever bowling figures in a Sheffield Shield final when he takes 8-89 against Western Australia. Those who know a little bit about Australian geography may have noticed that the venue for the match is in neither of the participating states. It is being held in Hobart because the preferred venue of the league-topping Victoria, the Melbourne Cricket Ground, is required for some other tournament until next Sunday.

March 23

WC Day 38. At my weekly session with my hand therapist, she informs me that I have the hand strength of an 80-year-old woman. My mother is 76, so, if she is average, she should be able to beat me at arm-wrestling. I had better keep doing those exercises.

History will be made tomorrow, as New Zealand are playing South Africa in the semi-final. Neither team has won a World Cup semi-final before — New Zealand in six attempts and South Africa in three. From a South African perspective it will either be The Greatest Day In History or The End Of The World As We Know It. Whatever the outcome any rational views somewhere within the continuum of these extremes will be as rare as a dot ball in the 50th over.

March 24

WC Day 39. South African born Grant Elliott turned 13 on 21 March 1992. I wonder what he was doing the next day as South Africa lost in the World Cup semi-final to England when their rain-reduced target meant they needed 22 off one ball (or at least that is what the scoreboard showed. It turned out that it was officially 21 off 1 ball). I wonder what 20-year-old Grant Elliott was doing when the famous Klusener/Donald run out ended South Africa's hopes in the 1999 semi-final against Australia. I suspect he was probably as distraught as most South African cricket fans on those days. Today, playing for New Zealand he is Man of the Match with 84* off 73 balls including a massive six to win the game off the penultimate ball from Dale Steyn. He will be going to the World Cup final. His former countrymen will not. Once again rain proved to be the Best Supporting Actor in South Africa's World Cup exit, as a break means that South Africa's 281-5 in 43 overs is adjusted to a target of 298 in 43 overs. New Zealand produce the highest successful run-chase in a World Cup knockout game, beating the 289-4 by Australia against New Zealand in the quarter-final at Madras in 1996. It is also the first time that New Zealand have won 10 consecutive ODIs. Brendon McCullum reaches his 50 off 22 balls. He is responsible for four of the nine World Cup fifties made off 22 or fewer balls. I am pleased to note that my prediction of much extreme opinion is wrong. In South Africa, most views on the game are entirely reasonable.

During South Africa's quarter-final match against Sri Lanka on 18 March, the conversation on Radio 2000 had turned to beards. When I mentioned that I last shaved in 1993, Mluleki Ntsabo challenged me to remove the beard if South Africa won the World Cup. It is kind of hard to disappoint all the radio listeners, so I felt compelled to accept the challenge. New Zealand's win over South Africa today means that at least my beard is safe. So, there is a silver lining to every Long White Cloud.

Colin Munro puts all the World Cup six bashers to shame by walloping 23 of them in a Plunket Shield match for Auckland against Central Districts at Napier. In over 56 000 first-class matches no one had ever hit more than 16 sixes in an innings. So, having suffered a jump of Bob Beamon proportions, the record must feel as smashed as the Central Districts bowlers did.

March 25

WC Day 962. Are we there yet? No, the World Cup is still going, but at least the end is in sight.

Victoria win the Sheffield Shield after a drawn final, but it is Western Australia's Adam Voges who has produced one of the finest Sheffield Shield seasons ever. His 1 358 runs at an average of 104.46 is the fourth highest aggregate in a season in the competition. This is the sixth time that a batsman has scored 1 000 at an average of over 100 in a Sheffield Shield season. One of the greatest Australian batsmen did it twice. No, not Sir Donald Bradman for a change (he only did it once), but Bill Ponsford who scored 1 091 runs at 136.37 in 1926/27 and the next season scored 1 217 at 152.12, famously including a century, a double-century, a triple-century and a quadruple-century in a four game sequence (though, sadly, not in that order).

March 26

WC Day 41. Australia post 328-7, becoming the first team to reach 300 in a World Cup semi-final. As per the pattern of the competition a score over 300 again provides a comfortable win as India subside gently to 233. The number of catches in the tournament passes 500. The previous most in any World Cup was 449 in 2003. India lose their first wicket during the batting powerplay in the tournament. They had scored 253 runs in 32 overs in that phase of the game before losing that wicket.

March 27

WC Day 42. No World Cup play today means there is time for a bit of contemplation. Bat has dominated ball in this World Cup to a far greater extent than ever before. Clearly there are a lot of fans who think this is a good thing, but I prefer a better contest between bat and ball. Test cricket has to maintain a balance between bat and ball: If batting becomes too easy then most games will end in draws and no one will watch. The limited overs game on the other hand has no specific need to maintain such a balance. It doesn't really matter how many runs are scored as you will still get a result on the day, although if there are really a lot of runs it may take a little bit longer as you have to keep fetching the ball after each shot. Assuming the view that some balance needs to be restored to the 50-over game is accepted (and it may be a wild assumption, but I am not really interested if the alternative view prevails), what can be done to achieve this? There are various aspects that need to be considered.

Firstly, modern bat technology has advanced to the point where the sweet spot is apparently two and a half times the size that it was. On this basis, you could take the view that current batsmen are the worst of all time. After all, a good total with the old bats used to be around 250 so with bats having a sweet spot two and a half times what they used to be you would expect totals to get up to around 625 (250 times 2.5) and they are only around 300. This is, of course, a bit facetious. A bit. But, maybe the thickness of bats needs to be regulated. And even if it is not, the ball is reaching the boundary quicker than it ever used to, so the rule allowing only four boundary fielders for most of the innings seems to be a cruel violation of natural justice. Restoring it to five is the minimum that should be done. Fielding restrictions in general may well be redundant and removing them completely is also something that should be considered.

Secondly, using two balls throughout the innings clearly favours the batsmen by keeping the ball hard for the last 10 overs and also virtually removing reverse swing from the equation. The problem, of course, is that in nearly 40 years of playing with a white ball it seems to have proved impossible to make one that lasts for 50 overs. The previous playing condition had a mandatory ball change after 35 overs as that is about how long the white ball lasts. Bearing this in mind, my suggestion would be to use two balls for the first 40 overs and then one of the two for the final 10 overs (preferably with the fielding team having the choice of which one to throw away). This will allow the ball to become a little softer and restore the possibility of a bit of reverse swing.

Thirdly, not only has reverse swing been largely eliminated, but the doosra is also on the way out with the crackdown on bowling actions. The number one and two ranked ODI bowlers before the tournament, Saeed Ajmal and Sunil Narine, did not appear in the World Cup as their actions did not fit the requisite maximum 15 degree elbow bend. This seems a bit of a waste to me. The laws against throwing were primarily introduced because of the danger posed by a fast bowler doing it. But spinners don't pose the same physical threat, so a bit more leeway for spinners which would allow the doosra back in would make the game better.

Finally, and I know this will offend some of the many 50-over traditionalists, but there has never been a really good reason for each individual bowler to be restricted to only 10 overs. Because of the restrictions, a wicket often means an opportunity to sneak in a few of the fifth bowler's allocation rather than opportunity to attack as would seem a more natural course of events. Allowing more overs per bowler will increase the overall standard of bowling and therefore allow the captains more attacking options. Conservative reaction means that there is next to no chance of getting agreement to bin the overs restriction on each bowler completely, but here is one of the better ideas I have heard to allow at least some additional overs to some bowlers: For each wicket that a bowler takes he is allowed an additional over. So, a bowler taking two wickets, for example, would be allowed 12 overs. It would make for a better game.

That's enough thinking for one day. Goodnight diary.

March 28

WC Day 43. The Lions had already secured the Sunfoil Series during the previous round of matches, but I manage to pop down to The Wanderers for the afternoon where they are playing Warriors. Neil McKenzie, having announced his retirement from the first-class game, scored 203* and he is just the 10th player to score a double-century in his last first-class innings. The only other South African to do this was Jack Siedle whose last three innings in first-class cricket were 105, 111 and 207 playing for Natal in 1936-37. McKenzie has always been known for his superstitions and so I found it mildly amusing that he was the 99th batsman to be run out on 99 in first-class cricket when he had that misfortune in the Test match against Australia in Cape Town in 2002. I have never told him that one, but it should be safe to let him know now that he has retired.

March 29

WC Day 44. And so, it ends. World Cup finals in many sports often prove to be a bit disappointing, except of course to the fans of the team that wins. Today is no exception. Australia dismiss New Zealand for 183. Although this is exactly the same total that India defended successfully in the 1983 World Cup final against West Indies times have moved on. New Zealand have no real chance and lose by seven wickets. Brendon McCullum is bowled by Mitchell Starc for a duck in the first over of the match. There is a lot of Twittering to the effect that he is the first captain to make a duck in a World Cup final, but I find the stat that this is the first time that a wicket has fallen in the first over of a World Cup final more interesting, not least because it is a bit more difficult to research.

Starc finishes the tournament with 22 wickets. Twelve of these were bowled and, even more astonishingly, eight were bowled for nought. Starc has only played one World Cup and he joins the great Wasim Akram, who played five World Cups, with the most batsmen bowled for a duck in a World Cup career. Starc's 22 wickets have come at an average of 10.18 and just 3.50 runs per over and he joins Courtney Walsh (1999) as the only bowlers to have had both the best average and the best economy rate in a World Cup. My personal choice for Player of the Tournament is Mrs S who has had to put up with me getting up at times when sensible people are asleep as well as having to take the kids to school more often than she usually does when I am around. If you had to give it to someone who actually played, however, Starc was the clear standout for the award.

Steven Smith becomes the first player to score 50s in five consecutive World Cup innings and he and Grant Elliott join Mike Brearley (1979), David Boon (1987), Javed Miandad (1992) and Aravinda de Silva (1996) as the only players to have scored a 50 in both the semi-final and final in the same year of a World Cup.

The World Cup has been long and hard work with unusual working hours for me and my overwhelming feeling is that I am just happy it is finished.

March 30

I don't think I am fully qualified to comment on whether there is rest for the wicked or not. But, I do know that there is definitely no rest for the cricket statistician. The World Cup may be finished, but there is still plenty else for me to do. The Sunfoil Series has ended and the stats need to be compiled for that. And there are six matches each in the finals rounds of the Women's Provincial 50-overs and 20-overs competitions which need to be captured and logs and averages distributed. More spreadsheets need to be sent to the Awards Committee. And so on and so on. It is another busy day.

March 31

Remarkably the live scores section on ESPNCricInfo says 'No matches being played at this time'. This is a very rare occurrence and undoubtedly not a Bad Thing. The cricket calendar would probably benefit from a few more days like this.

The rest of the world continues, however. The SA Cricket Awards evening always features some form of entertainment and one of the best in recent years was comedian, Trevor Noah. Today Noah is announced as the new host for the *Daily Show* in America replacing long-time incumbent Jon Stewart. So there's one for li'l' old South Africa.

The lack of actual cricket gives me the opportunity to spend a bit of time catching up with checking all the South African scores with the official scoresheets as I start to prepare for doing my part for the South African Cricket Annual, edited by Colin Bryden, a task that has occupied a fair amount of my time each winter for the past 20 years.

April 1

Simon Barnes has written an article on ESPNCricInfo suggesting the possibility that combination of T20 type batting with Test match field placings in the World Cup has made the ODI the leading form of the game. Or, to put it another way: The Piggy-In-The-Middle has become the Goldilocks option. It is an interesting point and I certainly approve the Test match field placings, although I don't agree with the overall premise. But April Fools' Day is not the time to get involved in a debate if you want to be taken seriously.

April 2

The English season starts (again). Yes, it started in Abu Dhabi a couple of weeks ago, but the first first-class matches actually in England begin today. To say that the start of the English season is understated is a bit of an understatement. It all begins with counties playing matches against the six university teams recognised as first-class. No opening ceremony, no cheerleaders, no dancers, no fireworks and no pop concerts. Just 15 people in white walking out onto the various fields. There is actually no good reason why the university teams have first-class status, but the matches give the county players an opportunity for a gentle warm-up and not so gentle padding of their averages, and the university players the opportunity to put 'first-class cricketer' on their CVs which will presumably impress at least some prospective bosses when they apply for real jobs after graduation.

April 3

It is a quiet day as the Easter Weekend begins. Apart from the English season there are some low-key T20 tournaments in India and Sri Lanka which need to be added to the database, but not much else.

April 4

In 2011, Barney Gibson became the youngest first-class cricketer in England when he made his debut as wicket-keeper for Yorkshire at the age of 15 years, 27 days. That is going to be his only appearance, as he announces his retirement from the game today. On the ACS mailing list, Keith Walmsley provides the information that Tasnim Akhtar of Sargodha at 13 years, 180 days is the youngest player to appear in his last first-class match, although Gibson obviously holds the English record.

April 5

Baseball's back! The Major League season starts today and I will be following as closely as cricket time allows. With a bit of luck I will be able to catch some games on TV as well as listening to live streaming audio coverage. Virtually every day for the next six months (and hopefully seven, if they make the playoffs) one of the first emails I will open in the morning is the one that tells me how the Boston Red Sox have done overnight.

Unlike cricket, baseball has retained the concept of a season. Each team plays 162 games in the regular season before the playoffs and this is how it has been since 1961 when the number of games was raised from the 154 that it had been since 1904. So, you know what each season looks like. On the other hand cricket, at international level at least (and this is the cricket that people actually watch and follow), is a continuous treadmill, devoid of season. You have to be a dedicated follower of domestic cricket to understand the concept of a season in modern cricket. Maintaining the concept of a season, as baseball does, gives the fan something to look forward to in terms of rhythms and tempos as well as a high degree of certainty of dates. So, you can say 'Baseball's back!' with a sense of excitement and anticipation.

April 6

It is party time as the family gathers to celebrate my father's birthday. It is not his actual birthday, of course. That is on the 12th, but I will be away by then so we need to do the party in advance.

April 7

The Red Sox have opened their season with an 8-0 win over the Philadelphia Phillies. Hanley Ramirez was brought up through the Red Sox farm system and played two games for the team in 2005, but has spent the past nine years at the Miami Marlins and Los Angeles Dodgers. On his return to the Red Sox yesterday he hit two home runs, including a grand slam (a home run with bases loaded, scoring four runs, for those needing an explanation). The Red Sox have gone worst to first to worst in the past three years. So, although there is no statistical basis to expect this, I am hoping that the pattern continues for one more year. Don't worry, dear reader, I am not going to bore you with baseball every day for the next six months, but there is nothing of interest in the cricket world today.

It is the final CSA Awards meeting with all the various competitions having finished. Again, some of the judging panel are away so contribute via Skype. Victor Mpitsang is in Bangladesh with South Africa Under-19s, while HD Ackerman is at home in Durban prior to leaving for a commentary stint at the IPL. Neil Manthorp 'attended' the previous meeting via Skype from Australia, but is there in person for this one. The cricket world is always busy.

April 8

It has been a lot of hard work for the three months so far this year and I could do with a holiday. Antigua, maybe? Grenada, perhaps? Barbados? Fortunately those are the places I will be heading to tomorrow. It won't be a holiday however as I will be there to work on England's Test matches for BBC's Test Match Special. So, there is some last minute planning for the trip to be done.

The IPL starts today.

April 9

The major sporting news of the day is that Jack Nicklaus has made the first hole-in-one of his career at the tender age of 75. He did this in the Masters Par 3 Contest at Augusta. It is good to know that there is hope for all of us.

I am flying to New York tonight on my way to Antigua and it is the usual busy last day before travel. The actual packing is not such a big deal, but there always seems to be so many other things to finalise before I go. Somehow travel days provide a deadline for all sorts of things on the To Do list, some of which have been lurking there for months. It is going to be a 16-hour flight.

April 10

I arrive in New York to the news (not very big in New York itself) that Richie Benaud, one of the great men of cricket, has died. So, it is a sad day for the game and the inevitable, but appropriate, hashtag '#mourningeveryone' soon appears.

I am sure some readers may be appalled by this, but today provides the highlight of the year so far as I go to Yankee Stadium for the Yankees v Red Sox game. This is one of the great rivalries of not just baseball but all sport, although the current teams aren't quite as star-studded as they were in the first decade of the 21st century. Disappointingly the stadium is only about three quarters' full, but most cricket games would be very happy to draw as many as 41 292 spectators. It turns out to be an extraordinary game. With two outs in the bottom of the ninth the Red Sox are leading (as they have done through the whole game) 3-2, but Chase Headley hits a home run to tie it up. At this point there is a major conflict between The City That Never Sleeps and The Cricket Statistician That Needs Sleep. It is already 10:15pm and I need to get back to my hotel in Newark which will take an hour and a half and then be awake at 6:00 to get to my flight to Antigua. I decide to watch the top half of the 10th innings in the hope that the Red Sox score and then I can watch the bottom of the 10th and with a bit of luck see the Red Sox win. No runs are scored in the top of the 10th so I head back to the hotel. (From my cricketing perspective, it is an honourable 3-3 draw, but baseball needs a winner). I arrive back at the hotel at 11:55 and switch on the TV to see that the 14th innings is nearly done. Eventually the Red Sox win 6-5 in 19 innings (while I am asleep, of course). At six hours 49 it is the longest Yankees-Red Sox game ever.

Earlier I spend the afternoon walking through Manhattan. New York is a great city to walk around, although it is a bit of a strain on the neck as you are always looking up at the various skyscrapers. Today I walk the Highline from 34th Street. The Highline is an interesting concept. It used to be a freight railway line elevated 30 feet above the ground. After falling into disuse, it was revived as a public walkway with various plants scattered around and provides a different view of the city. Admittedly early April (the end of winter) is not the ideal time to observe the plants as there is not much life in them currently. From the end of the Highline at 14th Street, I walk across to Broadway and then down all the way to the new World Trade Centre precinct and my first view of the new World Trade Centre buildings. Two of the four planned new buildings have been completed. But it has been cloudy all day and the top of one of them at 80 storeys is lost in the clouds. Then it is a sombre walk through the 9-11 Memorial Museum before heading off to Yankee Stadium but not before I have a lox (salmon and cream cheese) bagel at my favourite New York Deli. It proves impossible to get Sinatra out of my head while walking around the greatest city in the world.

April 11

I fly from New York into Antigua where it is a bit warmer than the 10 degrees centigrade that I have had the previous 24 hours. I had to pack a warm jacket for the New York visit and it will spend the next month cluttering up my bag without being needed again. I catch up with some of the members of the Test Match Special team. While I am not a great imbiber of alcoholic drinks, I have my first rum punch of the tour on the When In Rome principle. I am not in Rome, of course, although I have visited there as a tourist. My next visit to Rome will be when Italy play their first cricket Test, which may not be for quite a long time.

Dinner is snapper, my first fish of the tour. There is a lot of water and, therefore, fish in this part of the world. I am not a great expert on diets, but I have always understood that eating fish is good for the brain. On that basis I should be quite clever by the time I leave the islands in early May.

April 12

It is a quiet day lounging around the resort we are staying at, doing a bit of preparation for the Test starting tomorrow. I do this while taking in views of one of Antigua's 365 beaches. That's right — one for each day of the year. I am not sure what they do on 29 February.

The County Championship starts today. This is always a great time of the year, as the venerable competition begins another season. Although some of the gloss has been lost in recent times with the decrease in quality and quantity of overseas players specifically, it will provide lots of interest over the next six months. With up to eight games going on at the same time there will always be something fascinating happening in at least some of the games. Today I listen to a bit of the commentary from the Somerset v Durham game (Somerset collapse from 224-2 to 299 all out). Having scored centuries in his last two ODIs, Brendan Taylor becomes the first player to score centuries in his first two first-class matches for Nottinghamshire as he makes 106 v Middlesex at Lord's to follow his 105 against Loughborough Marylebone Cricket Club University last week.

In the Relegation match in Sri Lanka, Galle recover from making 31 in their first innings to beat Sri Lanka Air Force Sports Club by four runs. It is the lowest total made by a team which went on to win a first-class match since 1924 when Gloucestershire beat Middlesex after being bowled out for 31. Hampshire still hold the overall record having beaten Warwickshire in 1922 after being bowled out for 15 in their first innings.

April 13

It is great to have Test cricket back. I know this will sound really fuddy-duddy, but cricket just looks better in white clothes. Somehow the contrast of the white against the green background of the field is more pleasing on the eye than, say, green on green for example. Coloured clothing is pretty normal in most sports these days, but I do not know of any other sport that is played in kit that is quite as loud as cricket's.

This Test match is being played from Monday to Friday which does not seem to be an ideal time to attract spectators. At least today there is a pretty good crowd as the government has declared a half-holiday to encourage people to get to the cricket. While there is a lot of angst around the numbers of spectators actually attending Test cricket, it has to be noted that cricket owns the Office Hour Sports market. What other sport is played while people are at work? If you are looking for sporting entertainment at your office only cricket provides this. Think about it: If you are bored in a meeting you are unlikely to be able to check out any live scores of other sports while pretending to look at the important spreadsheet on your laptop. But, you can check out what is happening in a live cricket match. You just need to make sure that you don't shout 'Yes' if your team takes a wicket while the boss is waffling on about declining third quarter sales of widgets in the West Region. Especially not if you are the person responsible for the sales of widgets in the West Region.

Ian Bell has been playing Test cricket for 12 years and built up a fine record. This is the 16th time he has played in the first Test of a series on tour and he scores 143 which is, surprisingly, the first time that he has made a century in the opening match of a series away from home.

In the County Championship Paul Collingwood has done the double of a century and five wickets in an innings for Durham against Somerset at the age of 38 years, 322 days. Although there are many older players who did this in the good old days when many county players were still playing well into their 40s, Collingwood is the oldest since John Shepherd who was 39 years, 198 days when he scored 168 and took 7-50 for Gloucestershire v Warwickshire at Birmingham in 1983.

April 14

It is a gentle day, although England start it by collapsing to 399 all out. I look up a few obscure stats: Having lost their first three wickets for 34 and their last six for 58, England's 399 turned out to be the second highest total by a team losing the first three wickets for less than 40 and their last six for less than 60 behind West Indies' 431 v Australia at Kingston in 1999

(Brian Lara made 213 of those) and then Ed Smith challenges me to find a list of players who had spent half their lives playing Test cricket following the realisation that Shiv Chanderpaul had done this (he made his debut at 19 and is now closing in on 41). I manage to find 15 cases which I do by using a couple of my standard database queries, Youngest on Debut and Longest Careers. By merging the results from these two queries I can then answer the question by selecting those whose careers were longer than their debut ages. By the way, Chanderpaul is one of only three players to have played Test cricket as a teenager and also after the age of 40 along with Sachin Tendulkar and Brian Close (22 Tests in 27 years).

I also while away some of the time while West Indies consolidated quietly/blocked boringly by searching for Graeme Swann's only wide in Test cricket. Swann did not bowl a no-ball in his career — which is impressive Extras Discipline, unmatched in Test history by anyone else who bowled the equivalent of at least 2 500 six-ball overs. He bowled his only wide to Praveen Kumar at Birmingham in 2011. Swann lets us know that it was a deliberate attempt to get a leg-side stumping, which is an entirely plausible explanation given that Kumar whacked him for 36 runs off 11 balls in that innings.

April 15

There is a first for me today. I tend to sit in the seat in the least accessible corner of the commentary box, for the simple reason that I sit there all day while the commentators and summarisers rotate in the other chairs. When there is a special guest, however, I generally have to sacrifice my chair for that guest while the commentators remain where they are. Today I am evicted from my seat by a Prime Minister. Antigua's Gaston Browne has come into the commentary box for a lunch-time chat with Jonathan Agnew and Viv Richards.

April 16

Gary Ballance scores 122 as England set up their declaration. He now has four centuries in just nine Tests. At the end of the innings he has 861 runs at 61.50 in his career. Only Herbert Sutcliffe and Andrew Strauss have scored more runs in their first nine Tests for England.

Geoffrey Boycott has the most amazing memory of the innings he has played, unlike anyone else I have come across, so when he mentions that he scored 99 and 113 against West Indies at Port-of-Spain in 1974, I can't help pointing out that it was actually 99 and 112.

April 17

West Indies save the match with a remarkable performance. They end on 350-7 and become only the fourth team to save a Test match batting for more than 50 overs after the loss of the sixth wicket in the final innings of the game. Jason Holder joins Daniel Vettori, Ajit Agarkar and Matt Prior as the only players to have scored a century batting at number eight or lower in the fourth innings of a Test. It takes a bit of research to discover that Holder's previous best first-class score of 52 is the joint third lowest by a player making their maiden Test 100. His team-mate, Jerome Taylor holds that record with 40, while New Zealand's Bruce Taylor had a previous first-class best of 49 before his first Test 100 and South Africa's Tuppy Owen-Smith also had 52 (in his case not out).

Jimmy Anderson finally passes Ian Botham's England record when he dismisses Denesh Ramdin. He had needed four wickets at the start of the match, so it was a bit of a wait before he got there in the final session. Botham had held the record since 5pm on 1 July 1985 when he dismissed Australia's Graeme Wood at Lord's to pass Bob Willis' 325. I calculated the length of time that Botham had held the record at 10 882 days, three hours, 53 minutes. When I tweeted the longest time that anyone had been England's leading-wicket taker for, I made a typo. Instead of saying that Botham held the record between the years 1985-2015, I managed to type '1985-12015', leading to inevitable responses to the effect that that was a very, very long time. Only SF Barnes (14 949 days between 1912 and 1953) had held the record for longer than Botham.

April 18

It is a day off and much of it is spent with the Test Match Special team on Love Beach (we couldn't make it to the other 364 beaches on the island in the limited time available). The beaches really are stunning in this part of the world and this one is no exception. We play a bit of beach cricket and watch a spectacular sunset. I am reminded of what I consider as probably my greatest playing achievement in cricket. On my previous visit to Antigua I had managed to get a tennis ball to turn (with my loopy leg-spin) *up* the slope on a beach. I was very chuffed with that, and was still admiring it as the local batsman smashed it way into the sea.

April 19

I fly to Grenada at 17:30 with some of the Test Match Special team. The flight turns out to be a charter plane organised by one of the English supporter travelling parties. Travel around the West Indies on this tour has proved to be an interesting challenge for some. The thousands of English cricket fans on the tour means that there are rather more people moving around the islands than usual. This leads to stories of some of the media flying from Antigua to Grenada via places like Miami and one or two who have had to stop on five different islands on their way there. While boarding the plane Tony Cozier informs me that LIAT (the main airline in this part of the world) has just got a new fleet of planes. I verify this when, for the first time in my experience there are no 'No Smoking' lights above the seat. They have been replaced by 'No Laptops/Electronic Devices' lights, a true sign of the times.

There are quite a few security cameras at airports around the world that will have photos of me in various states from mildly frazzled to downright grumpy after a long international flight. The greeting at Grenada's Maurice Bishop airport is about as friendly as these things get, with steel bands, rum samplers, and smiles from officials. So the cameras probably actually have some pictures of travellers with smiles on their faces.

April 20

News comes through of an innings of 350 off 138 balls by Liam Livingstone in a club game for Nantwich v Caldy in the Cheshire League. This is originally claimed as a world record for any limited overs game. The problem is that there are no proper records kept for what is termed 'minor' cricket and not surprisingly the 'record' is soon debunked with a 358 and a 381 coming to light. AEJ Collins' famous 628* in a timeless match between Clarke's House and North Town House at Clifton College in 1899 remains the highest known score in all cricket.

Livingstone has played cricket for Lancashire Second XI, but has not played a first-class match. However, last year he appeared as 12th man during the Manchester Test match. I had been reliably informed that he was the 12th man, but, of course had no idea what he looked like. The commentators also had no idea who he was so when he first fielded the ball and they asked who the 12th man was, I couldn't resist saying 'It's Livingstone, I presume'.

April 21

The 150th Test match between West Indies and England begins at the National Cricket Stadium in St George's. Only the Ashes (336 matches) has seen more Tests between two countries. The ground is the 42nd that I have watched a Test match at. It turns out to be a fairly tedious day with West Indies finishing on 188-5 in 70 overs following a delayed start. The TMS commentary diverts away from the cricket more than usual with classical music, Great Gatsby, West Indian sunsets and the first cake we have received for the tour all getting attention amongst other things.

Meanwhile, the woodwork is being denuded as more big limited overs scores in minor games have appeared including at least three quadruple hundreds. We will probably never have a definitive list.

April 22

It is a fairly nondescript day as West Indies muddle their way to 299 and England reply with 76-0 at the close. The highlight is a 10th wicket partnership of 52 for West Indies in which Shannon Gabriel at number 11 scores 20*. Which is a pretty good effort for a man with a Test average of 3.00 and first-class average of 4.90. In 58 previous first-class matches his best score was 16. After his epic 20*, his averages increase to 5.50 in Tests and 5.36 in first-class.

April 23

Alastair Cook and Jonathan Trott put on 125 for the first wicket. It is England's first century opening partnership since Cook and Nick Compton added 231 against New Zealand at Dunedin in March 2013. The 40 innings in between these two is the longest run England have ever had without having a century opening partnership. Even more remarkable is that West Indies have had 67 innings against them without conceding a century opening partnership. You may have expected something like that in their finest days of great fast bowlers in the 1980s and 1990s, but it is quite a surprising achievement in the current, not so great, era.

Disappointingly, Cook gets out for 76 and it is another innings in his sequence without a century. It does however, allow the opportunity for Tom Hayward to get a mention in the commentary as Cook's 34 innings without a century is now the second longest by an England opener behind Mike Brearley's 41 and nudges Hayward, the first of Jack Hobbs' great opening partners, into third place on that list with 33.

April 24

When I wake the computer up I notice that my service provider's home page has a link to an article on the '20 Greatest Beaches In The World'. So, I sit looking out of my hotel room at the Grand Anse beach in Grenada and page through the beaches wondering where this one fits in. I am most disappointed to get through all of them without seeing the Grand Anse. There is only one from the cricket playing West Indian islands that makes this list. Whoever wrote the article needs to get out more and see more beaches. Now, now, don't all volunteer at once.

Joe Root becomes the second youngest to score 2 000 Test runs for England as his extraordinary run of form continues. This innings is 182*. He now has 1 101 runs in his last nine Tests at 110.10 including reaching 50 in each of his last six innings. He is, however, involved in three run outs. It takes a bit of research to confirm that he is the seventh player to have been involved in three run outs in one innings in Test cricket and the second Englishman, after Bill Athey, to claim this dubious honour. Athey's was in a manic run chase against Pakistan at Birmingham in 1987. On that occasion England were chasing 124 in 18 overs and finished on 109-7 with two balls remaining. You can't help thinking that most teams would chase a target like that quite easily these days.

Most attention, however, is not on the stats, but is reserved for Marlon Samuels who, having been involved in a sledging war with Ben Stokes, stands to attention, hat on heart, and gives a salute as Stokes walks past him having holed out with a horrible shot to the cow corner boundary.

April 25

England pull off an astonishing win. West Indies begin the day on 202-2 with a lead of 37. Early in the day, I point out that 118 teams had gone into the final day of a Test match batting in the third innings with a lead and two or fewer wickets down and only three of these had lost. Of these, one was when Garry Sobers made a bizarre declaration against England at Port-of-Spain in 1968 leading to an easy target which England chased down. The other two teams to have lost from this position were India v England at Delhi in 1984 and England v Australia at Adelaide in 2006. West Indies joined them today. Jimmy Anderson bowls a magnificent spell with the new ball and is involved in all six dismissals before lunch, with three wickets, two catches and a run out.

There are some stats that you think are quite good but don't get a great deal of attention, and vice versa. There are also some that you know will go down quite well. These often, but by no means exclusively, involve great names like Sir Donald Bradman. There is one such today. Joe Root has now made the highest score of a Test match seven times in his 24 Tests. His 29.16% in this category is second only to Bradman who made the top score of the match 20 times in his 52 Tests (which is 38.46%, in case you were reaching for your calculator). Root has knocked another great name, Graeme Pollock (six out of 23 — 26.08%), into third place.

Another stat that inevitably goes down quite well is Gary Ballance becoming the third quickest to reach 1 000 Test runs (17 innings) for England joining the likes of Herbert Sutcliffe (12), Len Hutton (16) and Wally Hammond (18) on that list.

April 26

It is a 'Me' day. With my various cricketing and family commitments I seldom get the opportunity to have a day totally to myself. Today is one:

Wake up late.

Do some reading (It is the autobiography of well-known West Indies broadcaster Reds Perreira, which I had obtained from the man himself during the Antigua Test).

Have a late breakfast.

Skype the family.

Have afternoon sleep.

More reading.

Long walk down the beach.

Room service in the evening while watching the Mets play the Yankees on the TV.

All pretty blissful.

Somewhere in between all this I manage to tweet about Oliver Robinson becoming just the seventh player to score a century on first-class debut batting at number nine. He made 110 for Sussex v Durham. More interestingly he shared a 10th wicket partnership of 164 with Matthew Hobden. After a fair bit of tapping the keyboard I am able to confirm that this is the second highest 10th wicket partnership involving a debutante in first-class cricket history. On his first-class debut for New South Wales v Victoria at Sydney in 1912 Cecil McKew shared a partnership of 169 for the last wicket with Australian Test cricketer, Roy Minnett. McKew's contribution was all of 29.

April 27

It is another quiet day off lounging around the beach resort. I have another afternoon sleep. It is the first time I have had afternoon sleeps on consecutive days since 2002, so that is the record for the day.

April 28

It is tourist time, as I do a trip into St George's, the main settlement in Grenada. It is a charming little port town full of narrow and very steep streets. A visit to Fort George proves disappointing. The fort has a fair amount of history, having been originally built in the 1660s and gone through the usual transfers from colonial powers. In 1983 it was the scene of the slaying of Prime Minister Maurice Bishop in a coup that led to the subsequent American invasion. However, it is not maintained as an historic building at all, so from that point of view it is overpriced at a US$2 entry fee. The major upside of visiting the fort is the spectacular view across the island. I am amused in the souvenir shops in town to discover 'Made in South Africa' signs on a number of items. I feel compelled to buy some, as it is not often on tour that you get to make a simultaneous contribution to the economies of both the country that you are visiting and the one that you are from. Well, nano-contribution, actually.

In the evening we fly to Barbados. It is another charter plane carrying English cricket fans, as the island's normal flight schedule does not have the capacity to cope with the demand. Over 5 000 English fans are expected to be at the Test match. Of course the famous Typically Tropical song *Whoa, I am going to Barbados* gets stuck in everyone's minds. Generally a trip to Barbados is regarded as a significant upgrade from wherever you are coming from. In this case I am not so sure it is. Although Barbados is regarded as the jewel in the Caribbean crown, especially amongst the cricket-playing world, Grenada has been wonderful with the spectacular Grand Anse beach and a clearly less commercialised tourist mind-set.

April 29

Daniel Lawrence has scored a century for Essex against Surrey at The Oval at the age of 17 years, 290 days, making him the third youngest player to score a century in the County Championship. He also threatened WG Grace's record of being the youngest Englishman to score a double-century, before getting out for 161. The reporting of the record is interesting. Godfrey Bryan is the youngest, having scored 124 for Kent v Nottinghamshire at Nottingham in 1920 at the age of 17 years, 247 days. However, he is generally given as being 17 years, 245 days in most reports I see. The discrepancy is because he made his century on the third day of the match, but most database programs, including mine, do the calculation of ages as at the first day of the match. This is mainly because it is much easier to program than to try and figure out programmatically which day of the match the century or other milestone was achieved. Not to mention that we don't always have full close of play details that are needed for these calculations. Not at first-class level anyway, although we do have it for Test cricket. So, whenever I do a query involving dates, I always then check the actual scorecard to see which day of the match the event happened. Dipak Patel is the second youngest, correctly reported at 17 years, 270 days for Worcestershire v Surrey at Worcester in 1976. He scored his century on the first day of the match.

April 30

Ah, Barbados. Palm trees, glorious beaches, sun, fun, and sand, a wonderful place to visit. I spend the morning in the library. The search for cricket information is endless and I am looking to find more details of things that don't appear in old scorecards but may be reported in the newspapers of the day — things such as innings timings and boundaries, fielders involved in run outs and any other little bits of extra information that can enhance the scorecard. I manage to plug a few gaps in some Test scorecards, but the main prize eludes me: In 1944 Frank Worrell scored 308 for Barbados against Trinidad in Bridgetown. This is the only first-class triple century for which no additional information is available. The match report in the *Barbados Advocate* is extensive ('... Goddard scored a single off Pouchet, and then Worrell hit him to the fine leg boundary. Worrell now had 258 and Goddard 131 ...'), but there are no details of how long he batted or how many boundaries he hit.

The afternoon is spent much more productively, as the doyen of West Indies cricket broadcasters and journalists and one of the great men of cricket, Tony Cozier, takes Ed Smith, Graeme Swann and me on a trip around the east coast of his beloved island. (I am sure Tony must be tired of being called a 'doyen', but it is as appropriate for him as anyone in world cricket). The east coast is much wilder and less developed than the more touristy west coast, and all the more spectacular for it. So, it is a very relaxing afternoon with stops at a number of rum shacks thrown in as we get ready for tomorrow's Test match.

May 1

Alastair Cook finally makes a century. For most of his previous 35 Test innings since his last one, there has been intense media scrutiny counting those innings and wondering when the next 100 will come. So, it must be a great relief to him. England finish on 240-7 after a good day of Test cricket, but one with limited statistical interest, although Cook's 100 is the

100th in Test cricket at the famous Kensington Oval in Bridgetown, one of the iconic venues for the game.

May 2

An extraordinary day sees 18 wickets fall, which is the most in a day of Test cricket in West Indies. It is an England Collapso, then a Calypso Collapso then another England Collapso which leaves the match delicately poised at the end of the day with England 107 ahead in their second innings with five wickets in hand.

Tino Best, summarising for TMS, asks on air how many different XIs Shiv Chanderpaul had appeared with in his 164 match Test career. This provides an interesting database challenge. To do it properly would need an 11 by 11 matrix for each team in each match and would be beyond the limitations of my software. So, I 'cheat' a bit. Each player is uniquely identified by a number in my database. By simply adding up the player numbers for each team in each match I can create a number that identifies the XI. There is a very small possibility of compensatory errors in this process (e.g. if players numbered one and four are in one XI and are replaced by players numbered two and three in the next team the team total number would stay the same even though the XIs are different). But I am confident that this is very unlikely and am therefore prepared to announce that Chanderpaul appeared with 149 different XIs in his 164 Tests.

My understanding of parenting is that it is essentially a process of transferring dependence. When a child is born it is 100% dependent on its parents. By the time he or she is 21 they are 100% independent, legally at least. I mention this because today Mrs S and I reach one third of our way through parenting, measured from the day of the birth of the first daughter to the 21st birthday of the second one.

May 3

The West Indies pull off a tremendous win by five wickets chasing 192. The match had shaped up to be a real classic, but turned on a missed stumping that would have made the score 87-5. The 21st century has been a far cry from the West Indies' great days of the 1980s and 1990s when they dominated the cricket world, and England especially, and today's win is just their second, set against 18 defeats, in the last 29 Tests between these teams. So the series ends at 1-1. From my perspective it has been fairly quiet statistically speaking.

May 4

Whenever a Test match or tour finishes early there is an inevitable scramble amongst all involved to change flights, especially if the option is to get home. Not surprisingly the scramble to leave Barbados isn't as intense as it is to leave most other places on the circuit. I make a dash for Boston to see an old mate and get to Fenway Park, home of the Red Sox. It is a long day. I wake at 04:00 to get to the airport for the 07:10 flight to Miami. Things get interesting at Miami. My 14:35 connecting flight to Washington is delayed by an hour, which means that with an 18:00 landing time in Washington I might struggle to get to my 18:30 flight to Boston. The airline is very helpful and moves me to a direct flight to Boston at 15:15 and then, having dashed to the new boarding gate, I am pleasantly surprised to be upgraded to first-class. This is a very rare occurrence for me. Although I don't keep statistics on it I think I have only been upgraded from economy five times in my flying career (all on domestic flights). At the time of typing I have yet to think of a title for this book, but today's experience makes me think 'First-class from Miami' may be something to consider. Of course, 'First-class' has been used in cricket book titles before, e.g. *First-class Cricket A Complete Record 1929* and variations on that, but I very much doubt that there has ever been a cricket book with 'Miami' in the title. Although I now get to Boston an hour and a half earlier than I expected, my bag steadfastly adheres to the original schedule, so I have to wait at Logan Airport for it anyway.

May 5

The day is spent walking through the city of Boston. I arrive at South Station and walk up through Boston Common heading towards the Charles River. Boston is a wonderful city with what I would call a nice level of busyness. It is not the hectic, commercially driven busyness of the major cities like New York and London. Nor is it too sleepy. Boston is home to some of the great academic institutions of America, if not the world, not to mention some of America's most important historical heritage. As such it has a much more contemplative air than New York. If New York is coffee, Boston is tea. So its busyness level is just right for me. Hello Goldilocks. Again. That's enough pretentious city waffle for now. I am off to the ballgame.

Tonight provides a rare sojourn into the world of sport's fandom for me. I go to Fenway Park for the Red Sox v Tampa Bay Rays game and it turns out to be a wonderful evening, trumping the game at Yankee Stadium as the highlight of the year to date. Fenway Park, having hosted its first game in 1912 is the oldest of Major League Baseball's current stadiums and as such, greatly loved. Boston's leadoff hitter Mookie Betts crunches two solo home runs over the famous Green Monster to provide the only run-scoring plays in the game for a 2-0 win. Apparently it is the first time that the Red Sox have won a game since 1940 where the only scoring plays were two solo home runs by the same player. You've got to love sport stats.

There were three bonuses at the game. Firstly, instead of the USA national anthem being sung it is played on the saxophone (perhaps the greatest musical instrument invented by mankind). Then there is a reunion of the 1975 Red Sox team with many of the players on that team being introduced to, and loudly cheered by, the crowd. The 1975 Red Sox team lost one of the more famous World Series to the Cincinnati Reds. Game 6 of that series is regarded as the greatest game of baseball ever played and was ended by a walkoff home run by Red Sox catcher Carlton Fisk. In one of the most iconic sporting images ever, Fisk was shown 'waving' the ball fair. And bonus number three: It was Carlton Fisk bobblehead day, so everyone who arrived early enough, including me, got a free Carlton Fisk bobblehead doll with their ticket. Yippee!

May 6

It is a tourist day in Boston. I am amazed to bump into my doctor's receptionist in a book shop in the main shopping centre in town. It is a small world, etc, etc. Lunch is New England Clam Chowder as you do in this part of the world, and then I go on one of the famous Duck Tours of the town. The 'Ducks' are amphibious vehicles, so you drive around looking at the various sights of town and also have a boat ride on the Charles River without the inconvenience of having to change vehicles.

Disappointing news has come via the ACS mailing list. The game mentioned on 12 April in this diary where Galle won after being dismissed for 31 has apparently been ruled not first-class by Sri Lanka cricket. So, a great stat disappears down the administrators' drain.

May 7

I choose to travel from Boston to New York by bus. Mainly this is because it is quite a bit cheaper than flying and at around four hours, not that much longer door-to-door (in theory anyway). But also it gives you a chance to see more of the countryside than you would if you fly or even go by train. You even get to stop, albeit briefly, in places you would never go to otherwise, like Hartford, Connecticut. Often, but not always, these stops remind you why you wouldn't visit these places in the first place.

In the evening I go to Yankee Stadium. I have already been to two baseball games this trip so I consider doing something different this time. However, the pull of potential history proves too strong. The Yankees hitter Alex Rodriguez is on 660 home runs, tied with Willie Mays for fourth place all-time and the chance to be there for number 661 is impossible to resist. Rodriguez missed the entire 2014 season as a result of a suspension for using performance enhancing substances. He duly delivers home run number 661 to go into fourth place on his own and I can claim 'I was there' for a bit of history, however flawed it may be in this instance. The level of excitement is relatively muted in the circumstances and the Yankees are insisting that as a result of his tainted past they will not be paying him a $6 million bonus that is in his contract for passing various home-run hitting milestones. Anyway I was there. I didn't stay for the whole game as my $5 seat (an appropriate price for a cheapened bit of history) in the 'nose-bleeds' induced a bout of vertigo that I needed to escape from, and I instead did a pleasant walk around central Manhattan in the evening watching the city stay awake, as it does. At around 10:30pm I witness an 'Only in New York' confrontation. A smartly suited businessman is standing with his briefcase in one hand and the other on the bonnet of one of the city's famous yellow taxis preventing it from sneaking any further into the intersection than it already has pending the traffic light changing to green and they are yapping away at each other in true New York style.

Willie Mays, by the way, is generally regarded as the best all-round baseball player ever. He is in the top echelon of hitters, but, unlike most of the other top hitters, he was also a great outfielder. A cricketing equivalent of Mays would be a cross between Graeme Pollock and Jonty Rhodes.

May 8

Time to fly home. The day is spent on the plane from New York to Johannesburg, most of it asleep. Plane sleep, if you know what I mean.

May 9

The main thing I need to check when I get home is whether Bangladesh's remarkable Mominul Haque has reached 50 in their second innings of the Test against Pakistan to continue his sequence of scoring 50s in Tests. I am pleased to note that he made 68 and has now scored a 50 in each of his last 11 Tests, just one short of AB de Villiers's world record of 12. The start of his Test career compares favourably with anyone ever. In 14 Tests to date he has 1 380 runs at an average of 60.00 with four 100s and nine 50s. The only Test in which he did not make a 50 was his third match and he scored 23 & 29 in that one. His score is always the first one I look for when Bangladesh are batting in a Test match.

At the other end of the run-scoring scale, Pakistan's Imran Khan has become the first player to fail to score a run in each of his first four Tests, having made 0* in his only innings to date. I suspect he is likely to fall someway short of his famous namesake's career 3 807 runs and 362 wickets in Tests.

The results of the UK election are quite interesting. Pre-election polls unanimously predicted a hung parliament, but the Conservative party wins an outright majority. It is amusing to see that the pollsters have got it wrong. Predictions were that Labour and Conservative would both get about 34% of the popular vote, but the Conservatives get 36.9% to Labour's 30.4%. So, there will be much discussion in the statistical community as to how they got it wrong. Sometimes statistics is more of an art than a science.

May 10

The excitement of the day, in statistical circles at least, is in Hove where Middlesex manage to collect 62 extras in their total of 269 against Sussex, but the best score by a batsman is 38. (Extras are helped a bit by the ruling for English domestic cricket that no balls are counted as two runs each and there were 30 no balls in the extras tally). There are numerous cases of extras being the top scorer in an innings. In this case the total seems quite high for extras to be top scorer and the difference between extras and the next best also seems quite high. So, to contextualise it we need to play around with the parameters. Eventually, I am able to reveal that this is the second highest total in first-class cricket with 60 or more extras and a best score by someone actually using the bat to compile runs of less than 40. The only higher one is 286 by Durham v South Africans at Chester-le-Street in 1998 (HS 39, Extras 69).

The Intercontinental Cup (colloquially known as the ICup for short. You try saying 'Intercontinental' often and you will understand why) begins today in Windhoek with Namibia taking on Hong Kong. As this is the only first-class cricket played by the Associates, I always follow this competition closely. With eight teams playing seven games each over a three-year period, it is cricket's most strung out tournament.

May 11

The Kevin Pietersen issue has been hanging around English cricket for a while. Last year, England management made it known that they were not going to choose Pietersen again. But earlier this year, incoming ECB Chairman Colin Graves seemed to suggest that Pietersen could be considered again. Pietersen then abandoned his IPL contract to play county cricket for Surrey in an attempt to revive his England career. Today, with rumours suggesting that the door was about to be firmly shut again, he scores 326* against Leicestershire.

May 12

Pietersen ends on 355* when Surrey are all out, but the door is shut by

ECB management. The most interesting statistic about the innings is that the next highest score in the innings is 36. In other words, he didn't get much help. Of all the triple-centuries scored in first-class cricket this is the fourth lowest second best score in the innings. Vijay Hazare's 309 out of 387 with a next best of 21 (by his brother, Vivek) for Hindus v The Rest at Bombay in 1943 remains the greatest of the 'stand-alone' 300s. With the chances of him playing for England seemingly ended it is quite likely that this will prove to be Pietersen's last first-class innings as it would seem that playing Twenty20 leagues around the world is the most likely course for the remainder of his career. If this is the case then his 355* is an extraordinary last first-class innings and easily the highest by anyone. Sam Aggarwal scored 313* for Oxford University v Cambridge University in 2013 and is not likely to play again. No one else has scored more than 241 in their last first-class innings. Norman Callaway famously scored 207 in his only first-class innings for New South Wales v Queensland in 1915, but tragically died in the War.

May 13

Namibia complete a comfortable win over Hong Kong by 114 runs. Apart from home ground advantage, their experience in playing three-day cricket within South Africa's provincial structures clearly helps them in the ICup. It is their 118th first-class match and Hong Kong's third.

At The Oval, Surrey are set 216 in 24 overs to win after stubborn resistance by Leicestershire. They chase it down, making 218-3 in 21.2 overs. Steve Davies stars with 115* off 69 balls. At 10.21 runs per overs it is the second highest run-rate recorded in an innings in first-class cricket, with a minimum of 20 overs. Often these records need to be qualified by excluding innings that were contrived (where 'joke' bowling is used to expedite a declaration) and where penalties are included (India had over-rate penalties in first-class domestic matches for many years, which could lead to inflated scores). This case is an example of this.

May 14

One of my main objectives to achieve during the 10 days that I have at home between the West Indies tour and heading off to England for the

New Zealand series is to finalise checking all the scorecards that need to be processed for the South African Cricket Annual. I manage to do this today and send them all in one big file to Ros Brodie (who is in India for the IPL) and she will get them into the format we use for the Annual, as she has been doing for the last 21 years. It is a nice tick on the To Do list.

May 15

The Gas Man Cometh by Flanders and Swann comes to mind today. I make an unintentional attempt, albeit on a much smaller scale, to emulate the events of their well-known song when the arrival of the gasman on Monday morning leads to a sequence of calamities around the house. In my case today, the plumber arrives in the morning to fix the geyser, a leaky toilet and some taps. When we need to switch the water mains off, we discover that the box for this has become a nice nesting ground for a swarm of bees. So, I need to call in the bee removal man as well.

Things take a turn for the better with my bridge hands in the evening. On one hand, my partner and I manage to get into a six no trumps contract, despite me having only two diamonds to the queen and him having two diamonds to the jack. A diamond lead would have seen us go down four. But, fortunately the lead was a club and we did not lose a trick.

The long and largely pointless (given that there will be only 10 teams in the main event) process to get to the 2019 World Cup begins today with Hong Kong taking on Namibia at The Wanderers Club in Windhoek. Namibia collect the first points of the ICC World Cricket League Championship with a remarkable win by one wicket. After Hong Kong score 194-9 in their 50 overs, Namibia slump to 13-4 then sneak home with four balls to spare.

May 16

Baseball enthusiasm levels are declining in direct correlation with Red Sox results. A 2-1 loss to the Seattle Mariners sees the Red Sox record slip to 17-19 (17 wins and 19 losses). Prospects of making it to the playoffs are declining.

May 17

Namibia's top order lets them down even more spectacularly than they did in the first game against Hong Kong. This time they slump to 15-7, the joint fourth lowest total at the fall of the seventh wicket in all List A matches. Although the tail wags them to 109, Hong Kong win easily by 8 wickets.

May 18

The outcomes of the ICC Cricket Committee meeting are revealed. The most significant one relates to ODI playing conditions. It took the administrators a while to realise what should have been blindingly obvious before they invented them that the fielding team did not want fielding powerplays so they were scrapped a few years ago. Less obvious was that batting teams didn't really want batting powerplays either. But this has finally become clear with teams not wishing to risk losing wickets in the batting powerplay. Between 2009 and 2011, the average number of wickets in the batting powerplay in ODIs was 1.68, but since the start of 2012 it has been 1.02. The average number of runs in this phase of the game was 37.81 between 2009 and 2011, but has declined to 31.45 since then. So it is proposed that the batting powerplay is done away with and that the number of fielders allowed outside the circle be two in the first 10 overs, four in overs 11 to 40 and five in the last 10. It is the five in the last 10 that will make the most difference with smashing boundaries all the time becoming a bit more difficult. Perhaps more should have been done to restore the balance between bat and ball, but at least it is a start. Generally the ICC's executive rubber-stamps the Cricket Committee proposals so it is reasonable to expect these changes to be implemented on 1 October.

May 19

It is seven degrees centigrade when I arrive on a late spring day in London and it barely warms up all day which added to the rain makes it fairly miserable, although I do manage to catch up on some sleep. I had left

Johannesburg on a late autumn day with cloudless skies and a temperature of 23 degrees centigrade. Still, we mustn't grumble about the weather.

May 20

Test match preparation is the order of the day. I do my normal stats pack and head into London to collect my accreditation at Lord's.

May 21

At Lord's, New Zealand are playing their 400th Test. New Zealand Radio commentator Bryan Waddle has been at 231 of them, a fantastic record. It is also New Zealand's 100th Test against England. They are the sixth pair of teams to play 100 Tests against each other. England recover from 30-4 to reach 354-7 by the close of play. Although it is an engrossing day of cricket with Ben Stokes counter-attacking 92 off 94 balls the highlight, I struggle to find much to excite stats enthusiasts. A sign of this is that the best stat that I came up with for the day was that England's fifth wicket partnership of 161 between Joe Root and Ben Stokes was the third highest fifth wicket partnership in Tests by a team that lost their first four wickets for 30 or fewer runs. No wonder the commentators think that I need to get out more.

May 22

England finish on 389 all out which is the highest total ever made by a team that lost their first four wickets for 30 or fewer in a Test match, beating Pakistan's 387-9* (from 22-4) against Australia at Adelaide in 1990.

Mark Wood, on debut, has Martin Guptill caught in the slips for what should have been his first Test wicket. But replays show that he had overstepped, so it is a no ball. His team-mate, Ben Stokes, had had a similar experience on his Test debut at Adelaide 18 months ago when what should have been his first wicket (Brad Haddin) turned out to be a no ball.

Keep those feet behind the line, folks.

Meanwhile, Zimbabwe take on Pakistan in a T20 International in Lahore. It is the first international match played in Pakistan since the terrorist attack on the Sri Lanka team in March 2009. We all hope that the tour goes off well.

May 23

At the end of each day's play in a Test match both teams produce a player (or coach) to talk to the media. The identity of this player is a function of various factors. The ideal choice is the player who performed best on the day, but things like whether he is not out, possibly injured, whose turn it is, the mood of the player(s), and probably the mood of the media manager as well also come into play when making the decision. Today there is a case for Mr Extras to do the interviews. There are 67 of them in the New Zealand innings. This is the fifth most ever in Tests and the second most conceded by England. Particularly impressive are byes (26) and leg-byes (34). When there are lots of extras in an innings no balls are usually a major contributor, but this time there was only one – the one Mark Wood would have taken his first Test wicket with if he had managed to keep some part of his foot behind the line.

In the end, I was disappointed with leg-byes. After a steady performance to reach 34 by the 112th over with only five wickets down I was convinced that the world record of 35 (which England conceded against South Africa at Birmingham in 2008) was inevitably going to go. But they stubbornly refused to budge for the remaining 20 overs and five wickets in the innings. There were a couple of other observations around leg-byes. Firstly, I remember being at Birmingham in 2008 and there was almost complete lack of interest in the world record at the time (quite appropriately actually, as the most leg-byes in a Test innings is hardly Oscar-winning material in the field of cricket records), but just seven years later, there is much excitement on Twitter and ball-by-ball commentaries as the record approached. Secondly, when I am scoring I do a regular manual check to see if the bowling figures add up. So, I add the runs conceded by the bowlers and then add the byes and leg-byes and this should be the same as the team total. In this innings I found it was quite disconcerting when doing this calculation. Generally the total number of runs conceded by the bowlers is pretty close to the overall total as byes and leg-byes are not that many. But this innings I was finding even with the total well into the 400s that the runs conceded by the bowlers was still stuck in the 300s and I kept double-checking to see if the bowling figures were actually correct.

More significantly, Kane Williamson is out for 132, meaning that he has made 374 runs since his last dismissal in Tests, a New Zealand record. New Zealand also produce just the second occasion in their 400 Tests of each of the first four batsmen in an innings reaching 50. I have a bit of fun getting Jeremy Coney trying to guess who the four were on the previous occasion: v Pakistan at Lahore in 1965. To add to the fun, on that occasion the top *five* all made 50s.

Meanwhile, it is Sports Day at school back at home. Sadly, the five-year-old is sick so misses it. Our daughters have inherited their parents' sporting genes, so it is no great surprise that the seven-year-old finishes last and sixth out of eight in her two individual races, but she manages to be part of a winning team in the relay race. I am sad that I am not there to watch it, but happy that I get to avoid embarrassing myself in the Father's Race.

May 24

Having played a special innings on the first day, Ben Stokes goes one better with 101 off 92 balls, reaching his 100 off just 85 of them. This is the fastest ever Test 100 at Lord's, beating the 87 balls by Mohammad Azharuddin for India in 1990, and the second fastest in all Tests for England. Cricket's greatest ever hitter, Gilbert Jessop (known as 'The Croucher' because of his stance when facing) still holds that record. His match-winning fourth innings century against Australia at The Oval in 1902 which came off 76 balls is one of the very great Test innings.

It occurs to me that it is unlikely that anyone has scored as many runs in each innings as quickly each time as Stokes has in this match. I do some research, defining the parameters as a score of 80 or more at a strike-rate of 95 or more in each innings and can only find one comparable performance: Ricky Ponting scored 105 off 100 balls and 86* off 84 balls for Australia against New Zealand at Auckland in 2005. The match situations this time (coming in at 30-4 in the first innings and with a lead of 118 and 4 wickets down in the second innings) are much more challenging, so Stokes' astonishing efforts trump Ponting's.

Stokes was born in Christchurch, New Zealand and becomes the sixth England player to score a Test century against the country of his birth. The others are Colin Cowdrey and Nasser Hussain (born in India), Andrew Strauss and Kevin Pietersen (born in South Africa) and Zimbabwe-born Graeme Hick.

Dental triumphalism over Mrs S from the dentist visit a few months ago disappears in one crunch in the mouth as I manage to lose a bit of tooth at lunch.

The IPL finishes today.

May 25

England win a wonderful Test match by 124 runs with 9.3 overs to spare as New Zealand subside to 220 all out chasing 345 in 77 overs. It has been a match of fluctuating fortunes, plenty of runs (the last wicket for New Zealand manages to ensure that the aggregate of 1 610 in the match sneaks past the previous most for a Lord's Test of 1 603 in the famous 1990 match against India) and 40 wickets. The aggregate also turns out to be the most in a Test in which all 40 wickets fell and there was a time limit in the match. The four cases where more runs had been scored and all 40 wickets fell were all in timeless Tests in Australia. In short, there is virtually nothing to be unhappy about, especially if you are a neutral observer.

Perhaps the most telling of the 'turnaround' stats for England is that they have only once previously won a Test match from a worse position at the fall of the third wicket in the third innings of the match. In this Test they were still 60 behind at that point and the only time they have won from a worse position when three down in the third innings of the match is the famous Headingley Test of 1981 when they beat Australia after following on. In that game they were still 190 adrift when they lost their third wicket in the third innings of the game. Ben Stokes nails down the man of the match award (if he hadn't already) with a magical over which snuffed out a potential rally. New Zealand, were 61-3 at the start of the over with Kane Williamson and BJ Watling providing good resistance after New Zealand started with 12-3. Stokes got Williamson out and then Brendon McCullum first ball, to much excitement from the big fifth day 'people's crowd' who had been lured in by cheap tickets and the state of the game. Stokes now has 648 runs and 28 wickets in his first 10 Tests. I look up all those who scored 600 runs and took 25 wickets in their first 10 Tests. And Stokes has joined an interesting list: George Ulyett (who played for England in the 1870s and 1880s), South Africa's first top quality all-rounder Jimmy

Sinclair, India's Dattu Phadkar and Dwayne Bravo. It is of course mostly interesting not for the names on it, but the ones missing. Stokes' start to his Test career is well ahead of most of the game's really great all-rounders.

I was most disappointed when Alastair Cook was seventh man out in England's second innings to be replaced by number 9 batsman Stuart Broad. Had Broad come in while Cook was still there it would have been the first time in the 78 Tests they have played in the same team that they would have batted together. I was hoping that they would bat together for the first time so that I could produce this wonderful, arcane stat. Next Test, perhaps? Only Sanath Jayasuriya and Muttiah Muralitharan (90) have played more Tests together without a single batting partnership between them.

May 26

So what do you do after a busy five days of Test cricket? If you are me, you go to watch cricket, of course. I pop down to Beckenham to catch some of the Kent v Surrey County Championship match. The main incentive is to collect another ground. This is the 90th venue at which I have watched first-class cricket. It is a pleasant day, spent mostly in the company of the world's leading cricket statistician, Philip Bailey, who maintains CricketArchive's excellent database. I forgot to pack a cap when leaving Johannesburg, so I buy a Kent sun hat at the ground which results in some sledging from Surrey man Alec Stewart when I see him on the field during lunch.

May 27

It is a catch up day as various emails and not very urgent bits of work (not to mention this diary) tend to get neglected during Test matches. I am disappointed to see that AB de Villiers will not be playing in South Africa's Test series in Bangladesh in July as he will be on paternity leave. While congratulations for the pending fatherhood are in order, there is a statistical milestone that gets knocked on the head as a result. De Villiers has played 98 Tests since his debut without missing one and is thus on course to be the first player to appear in 100 Tests consecutively from debut. Brendon McCullum might now be the first to do this. The Lord's

Test was his 93rd and he is yet to miss one.

May 28

It is another travel day as I catch the train up to Leeds. The weather is pretty clear all the way up, but as the mellifluous tones of the conductor waft over the tannoy letting us know that we are about to arrive at Leeds, the first spots of rain appear on the windows of the train. Welcome to Leeds!

May 29

Not all that long ago most fans would have thought 297-8 was a good day's Test cricket. Today we lose the first session and New Zealand still score 297-8. In 65 overs. After 50 overs they were 237-4 which I note is higher than the historical average for 50-over ODIs of 236. Luke Ronchi threatens both New Zealand's fastest Test century (74 balls by Brendon McCullum v Sri Lanka at Christchurch six months ago) and Shikhar Dhawan's fastest Test century on debut (85 balls v Australia at Mohali in 2012), but gets out for 88 off 70 balls. This means that statisticians need to scramble for slightly lesser stats to contextualise the innings, and so the stat becomes that Ronchi ends up with the highest strike rate (125.71) in a score over 80 on Test debut.

Jimmy Anderson wasted little time getting to 400 Test wickets (he is the first for England and 12th overall), dismissing Martin Guptill with his eighth ball of the day.

Brendon McCullum hits the first ball he faces for six, a rare occurrence in a Test innings. There is a good quiz question on this particular performance: 'Who is the only player to hit the first ball he faced in a Test innings for six on three separate occasions?' Chris Gayle, perhaps? Viv Richards? Ian Botham? McCullum, for that matter? All wrong. The answer is Muttiah Muralitharan.

May 30

It is FA Cup final day. We are in Leeds, where Test crowds have not been good recently. England are playing New Zealand, who are traditionally not a massive drawcard in cricket. It is still May and temperatures don't get above 14 degrees centigrade. And yet, Headingley is sold out today. Maybe, just maybe, Test cricket isn't quite as dead as some people seem to think it is.

England bowl poorly to the tail and Stuart Broad produces the extraordinary figures of 17.1-0-109-5. At 6.34 runs per over it is the worst economy rate by a bowler taking five wickets in an innings in a Test. Only Dale Steyn (13.1-1-82-5) v Sri Lanka at the P Sara Oval in Colombo in 2006 has also conceded over six an over while taking a five-for before.

Sky stats man Richard Isaacs comes up with the best stat of the day. Alastair Cook has passed Graham Gooch to become England's leading run-scorer in Tests. With Jimmy Anderson also playing in the same team it is, remarkably, the first time since 1914 that England have had their leading run-scorer and leading wicket-taker playing in the same Test XI. Two of the greats, Jack Hobbs and Sydney Barnes were the men back then. In checking this I find a near miss. In 1992 David Gower became England's leading run-scorer in the game after leading wicket-taker Ian Botham played his last Test.

May 31

England are bowled out for 350 to provide just the eighth instance of teams being equal on the first innings in a Test match. New Zealand get themselves into a good position at 338-6 by the close on the back of a fine 100* by BJ Watling. For the first time in the series Brendon McCullum plays what might be termed a 'proper' Test innings with 55 off 98 balls. His 83 prior runs in the series had come off 67 balls. He even faces a maiden from Jimmy Anderson which is the first time he has played out a maiden in a Test match since Mohammad Hafeez bowled him one in Sharjah in November 2014, four Tests, 340 balls and 374 runs ago.

In a bit of a surprise Kevin Pietersen turns out for Surrey in a County Championship game, thereby ruining the possibility of 355* being his final first-class score.

I miss watching the Comrades Marathon again. The great South African ultra-marathon is an up run this year from Durban to Pietermaritzburg, with the finish at Pietermaritzburg's lovely Oval cricket ground — my old home ground when growing up. I used to watch the race all day every year, but seldom get the chance to do so these days and it certainly isn't on my TV in Leeds this time. This year, it is one for the statisticians as they say, as Gift Kelehe is the winner, so he and brother, Andrew, who won in 2001, become the first pair of brothers to win the famous race. And Caroline Wöstmann is the first South African to win the Women's race since 1998.

June 1

Some stats are prepared well in advance, while others just kind of happen. When Mark Craig hits a six today I decide it is time to check how many sixes there have been in the match. A glance at the New Zealand second innings shows that Craig's is the seventh six of the innings, but they have been hit by seven different batsmen. This throws me in a different direction: What is the most number of batsmen who have hit a six in one innings? It is a pretty easy query to write quickly and as I am checking the results which reveal two other cases of seven batsmen hitting a six in an innings (including New Zealand themselves six months ago) Matt Henry joins the club. So, I can happily let the listeners know that this is the first time that eight different players have hit a six in a Test innings. New Zealand end the match with an aggregate of 804 runs scored at 4.92 runs per over, comfortably the fastest run-rate by a team scoring 800 runs in a Test.

England get to 44-0 chasing 455 to win when rain sets in shortly after lunch and ends the entertainment for the day.

June 2

The freezing weather in Leeds seems appropriate given that today is the 40th anniversary of the famous day on 2 June 1975 when snow stopped play in a County Championship match between Derbyshire and Lancashire at Buxton. Which is a good effort by the snow given that June is early summer in England. Five days after this, the first cricket World Cup began in England and was played in glorious sunshine over the next two weeks. Inevitably, Dickie Bird was one of the umpires in the snowed out match and he visits the TMS box at teatime to reminisce about the day.

England lose four early wickets and never really recover as New Zealand win by 199 runs. At 30 years, 159 days, Alastair Cook becomes the youngest player to score 9 000 Test runs, beating Sachin Tendulkar's record by 94 days. I try to extrapolate what Cook could finish up with. The players with 5 000 or more runs made on average 47.5% of their runs after the age of 30. On that basis, Cook could get to 16 000. So, Tendulkar's Test record of 15 921 may be beatable. Just.

And Jimmy Anderson reaches 1 000 Test runs at last in his 104th Test. He is the slowest to this mark. Which is good news for Muttiah Muralitharan, who used to hold this dubious record with 95 Tests.

In Dublin, Ed Joyce makes 229* for Ireland against United Arab Emirates as the home team make a confident start to their ICup campaign that they hope will lead to Test status in 2018. It is the highest individual first-class score for Ireland, who finish the day on 420-3.

June 3

Good news for England is that their defeat is not getting much public attention as Sepp Blatter's resignation as FIFA President dominates not just the sports news but all headlines. On my way back from Leeds to London for my flight to Johannesburg tonight, I notice the pun-loving British headline writers are in good form as usual, with the likes of 'Blatt's All Folks', 'Blatt's your lot', etc.

In the County Championship, Leicestershire have beaten Essex for their first win since 2012. Their 37 matches without a win is the fifth longest streak in County Championship history. Northamptonshire's run of 99 games without a win between 1935 and 1939 may still stand for a very long time.

June 4

It is a bad day. I expect to be able to watch some of the Test match between West Indies and Australia at Roseau in Dominica on the satellite TV channel in South Africa. However, they are not showing it. Test cricket doesn't seem to be very important. And, it seems even less important when the headline 'NZC mulls scrapping Test for Chappell-Hadlee ODIs' appears on ESPNCricInfo. This means that inevitably there will be a schedule announced shortly with the originally planned third Test being replaced by three ODIs. All of which makes me very grumpy. Cricket continues its relentless pursuit of the mass market, increasingly at the expense of its niche market. While mass markets are, by definition, larger than niche markets, they are also generally a lot more fickle.

In the Test match which I can't watch, Adam Voges becomes the oldest player to score a century on debut, beating Dave Houghton who made one in Zimbabwe's inaugural Test against India in Harare in 1992.

June 5

Ireland complete a comprehensive innings and 26 runs win over the UAE to steal an early lead over their two main ICup rivals, Afghanistan and Scotland, who play out a rain-affected draw in Stirling in which there is only just enough play for both teams' first innings to be completed.

One thing Ireland wouldn't have a problem with should they play Test cricket is first-class experience. The XI who played against the UAE have a total of 838 first-class matches between them, thanks mostly to a lot of county cricket. Only one of the 10 Test playing countries, England, had more first-class caps between them in their inaugural Test XI.

There is an interesting view of polling in the *Financial Times* today as the fall out and analysis of how the pollsters got the UK election results wrong continues unabated. Researcher Philip Graves' view of traditional polling methods boils down to the idea that there is no point in asking people what they want or what they are going to do, because they do not even know themselves.

This no doubt does not apply to everyone, but there are obviously enough people to whom it does apply to mean that (fortunately) opinion polls will probably never be entirely accurate at predicting things like election results. But the election may lead to a wholesale review of the polling processes which will keep the numbers' people busy for a while.

June 6

My seven-year-old daughter loves soccer. Playing it, mostly. Today she actually watches some soccer: reruns of the European Champions League semi-finals. She hasn't watched much before so is under the impression that there are goals scored all the time. After watching some real matches for a while without seeing any goals she exclaims, much to my amusement, 'These guys are slower than cricket.' Paradoxically, considering the length that the game takes to play, I think cricket fans have the shortest attention spans of all sports' followers. If there is 10 to 15 minutes of play without a four, a six or a wicket, most cricket fans seem to be reaching for the remote to change channel or, if they are actually at the game, finding something else to watch or do. A soccer fan, by comparison, can watch 90 minutes of play without seeing a single goal and be riveted throughout.

June 7

The first thing I am alerted to when my computer wakes up is a game in Czechoslovakia where Prague CC Second XI are all out for 54 including nine ducks. Aditya Jaiswal makes 43*, one other player scores one and there are 10 extras. This is in reply to Bohemians CC First XI's 126-8 which included five ducks. The scorers must have been really troubled at that game.

The last thing I do in the day before going to sleep is to listen to the audio commentary of the Red Sox game against Oakland Athletics (while typing up this diary) and it is a happy ending as Boston produce their best win of the season. They score seven runs in the eighth innings to win, having trailed by 4-0 for most of the game. It is the first time they have won this season when trailing after seven innings. Pat Venditte, the 'switch-pitcher', makes an appearance in the game for Oakland. Will cricket see an ambidextrous bowler at top level any time soon?

June 8

One of the things (people? handles?) I follow on Twitter are the QI Elves. Today they report, amusingly, that 'A 2000 poll found that 19% of earners in America thought they were in the top 1% of earners in America'. I suspect that most of the actual top 1% of earners are too busy earning money to answer poll questions which means approximately 19% of

Americans have no idea of where they are in the money-making league table.

June 9

It is the greatest day in the history of the world. Again. This time it is England's turn to smash 400 in an ODI. It is the first time that they have done it, reaching 408-9 in their 50 overs against New Zealand at Birmingham. They go on to win by a record margin for England of 210 runs. It is an extraordinary turnaround in their first ODI after their abysmal World Cup campaign. Ironically, after all the call for change, the main stars for England are players who were actually at the World Cup. Jos Buttler (66 balls) and Joe Root (71) produce England's second and fourth fastest ODI 100s, captain Eoin Morgan makes 50 and Steve Finn (he of the 2-0-49-0 in the World Cup encounter between these teams) takes 4-35. Of the 'new' non-World Cup players, Adil Rashid is the only one to make an impression, but it is a fine impression as his 69 and 4-55 makes him just the eighth player to score a 50 and take four wickets in an innings in an ODI for England. Buttler and Rashid collect the world seventh wicket ODI record along the way with a partnership of 177. Five of the 10 partnership records in ODIs have come in the last 12 months. No doubt reaction tomorrow will be along the lines of 'The Cricket World Cup is coming home in 2019', etc., etc.

Meanwhile in County Championship's Second Division, Derbyshire beat Kent by eight wickets, which is an astounding turnaround after they slumped to 0-3 in their first innings. They are just the eighth team to win a County Championship match after losing their first three wickets in an innings without a run on the board, and the first since 1989. And there have been a lot of County Championship matches.

Also in the Second Division there is much excitement among the commentators at Grace Road as Leicestershire approach their millionth run in first-class cricket. They need to get to 180 in their second innings against Surrey to reach it in this match, but they fall three runs short. So that will have to wait for their next game. By my calculations Surrey are the team that have scored the most runs in first-class cricket. They are currently sitting on 1 408 153.

Even further down cricket's food chain there is news of a remarkable Minor Counties Championship match. Two days ago, Douglas Miller, former Chairman of the Association of Cricket Statisticians and

Historians, and Buckinghamshire historian, alerted the ACS email group to the highest ever Minor Counties Championship partnership. Eddie Ballard and Tanveer Sikander added an unbroken 431 for the second wicket for Hertfordshire against Bucks. Today, possibly even more amazingly, news comes through that Bucks won the game by six wickets chasing 490 in the final innings. All told there were 1 559 runs and 23 wickets in the three-day game. The Minor Counties Championship has been renamed (or re-branded as the marketing gurus will say) as the Unicorns Championship. I find this a bit odd. Between 2010 and 2013 a team called 'Unicorns' consisting mostly of Minor Counties players had appeared in the List A limited overs competition in England. To rename the competition after that team now that the team no longer plays is incongruous to say the least. Especially as 'Minor Counties' has served the competition pretty well since it was first played in 1895.

June 10

All good things come to an end. While catching up with the BBC's famous radio show *The News Quiz*, I discover that Sandi Toksvig's nine-year reign as chair of the show will finish after the current series. One of my favourite writers is long-time *News Quiz* panellist and leading English humourist Alan Coren, whose last book before his untimely death was called *69 for One* with a cricket scoreboard on the front cover.

Things beginning today include the one-off Test between Bangladesh and India at Fatullah. India are an untroubled 239-0 in the 56 overs available for the day as Shikhar Dhawan and Murali Vijay become just the second pair of Indian openers to have two double-century stands in Tests after Virender Sehwag and Gautam Gambhir.

June 11

It should be fairly obvious that if you schedule a Test match during monsoon season there is a very good chance of monsoon stopping play. To the surprise of absolutely nobody there is no play today in the Test at Fatullah.

I spend rather more of the day than I should writing a program to calculate runs scored by an individual in a day's play. It is quite a complex process involving scores, close of play details and figuring out on which day within the match the player scored which runs. I get it about 98% right by the end of the day. Bradman famously scored 309 in a day at Leeds in 1930. It is always a relief when computer written programs produce the same results as known facts.

In the Test match which is not on our TV screens, Steve Smith scores 135* against West Indies at Kingston. This is the eighth time in his last 14 Tests that he has made a century in the first innings, a sequence which only Sir Don Bradman had previously achieved. The Test in Bangladesh is being shown on TV in South Africa, or actually not being shown with all the weather about. So, the TV company will be digging into the archives to cover the masses of time when there is no play in Fatullah with old highlights' packages.

June 12

I forget to check the electricity load-shedding schedule in the morning, an elementary error in South Africa in 2015. So, when our electricity is switched off at 10am while my computer is in the middle of running a pretty complex and time-consuming program I use a few words that would not be considered appropriate on radio.

Australia are dismissed for 399 in their Test against West Indies in Kingston. Jerome Taylor, who began with 6-6-0-2 yesterday, finishes with figures of 25-10-47-6. The question is how to quantify this performance. It is probably the equivalent of a batsman scoring, say, 200 out of a total of 300. Stand-alone batting performances have standard measurements: Lowest Total To Include A Century or Double Century, etc. (Clive Rice's 105 out of 143 for Nottinghamshire v Hampshire in 1981 remains the lowest total in first-class cricket to include a century, along with Rizwan Malik's 100* out of 143 for Gujranwala v Bahawalpur in 2002) and Highest Percentage Of Team Total (Charles Bannerman's 67.34% — 165 retired hurt out of 245 in the first ever Test match remains the Test record). But stand-alone bowling performances are not easily categorised. Bowlers have taken as many as six and more wickets relatively frequently in high totals. But to do so, while conceding so few runs has to be pretty rare. After a bit of playing around with the numbers and trying to keep it relatively simple, I come up with the stat that this is the highest Test total in which a bowler has taken six or more wickets while conceding fewer than 50 runs. The previous best was when South Africa's Reggie Schwarz coincidentally took 6-47 out of Australia's 364 at Sydney in 1911.

Amazingly, in the ODI at The Oval nobody scores 400. In what might be considered a good day for bowlers by 2015 standards, New Zealand make a mere 398-5. Unlike the previous massive scores by teams batting first this year this one at least produces a relatively close finish as 'new' England fall 13 short of a Duckworth/Lewis adjusted target.

June 13

At Roseau, Adam Voges had become the 99th player to score a Test debut century. So I am on the lookout for number 100. In the West Indies second innings at Roseau, Shane Dowrich threatened to become number 100, but was out for 70. The only debutante at Kingston is West Indies' Rajindra Chandrika. Could he be number 100? No, he falls short. As short as you possibly can, in fact. He collects his second duck of the match to become just the fourth player to make a pair on Test debut as an opening batsman after Ken Rutherford, Saeed Anwar and Zimbabwe's Dirk Viljoen. Australia have made a confident declaration, setting West Indies 392 to win in effectively 188 overs.

June 14

The soggy Test at Fatullah comes to an end today with a total of 184.2 overs being bowled in the match. At 37 overs per day, if you really want to play Test matches in monsoon season you will need to schedule them for 13 days to have the equivalent of 450 overs available as you normally have in five days. South Africa are due to play two Tests in Bangladesh at the end of July, a month which is traditionally even wetter than June in that part of the world. Ours is not to reason why.

Mominul Haque scored 30 in Bangladesh's first innings and doesn't get a chance to bat in the second innings, so AB de Villiers' 12 consecutive Tests with a 50-plus score remains the record for now. We need to reset our sights for Mominul. In all 15 Tests he has played to date he has made a score of 25 or more. So, I check what the best such sequence is from debut and the record is held by the West Indies great, Everton Weekes, who made a score of at least 25 in each of his first 16 Tests. So, in the unlikely event of monsoons permitting enough play during the South

African series, Mominul will have a chance to knock that one off.

Australia duly complete a comprehensive win over West Indies by 277 runs as the hosts subside to 114 in their second innings, while the ODI in Southampton features a mere 302 from England, a pretty comfortable win for New Zealand and a bed in the TMS commentary box as the new facilities are in the hotel that has been built at the ground.

There is a horrible collision between fielders Rory Burns and Moises Henriques in a Twenty20 game at Arundel. It is something you never want to see in the game, especially not at a place like Arundel, which is probably the most idyllic setting for the game, and my favourite first-class ground.

It is reported that the first Test against India later this year will be Kumar Sangakkara's last Test. Seriously Kumar, don't go! He is still playing as well as ever and is only 37, which may seem fairly old for a cricketer, but I wish I was that young myself.

The ultimate performance in baseball is a perfect game by a pitcher. This is when a pitcher pitches an entire game without letting an opponent get on base. It is very rare, having happened only 23 times in well over 200 000 Major League games to date. When I abandon listening to the Red Sox's game as they are getting clobbered again I notice that the Washington National's Max Scherzer is perfect through six innings against the Milwaukee Brewers so I switch to listen to that. Now, I know as well as anyone that commentator's curse is a figment of the sports fan's imagination and so is statto's curse, but it is still disappointing that the first batter I listen to Scherzer pitch to gets a hit to break up the perfecto. So, I switch off and go to bed.

June 15

I wake up to discover that the only hit Scherzer gave up was the one I heard. He also gave up only one walk and collected a massive 16 strikeouts in one of baseball's great pitching performances.

The Magna Carta is 800 years old today (which is a lot older than both me and Kumar Sangakkara) and it manages to get into cricket reports in a punny kind of a way as 19-year-old Matthew Carter takes 7-56 on his first-class debut for Nottinghamshire v Somerset at Taunton. With England looking for a top class spinner, there is bound to be much excitement around this off-spinner. His return is the best by a spinner on County Championship debut since Jack Walsh took 7-46 for Leicestershire v Northamptonshire at Leicester in 1938. Walsh was an Australian left-arm wrist-spinner who went on to have a very successful county career. In those days, however, he had to forfeit his right to play for Australia in order to play county cricket. These days, no doubt, he would have gone on to have a successful international career for England.

June 16

It is a public holiday today: Youth Day in South Africa. So, it is a very lazy one. I do still have to update the database with a few matches as well as do some other small cricket-related things. But for a change (and a pleasant one, at that) cricket forms a very low percentage of the day. Still, there is nothing quite like doing cricket statistics in your pyjamas.

Another new team is added to the first-class list, as Papua New Guinea play their inaugural match. They are up against Netherlands in Amstelveen in the ICup. They start well, dismissing the hosts for 209, but subside to 103-6 in reply by the close.

June 17

Today provides the worst pun in this diary to date: Glamorgan's tail Waggs against Surrey at Guildford. Yes, Graham Wagg scores 200 in Glamorgan's first innings batting at number eight and shares a 10th wicket partnership of 105 with Michael Hogan. Wagg's is the 13th double-century by a number eight batsman in all first-class cricket and equals the highest (200* by Dominic Cork for Derbyshire v Durham at Derby in 2000) by a number eight in a County Championship match.

In Galle, not a ball is bowled on what is supposed to be the opening day of the first Sri Lanka v Pakistan Test. Not that I would have been able to see it anyway as it is yet another Test series that is not making its way to South African television sets. So, Kumar Sangakkara is going to play his remaining Tests without me being able to watch. I was lucky enough to be at his Test debut, also at Galle, in 2000 against South Africa. He did not make a lot of runs in that series (23, 24, 5, 25 and 6 to be precise) but it was clear to all observers even then that he was going to be a special player. Anyway, that is enough obsequious Kumar waffle for now, what's happening in the ODI at Trent Bridge?

Quite a lot actually. It is yet another run-fest as New Zealand make 349-7 and England win by seven wickets with six overs to spare, easily their highest successful ODI run-chase. Captain Eoin Morgan leads the way with 113 off 82 balls and becomes the second England captain after Alastair Cook (remember him?) to reach 50 in four consecutive ODI innings. The propensity for producing close finishes is what got fans excited about the one-day game in its early days, but these massive scores in the 2015 ODI avatar hardly ever produce any close games, even, oddly, when the team batting second chases the target down.

June 18

It is quite a pleasant cricketing statistics day. I do a number of what might broadly be categorised as Match Situation stats. I enjoy these kind of stats as they put a team achievement into perspective for me, although there is often not much general public enthusiasm for this kind of stat as they can sometimes appear to be fairly complicated. There are three that I do today to keep myself entertained.

Firstly, Somerset's two-wicket win over Nottinghamshire yesterday chasing 401 to win came after conceding a first innings lead of 210 and then not being asked to follow-on. There are lists of teams winning matches after being asked to follow-on, one of the greatest turnaround performances in all sport. But, I have never seen a list of teams winning after not being asked to follow-on when they could have been. This is, arguably, the worst of all faux pas a cricket captain can make. So, I set about compiling the list. This is not a simple task and involves a fair amount of programming as well as applying various rules to the list, e.g. excluding cases where teams have declared behind in order to set up a fourth innings chase. In the end I find 66 cases since 1900, when a 150 run deficit became the primary follow-on norm. I suspect that the list is only about 95% accurate as there have been various changes to this Law over time and different playing conditions in different countries. But it is a worthwhile exercise as at least it provides the bulk of the list which can then be amended to add any others that should be included or delete some that have been mistakenly included when variations on the Law have been used. By the way, Matthew Carter, who if you were paying attention to the June 15 entry you will recall took 7-56 in Somerset's first innings, ended up with 10-195 in the match, leading to another slew of debut and 10 wickets in lost matches on debut stats.

The second case is the Surrey v Glamorgan match (the tail-Wagging one

I mentioned yesterday). When Wagg came to the wicket in Glamorgan's first innings they were 106-6 in reply to Surrey's 406. Today they ended up winning the game by 7 wickets. So, I check how this compares with other similar match situations and Glamorgan have equalled the biggest victory margin by a team that was 300 or more behind at the fall of the sixth wicket in their first innings. The only other team to do this was WG Grace's London County team against the MCC in 1903. They were 23-6 in reply to MCC's 360 before recovering to 204, bowling MCC out for 86 and knocking off the target of 243 for just three wickets. All told it has been a cracking round of Championship games.

And number three in the list involves Papua New Guinea, who are already the only team to win each of their first two ODIs. They did this against Hong Kong in Townsville last year. (To save you reaching for your atlas, Townsville is in neither Hong Kong nor Papua New Guinea, but is in Queensland, Australia). Today they beat Netherlands by five wickets chasing 305 to win their inaugural first-class match. A bit of checking on the database reveals this to be the highest successful fourth innings' run-chase by a team on their first-class debut, beating East Zone's 284-8 against Australian Services in 1945.

June 19

CricketArchive is, I suspect, the primary Internet resource for many of the world's more serious cricket statisticians. Their server crashed three days ago and it is still down today. CricketArchive shedding is undoubtedly worse than electricity shedding and I am having withdrawal symptoms.

In Galle, Sri Lanka make up for a lot of lost time by reducing Pakistan to 118-5 in reply to 300 by the end of day three of a Test that has yet to produce much statistical excitement, but now may yet produce a result despite the weather.

The All-Rounders' Ratio (dividing batting average by bowling average) is sometimes used as a measure for all-round performance. There are arguments about the validity of the measure, but it does give some indication of ability if used carefully. A decent all-rounder would want his batting average to be higher than his bowling average and a ratio in excess of 1.50 is exceptional. The best in Test cricket are Garry Sobers and Jacques Kallis who are both on 1.69. In first-class cricket the 'Big Ship', Australia's Warwick Armstrong is a surprise leader with 2.37 and there are a few others over 2, including WG Grace at 2.17. Dolphins' player Daryn Smit has been plying his trade for Ramsbottom in the Lancashire League for the past few seasons. I notice at this stage of the season he has scored 614 runs at an average of 153.50 and taken 38 wickets at 8.65. This gives him a not-too-shabby all-rounders' ratio of 17.73 for the season to date.

June 20

Pakistan storm back into contention in Galle. Having been 96-5 yesterday they recover to 417 and nip out two Sri Lankan wickets, including Kumar, before the close. Asad Shafiq is last man out for 131, but the main catalyst for Pakistan's advantage in the game is provided by wicket-keeper, Sarfraz Ahmed, who hits 96 off 86 balls. In his last 10 Tests he has 826 runs at 91.77, an average beaten only by Andy Flower in a 10-Test sequence by a keeper. (Flower averaged 122.90 in his best 10-Test sequence). Most modern cricket fans love seeing attacking batting, but there are still a few old fuddy duddies like me who think that it can be a bit reckless at times. Fortunately we are a dying breed so there is not a great deal of negative reaction to Sarfraz's dismissal which ESPNCricInfo recorded as 'Prasad to Sarfraz Ahmed, **OUT**, he's tried one stroke too many and has given away a Test 100, *trying to sweep a fast bowler from several feet outside off*, got to the ball just on the full, and only underedged it on to his stumps, he is walking back slowly, placing his bat on his helmet in frustration'. The italics, as they say, are mine.

At Chester-le-Street, England complete a 3-2 ODI series in dramatic fashion. New Zealand make 283-9 (remember when that was a good score?), and after England collapse to 45-5 chasing a reduced target of 192 off 26 overs Jonny Bairstow swats (I think that is the first time I have used 'swats') 83* off 60 balls to help them to a three wicket win with an over to spare. The series has produced plenty of ODI records, none of them by bowlers. 3 151 runs and 390 boundaries are records for a 5-match series and 7.15 runs per over is the highest in any series. There won't be many answering the 'Bowlers Wanted' ads in the papers tomorrow.

June 21

I wake to news that, in his first start since the game I mentioned on 14 June, Max Scherzer has come within an elbow of a perfect game. With two outs in the bottom of the ninth and the Pittsburgh Pirates down to their last strike, Jose Tabata leans into a pitch and it hits him on the elbow. In baseball, a hitter is awarded first base if he is hit by the pitch, with the proviso that he needs to be attempting to avoid getting hit. So, there is a lot of discussion as to whether Scherzer was robbed of a perfect game by the umpiring call, but the reality is that it is very rare for a hitter not to be allowed a 'hit by pitch' and the Tabata type is generally allowed. And, as any good umpire will tell you, sports officials should not base their decisions on game situations. In any event, Scherzer has produced almost certainly the best back-to-back performance by a pitcher in Major League history.

Later in the day, Pakistan pull off a tremendous win. They bowl Sri Lanka out for 206 and win by 9 wickets. Legspinner Yasir Shah continues the impressive start to his Test career with 7-76 and his 46 wickets to date are the most by any Pakistan bowler in his first eight Tests. There is another match situation stat to look up. Pakistan were 204 behind when their fifth wicket fell in their first innings. 34 teams have now won a Test having been 200 or more behind when their fifth wicket fell in their first innings, but Pakistan are the first to do so by 10 wickets.

Bangladesh beat India in the ODI to complete a series win (2-0 with one to play) and, more importantly qualify for the ICC Champions Trophy in England in 2017. Pakistan and West Indies will have to fight it out to see which of them misses out on the eight-team tournament. For all of their international cricket history, Bangladesh have been largely disregarded, not least by statisticians. Many of the more analytical type 21st century cricket statistics have been produced as '... excluding Zimbabwe and Bangladesh'. So, it is fantastic to see Bangladesh disrupt the Top Eight Teams Club. The top eight teams in the rankings will qualify for the 2019 World Cup with the next best having to play in the World Cup Qualifier in 2018. Some cynical people think that the Qualifier has been scheduled in Bangladesh to increase that country's chances of making it into the elite 10 for the actual World Cup. However, if they continue their current improvement they may very well qualify automatically leaving some other anxious Full Member team to fight out for qualification with the top Associates in unfamiliar conditions in Bangladesh. Or, as some cynical people might expect, the qualifying tournament may be moved to whichever other Full Member finished outside the top eight.

June 22

The US Open golf finishes in the early hours of the morning in South Africa, while I am fast asleep, but Jordan Spieth is clearly the Max Scherzer of golf at the moment. Having collected the Masters in April he has now won both majors this year and he is still 21 years old. Comparisons may be odious, as the saying goes, but most of us still enjoy the smell of them. I hope young Mr Spieth will not soon be hailed as the greatest golfer ever as Tiger Woods was in his early days. Woods was undoubtedly the best and most exciting golfer in the world for most of his career, but unlike other sports, golf has, I think, a clear measure when it comes to the best ever: Number of majors won. There have been four majors a year since 1934, so it is a consistent standard. Jack Nicklaus won 18 majors in his career and while Tiger seemed to be on course (excuse the dreadful golfing pun) to pass that, he has been stuck on 14 since 2008. He turns 40 this year and is in the worst form of his life, missing the cut this weekend, so Nicklaus' record is looking safe for a while. By the way, cricket has a propensity for using initials in scorecards, so if he was a cricketer, Woods would be known as ET Woods (for Eldrick Tont).

Meanwhile news has come through that Shane Warne has booked some Major League baseball parks for T20 exhibition matches involving retired players in November: Dodger Stadium in Los Angeles, Yankee Stadium in New York and Wrigley Field in Chicago to be specific. One can't really complain about attempts to spread the game around the world, but a number of amateur meteorologists, including me, are quick to notice a potential flaw. New York gets cold in November and Chicago even colder. Snow is distinctly possible in Chicago, which is also not known as The Windy City for nothing. All of which could make outdoor cricket decidedly unpleasant. Any Chicago Cubs fan will no doubt be able to tell Warne that he should have booked Wrigley Field in October. I feel the need to explain that reference, so if you understand it I suggest that you jump to tomorrow's entry. For the rest of you, the Cubs are notorious for being one of the losingest (pardon the American terminology, but I am sure you will understand) teams in all of baseball. They last won the World Series in 1908 and have not appeared in the World Series since 1945. So, expectations are always low and the reference, cruel as it may be, to Wrigley Field being available in October implies that the Cubs can be pretty much guaranteed to fail to make the playoffs yet again.

The ICC's Annual Conference begins in Barbados today. I suspect that the list of apologies from delegates will be shorter than usual this time, given the location.

June 23

There is some excitement amongst the commentators as Surrey's extras get into the 60s against Derbyshire, but I put a bit of a dampener on it by tweeting the world and county records for most extras in an innings of 99 conceded by Gujranwala v Lahore City in 1997 and 98 by Essex v Northamptonshire in 1999, respectively.

June 24

There is a huge sigh of relief in Statsville's Cricket suburb as the Great CricketArchive Blackout Of 2015 finally comes to an end. It has been eight days since the website suffered what must have been a spectacular server crash, but it is good to have it back.

Stuart Broad takes 7-84 for Nottinghamshire v Yorkshire on his birthday which inevitably leads me to wonder about best bowling performances on a birthday. I am confident that there will be better ones than Broad and I start by restricting the search to County Championship matches. It is fairly tricky mainly because I have to try and figure out what day of the match a specific bowling performance took place which as I may have mentioned before is not that easy programmatically. So, it is a case of finding performances that took place in matches which started a few days before, or on, a player's birthday and then checking each case individually. Quite early in the process I come across the great left-arm spinner Hedley Verity taking 10-36 on his 26th birthday for Yorkshire against Warwickshire at Leeds in 1931. There are few better bowling figures in first-class cricket than that on any day, never mind a birthday. (Verity's own 10-10 for Yorkshire v Nottinghamshire in 1932 is the best). I can quickly check the few better than 10-36 to confirm that none of them was on a birthday and can therefore happily proclaim Verity's as a birthday best.

The ODI series in Bangladesh finishes with a consolation win for India, bringing to an end an impressive 10 match winning sequence for Bangladesh in home ODIs. Apart from a brief interruption in the second match the monsoon rains have stayed away from the ODI series. So the monsoons have clearly indicated their preference for the shorter format of the game.

June 25

They are underway at the P Saravanamuttu Stadium in Colombo as the second Test between Sri Lanka and Pakistan starts today. This stadium is known as the P Sara for short and once on an England tour, in a classic clash of pronunciation and accent, some of the English journos requested a ride from an auto rickshaw driver to the 'P Sara' and were disappointed to end up at the nearest Pizza Hut. It is a good day for the hosts as they bowl Pakistan out for 138 and finish in command at 70-1. Younis Khan becomes the 62nd player to appear in 100 Test matches, a number of colleagues that Colin Cowdrey probably never imagined joining him when he became the first to reach 100 Tests back in 1968.

June 26

As expected the ICC Annual Conference has ratified the Cricket Committee's recommendations with regards to fielding restrictions in the ODI Playing Conditions. I am sure you will remember all the details, having diligently absorbed them on the May 18 entry in this diary. The changes mean that there will be an overall average of 3.8 fielders allowed outside the circle during the 50 overs compared to an average of 3.5 in the last set of Playing Conditions. Will an 8.5% increase in outfielders result in a similar percentage reduction in scoring rates? In ODIs to date this year the overall run-rate has been 5.67, a massive 7.1% higher than any other year, with the previous highest being 5.29 which was set last year. With the new regulations, bowlers could be dancing in the streets like it is 2014 all over again.

I am amused when perusing the new Playing Conditions (which, by the way, are being implemented immediately, rather than the usual first of October cutoff date). Having got rid of voluntary power players, the three new fielding regulations are all called powerplays in the document. So that presumably ends all 'Block Plays', 'Normal Plays' and 'Nudge and Nurdle Plays' that used to be part of ODIs' rhythms and tempos. From now on it is Power, Power, Power all the way.

It is Market Day at school again and this time it is the seven-year-old's turn to do some selling. She has made 40 aeroplanes out of clothes pegs and I am quite chuffed when she manages to sell all 40 (and not all to various grandparents). Attempts to get the five-year-old to buy anything with a sugar content below 95% are as futile as last time.

There is domestic drama in the afternoon as a plate on the stove randomly switches itself on and sets fire to a package of books and papers. Fortunately a couple of bowls of water put the fire out quickly, but we are heading into what will be Johannesburg's coldest weekend of the winter so we can't leave doors open to remove the burning smell for very long.

June 27

It is Scherzer-watch again as the first thing I check in the morning is what he did last night. It is another great start as he is perfect through five and a third innings before actually giving up a couple of runs. He does, however, extend his hitting streak to six games, which is a lot for a pitcher. A bit like Glenn McGrath reaching 20 in six consecutive innings, I suppose.

Browsing the scorecard of the match between North Island and New South Wales at Wellington in 1894, as one does, I come across an interesting player called James McDonogh. Born in Ireland, he played six first-class matches: the one in New Zealand in 1894, two for Europeans in India in 1903 and three on tour for Philadelphians in Jamaica in 1909. That is a good effort to get around as much as he did in those days, and I am sure his life story must be more interesting than his cricket career, which produced 203 runs at 18.45 and 10 wickets at 25.70 in those six matches.

Kumar Sangakkara has announced that the second Test of the home series against India in August will be his last. So, it is official now. He is going.

The ICC Strategy 2016-19 in their press release following the Annual conference reveals a vision to become the 'world's favourite sport'. This is, of course, a good vision and one that you would expect governing bodies to aspire to. How do you define the world's favourite sport, however? Ticket sales? By my estimation (and it must be an estimation as very few official figures find their way into the public domain), cricket sells about 15 million tickets annually world-wide. Our friends at Wikipedia have an interesting list of attendances at sporting leagues. Football's Premier League in England sold 13 942 459 tickets in 2013/14, roughly the same as the whole world of cricket. North America's favorite (note clever use of

American spelling) sports sell a lot of tickets. 254 NFL games in 2013 drew an attendance of 17 372 838, and average of 68 397 per game. Both the NHL and NBA drew over 21 million in their most recent seasons. Not bad for sports played indoors. Never mind Major League Baseball which easily tops the attendance league selling in the region of 75 million tickets a year, even Japan's Nippon Professional Baseball draws over 22 million fans a season. But ticket sales certainly aren't the only metric to define the world's favourite (or indeed 'favorite') sport. Another important factor would surely be that you need to have a broad-based presence across the world. The world's current favourite sport, football (the Association version thereof), has 209 member countries of FIFA, of which 32 teams play in the World Cup. Yet, even that is not the most. FIBA, the International Basketball Federation has 215 member countries. Rugby Union's IRB has 117 members, with 20 of them to play in the 2019 World Cup. Baseball has 124 countries affiliated to the IBAF. With the addition of Serbia, who was awarded Affiliate Member status yesterday, the ICC has 106 Members. Of these, only 10 are allowed to play Test cricket (the premier form of the game, as we are still occasionally told) and only ten will play in the next World Cup. It would be great if cricket were to become the world's favourite sport, but it has a very, very, very long way to go before that happens.

June 28

The Caribbean Premier League is wildly popular in the West Indies and, unlike Test matches from that part of the world, is actually on South African TV screens, although given that they are played sometime in the middle of the night South African time it seems unlikely that the TV audience in this part of the world is particularly massive. Tonight the St Lucia Zouks are playing the Jamaica Tallawahs. This will be the 5 000th T20 game. It has taken the micro format 12 years and 15 days to reach this number. It took first-class cricket 126 years to see its 5 000th match and the full day limited overs game 23 years.

June 29

Kumar Sangakkara is out first ball in Sri Lanka's run-chase of 153-3 to beat

Pakistan. Maybe it is time to go, Kumar.

There are a lot of runs in county cricket today. At Birmingham batsmen numbers four to seven all score centuries as Sussex pile on 601-6 against Warwickshire. It is the third time that numbers four to seven have all scored centuries in a first-class innings after Pakistan did it against India at Faisalabad in 1983 and Middlesex inflicted it on Warwickshire (again) at Lord's in 2001.

Up in Chester-le-Street, Jonny Bairstow and Tim Bresnan add 366* for Yorkshire's seventh wicket against Durham. It is the highest seventh wicket partnership ever in first-class cricket in England and the third highest overall. It is also the third highest partnership by two players with surnames beginning with 'B' for any wicket behind the famous 405 between Don Bradman and Sid Barnes for Australia against England at Sydney in 1946 (mostly famous because both batsmen made 234 and Barnes claimed he was deliberately out for the same score as Bradman, being of the opinion that he was more likely to be remembered for making the same score as Bradman rather than making a higher score) and the rather less famous 441 by Carl Bradfield and John Bryant for Eastern Province v North West at Potchefstroom in 2002.

Cricket Australia announces that the Adelaide Test against New Zealand in November will be played as a day/night affair. There have been attempts to get Test matches played at night for some time now with ICC encouragement. Concerns over whether the pink ball that will be used is actually good enough don't seem to have been fully resolved, however, despite numerous first-class matches where it has been used. Dean Jones, by the way, is the only player to score a triple-century in a day/night first-class match having made 324* for Victoria v South Australia at Melbourne in 1995. In those days the ball they used was yellow. The primary purpose of playing games at night is to get more people to watch, or 'make the game more accessible' to be more accurate in marketing-speak. While I am not terribly enthusiastic about the concept of playing Tests at night (especially if they go on after my bedtime) it will be interesting to see whether it has the desired effect on attendance and TV audiences. At least the game will be more accessible than what was supposed to be the third Test between New Zealand and Australia which will no doubt have disappeared from the fixture list when it is announced as mulled by Cricket New Zealand earlier this month (see June 4). The best way to make any game inaccessible is to not play it at all.

June 30

One of cricket's oldest fixtures starts today as Oxford and Cambridge Universities meet at Fenners in Cambridge. They first met in a first-class match back in 1827 and have played an annual match pretty much every year since then. The game has nowhere near the status (cricketing or social) it had in the early days, although it was still played at Lord's until 2000. Its status as a first-class match is more a function of history and tradition than current playing standards. In case you are interested in the score, Cambridge finish the day on 99-3 in reply to Oxford's 156 all out. Pollock (that's AW, not RG, PM or SM) took 4-43 and Crichard 5-62.

Meanwhile Miles Jupp has been announced as the new chairman for *The News Quiz*, replacing Sandi Toksvig. Apart from probably never being able to shake his primary claim to fame which is playing the inventor, Archie, on the kiddies' TV program *Balamory*, Jupp's cricketing claim to fame is his failed attempt to become a cricket journalist which he wrote about in *Fibber in the Heat*. It is well worth a read.

July 1

Warwickshire manage to get to 612-6 in reply to Sussex's 601-6* at Birmingham, providing the 10th highest first innings score that has been overhauled in first-class history. No doubt the write-ups will suggest that this game is 'one for the statisticians'. That may have some truth to it, but most statisticians are actually cricket lovers as well and would recognise that it was actually a terrible game of cricket. Here is something I have never understood: If a game is over in a day and a half and especially if the pitch is turning square, the inspectors are immediately summonsed and the home team docked points or money. Yet, pitches that are so flat that there is never any prospect of producing a result have never, to my knowledge, produced any form of sanction. While a pitch which produces a game where, say, 100 and 110 plays 90 and 121-9 might not be entirely desirable, it is a whole lot better than 601-6 plays 612-6.

But the good news is that all those stats provide a soothing balm to the rest of the day. I am very fortunate to travel quite a lot, but a consequence is that my passport is getting full and will need replacement soon. I spend most of the day frustratingly standing in the queue applying for a new one and am thus in need of soothing balm by the time I get home.

July 2

It is day 183 of the year. So we are halfway through. Much to my own amazement, I am still doing this diary. So, I suppose I had better finish it now.

Having strolled to 562 at five runs an over in their tour match against Essex, Australia find things a bit tougher with the ball. Essex are 299-3 by the close with opener Tom Westley's 144 drawing comparisons with a young Alastair Cook scoring a double-century for Essex against the Australians in a two-day tour match in 2005.

To general lack of interest in the broader cricketing world Cambridge complete a five wicket win in the Varsity match.

July 3

Roelof van der Merwe makes his debut for Netherlands today in a T20 International against Nepal. He was a South African last week, but has just got his Dutch passport (his mother is Dutch). Van der Merwe had played 13 ODIs and 13 T20 Internationals for South Africa between 2009 and 2010. There are now 25 players who have appeared for two different countries in official internationals. Apart from Van der Merwe, four others of these have played for South Africa: Frank Hearne and Frank Mitchell both also played for England back in pre-World War I days, while Kepler Wessels played for Australia and John Traicos also played for Zimbabwe.

One of my current projects is checking statistical details of Ali Bacher and David Williams' book on South Africa's best batsmen. When David phones tonight, I am too polite to tell him I am in the middle of playing a bridge hand and dutifully answer his questions. Having been distracted by the phone call however, I forget where the king of diamonds is and go one down on a contract which I should have made with a simple finesse for said king.

July 4

Dunedin is one of my favourite places in the world, despite it being fairly low in the league table of 'Cities With The Best Weather In The World'.

There will be much joy in that city tonight. While out with the kids watching a *Beautiful Creatures'* performance at an open air theatre, I am distracted (like many of the other dads) by the big screen which is showing the Super Rugby final and the Highlanders beat the Hurricanes to collect their first Super Rugby title. For a place with a population of just 125 000, Dunedin has a tremendous sporting record. Apart from rugby they have also produced a number of notable cricketers, none more so than Brendon McCullum, who would currently be very high, maybe even top, in the league table of 'Leading Cricketers In The World'. Given New Zealand's deep love of rugby, I suspect that McCullum will be more pleased with today's rugby result than the 158* he whacked off 64 balls for the Birmingham Bears (The Team Formerly Known As Warwickshire County Cricket Club) in a NatWest T20 Blast game last night.

The Rhino announces his retirement. Like many others, I have always admired Ryan Harris as a cricketer. Despite incessant injury problems he managed to fight his way through 27 Test matches as a highly skilled quick bowler. Having been ruled out of the Ashes series with yet another injury, he has finally packed it in. He retires as the only seamer to have taken 100 Test wickets having made his debut after the age of 30 (five spinners have also done this, in case you are wondering). During his Test career Australia played 54 Tests in total. Of these, they won 16 and lost 6 of the 27 Harris played and won 9 and lost 13 when he didn't play.

In Pallekele, Yasir Shah picks up his customary five wicket haul (three in four innings now) as Pakistan bowl Sri Lanka out for 278 on the second day of the third Test of what has been a well-contested series. By the close Pakistan are 209-9 in reply.

July 5

It is time to travel again. I am off back to London tonight to do the Ashes for Test Match Special. So, it is the usual busy pre-travel day, but I keep an eye on the scores of the Test in Pallekele. It remains a tight contest without producing much of great statistical significance as Sri Lanka finish the day in the ascendancy leading by 291 with five wickets in hand.

July 6

Bad light stops play and causes draw is a fairly regular occurrence in cricket. Today it happens at Wimbledon. Being in London, I suppose I should have made an effort to get down to SW19, but instead I watch Kevin Anderson take on Novak Djokovic in the fourth round on the TV. Patriot fervour flares as South Africa's Anderson takes the first two sets on tie-breakers. But Djokovic takes the next two and bad light stops play with the match 'drawn'. They will come back tomorrow to finish it. By the way, it is interesting that Wimbledon is instantly recognisable by its post code 'SW19'. You do not often hear Lord's referred to as 'NW8'. And you are even less likely to hear The Oval referred to as 'SE11'.

There is a big turnaround in Pallekele as Pakistan, having lost their first two wickets for 13 chasing a victory target of 377 finish the day on 230-2 with Shan Masood on 114* and Younis Khan, who becomes the first player to make five fourth innings centuries in Tests, on 101*. There could be some statistical significance tomorrow if Pakistan chase down the target.

July 7

Djokovic wins the fifth set and the match, so they won't be dancing in the streets in Johannesburg today. Or, if they do, it won't be because of any tennis result.

In Pallekele, Pakistan go on to win easily by seven wickets. Younis Khan's fifth fourth innings' century proves to be his first in a match-winning effort as he finishes with 171*. It is the fifth highest individual score for a winning team in the fourth innings of a Test (Gordon Greenidge's 214* for West Indies against England at Lord's in 1984 is the best). Pakistan finish on 382-3 which is the sixth highest fourth innings total to win a Test and the second highest while losing three or fewer wickets behind Australia's 404-3 v England at Lord's.

Tomorrow I will be at my first Ashes Test in England. Or at least it would be but for the minor technical detail that the match is actually being played in Wales. On the train down to Cardiff there are notably more Australian accents than Welsh ones, and this is even more noticeable when I get to my hotel. England and Australia are the only countries that have fans travel with them in any numbers to overseas Test matches. This is a pity as having a decent number of supporters from both teams at a game

119

greatly enhances the atmosphere. While I am aware that travelling overseas to watch your team play Test cricket is not terribly cheap, I can highly recommend it. Although I have visited the SWALEC Stadium before, this will be the first time I have actually seen cricket there and it will become numbers 43 and 91 on my lists of grounds at which I have watched Test and first-class cricket, respectively.

Sadly, I am beyond the age of having sporting heroes, unless you count the Red Sox slugger David Ortiz. But when I was growing up in the 1970s in Natal (as it then was) my heroes were naturally Barry Richards and Vince van der Bijl. The reading material on the train to Cardiff is Andrew Murtagh's biography of Barry: *Sundial in the Shade*. Nostalgia may not be what it used to be, but it still kicked in during the read.

July 8

One of the discussions that sometimes comes up amongst those of us lucky enough to travel a bit to see Test cricket is which grounds have the best approach. Adelaide is always mentioned as the walk from town across the Torrens River is very pleasant. A stroll through Queens Park on the way to the WACA in Perth is thoroughly enjoyable. And of course the walk from St John's Wood tube station to Lord's is right up there with the general buzz of anticipation. I also rate the walk through the old University buildings and the sleepy suburbs of Dunedin (Sleepy, I suspect, mostly because the students are recovering from their previous night's activities. Activities which, being Dunedin, probably included burning old sofas. It is their 'thing'). I do like a good walk to a ground and the one to the SSE SWALEC Stadium (Known as Sophia Gardens in the Pre Naming Rights Era) has to be one of the best. The walk takes you past Cardiff Castle (They love a good castle in this part of the world, and Cardiff's is as impressive as most), the Millennium Stadium (the Stadium Formerly Known As Cardiff Arms Park before it was rebuilt, and a first-class cricket ground in its previous avatar), and through Sophia Gardens with its impressive tree collection and the River Taff. Even the rain is soft and gentle.

That's enough pretentious cricket ground walk waffle for now. In the actual play England are 43-3 when Joe Root faces his second ball. He is dropped by Brad Haddin and England finish the day on 343-7 with Root making 134 of them. He reaches his 100 off 118 balls which is the quickest century by anyone for either team in the first Test of an Ashes series. Steve Waugh used to hold the record with his 124-ball effort in 1989, while good old Charlie Barnett (127 balls in 1938) was the previous fastest for England.

Every time I see veteran Pakistan cricket journalist Qamar Ahmed the first thing I ask is how many Tests he has been at. I do this as usual at lunch today and the reply is that this one is number 411. Richie Benaud was reported has having done his 500th back in 2004. Qamar is always quick to point out, with a slight hint of disapproval, that Richie included the 63 that he played in. I think it is probably fair enough to include the ones you played in, but either way Qamar must be very near the top of the all-time list of Test match attendances.

July 9

It is another closely fought day at Cardiff although England are probably slightly ahead with the visitors 264-5 at the close in reply to 430. Having blown England away in the series in Australia in 2013/14 with 37 wickets at 13.97, Mitchell Johnson finishes with his worst figures in a Test innings of 0-111. The loudest cheer of the day was when he reached his 'century'. He has now conceded 100 runs or more in a Test innings 21 times which puts him joint second on this undesirable list for Australia with Clarrie Grimmett and behind only Shane Warne's 40.

Chris Rogers makes 95 and equals the world record of 50s in seven consecutive Test innings. He is the first opener to do this, the first Australian and the first to do so without going on to reach a century. Everton Weekes ('Wallop' to Frank Worrell's 'Wonderful' and Clyde Walcott's 'Woe' of the famous West Indies' 'Three W's') was the first to do this back in 1949. I suspect that I am almost certainly the only person to have been at the ground on each of the four occasions that this record has been equalled since then. There certainly weren't many at Queens Club in Bulawayo when Andy Flower scored his seventh consecutive 50 against Bangladesh in 2001. It is hard to imagine that any of those who were there apart from me were also at Port Elizabeth in 2007 when Shiv Chanderpaul equalled the record and at Leeds last year when Kumar Sangakkara joined the club. Can Rogers be the first to get eight?

July 10

There is quite a bit of emphasis on starting a series well, and especially so for the Ashes. Whether this necessarily has a significant impact on the result of the series is a matter of debate (or, if time ever permits, statistical research). But it is certainly interesting when Australia are bowled out for 308 to note that this is the first time in 10 Ashes' series that England have taken a first innings lead in the opening encounter. The last time was in 1997 at Birmingham. On that occasion England replied to Australia's 118 with 478-9*. They went on to win the match by nine wickets, but still lost the six-match series 3-2.

When Shane Watson is lbw for the 28th time in his Test career (his 26.66% is the highest of all players with 100 or more dismissals in Tests) Australia's batsmen number three to six in the order have produced the first instance in Test cricket of all being out in the 30s. They all got in and they all got out. By the end of the day England are all out in their second innings and Australia will need 412 to win in the remaining two days of the match.

There has been much excitement in South Africa about the development of young quick bowler Kagiso Rabada. Last year South Africa won the Under-19 World Cup with Rabada taking 6-25 against Australia in the semi-final. He also has a first-class best of 9-33 (14 in the match), as you will know from having absorbed the details of the February 22 entry in this diary. Today he makes one of the most impressive ODI debuts ever. He takes wickets with the fourth, fifth and sixth balls of his second over to join Taijul Islam as the only bowlers to have taken a hat-trick on ODI debut. Coincidentally, Taijul Islam took his last year against Zimbabwe at the same ground as Rabada: Mirpur. Rabada goes on to take 6-16 which are not only the best by any bowler on ODI debut but also the best for South Africa ever. Expectations are going to be high.

It is a good day for South Africa over Bangladesh as the Under-19s also win in the third ODI in Pietermaritzburg. This is a more impressive achievement than it might seem. Bangladesh's recent progress has not just been at the senior level. In April their Under-19s clobbered their South African counterparts 6-1 in a series in Bangladesh. That may have been relatively predictable as the South Africans would not have been used to Bangladesh conditions, but you would expect South Africa to come out on top at home. Not so: Bangladesh have won the first two matches of the current series.

Have a quick look at the March 13 entry where I used the old busses coming along at the same time joke in reference to Mahmudullah becoming the first player to score his first two ODI centuries in consecutive games having waited over 100 games for his first. Well, players scoring their first two centuries in consecutive ODIs having waited over 100 games for their first are now coming along like busses. Elton Chigumbura scores 104* for Zimbabwe against India in Harare today, having made his first ODI 100 (117) in his previous game, his 174th, against Pakistan in Karachi in May.

July 11

A photo appears in the press box of an Australian touring team to England. The trick is to figure out which year it was. Identifying old players in photographs is not actually one of my fortes. And I can't name a single one of the players in this one, but you will be pleased to hear that I instantly recognised the scorer. WH Ferguson ('Fergie') was the original 'Mr Cricket' and went on many tours in the first half of the 20th century as scorer and baggage master (there was proper multi-tasking in those days). In fact he did 204 Test matches worldwide between 1905 and 1954. Not bad considering there was only a total of around 300 in that period. Ferguson was quite a pioneer in scoring terms, keeping wagon wheels, linear sheets and balls faced long before they were fashionable. Anyway, Australian radio doyen Jim Maxwell comes to the rescue with the date of the photo. He spots ECS (Ted) White straightaway as White used to play in the same team as Jim's father. White did not play Test cricket but his only tour was 1938, so that seemed to solve the problem, even though Bradman was not in the photo.

Chris Rogers fails to reach 50 for the first time in eight innings. He does, however, get off the mark, making 10 and this keeps him on course for another potential record. Countryman Jim Burke holds the record for longest career without a duck — 44 innings. Rogers is now up to 41 and, having announced that this is his valedictory series could well claim that record for himself.

One of the tricks of the trade in cricket statistics is to store up potential stats. While David Warner is batting I look up his second innings record, knowing that it is better than his first innings record. He currently has six 100s in the first innings and six in the second. So, if he reaches 100 today he will have more 100s in the second innings than the first. I research which players with at least 10 Test 100s have more in the second innings than the first. There are only two of them: Mark Taylor with nine in the first innings and ten in the second and Mohinder Amarnath (five and six). Warner is dismissed for 52 in the last over before lunch so does not join them, but I will be on the lookout if he does in future.

Warner's dismissal precipitates a collapse as Australia go from 97-1 to 106-4 then 122-5. They never recover and are bowled out for 242. Going into the match, Joe Root had a remarkable bowling record in Tests: Against batsmen in the top five in the order he had seven wickets at an average of 29.00, but against batsmen six to eleven in the order he had just one wicket for 159. He ruins it a bit by getting numbers eight and nine out. But he takes the final catch to complete England's unexpected and emphatic win. So, he completes a useful match triple: 134 & 60, 2-28 and two catches. The only other England players with 190 runs, two wickets and two catches in the same Test are Ted Dexter (205, 2-48 & 3-86 and 2 catches) v Pakistan at Karachi in 1962 and Ian Botham (50 & 149*, 6-95 & 1-14 and 2 catches) in the famous match against Australia at Headingley in 1981.

Shane Watson is lbw for the second time in the match and his percentage of lbws in Ashes Test is up to 40 (14 out of 35). In the light of this, I am amused to discover that he has been dismissed most often in Ashes Tests for either team (35) without being out 'bowled'.

July 12

My Welsh is not very good — non-existent in fact. They do love the double 'L' though, and I notice on the boards while waiting for the train that the Welsh name for London is 'Llundain'. So there is the bit of useless information for the day.

I haven't paid much attention to Wimbledon due to the cricket, but I get back to London in time to see the last few sets in the Men's final. The dream of Roger Federer (and I suspect most tennis fans) for an eighth title, just short of his 34th birthday, are destroyed by Novak Djokovic. Federer had twin daughters the day before my second daughter was born which immediately made me reduce my ambitions for my daughter to a semi-final at Wimbledon. The cricket yesterday meant that I saw none of Serena Williams completing her second 'Serena Slam' in the Women's final. She currently holds all four Grand Slam titles and just needs the US Open later this year to complete a proper Grand Slam of all of them in the same year.

July 13

Last year Middlesex had a County Championship match scheduled at Merchant Taylors' School in Northwood. It was meant to be the first first-class match at the ground. Sadly not a ball was bowled. This year the match against Somerset started on the 11th and thus the ground joined the first-class list. I was all set to go there today, but guess what? It rained all day. Not heavily at all, but enough to ensure no play. So, instead I catch up on some stuff that got neglected during the Test.

July 14

Although it is overcast all day there is only a little bit of rain, so I manage to add Merchant Taylors' School to the list of grounds that I have watched first-class cricket at. It joins Technikon Oval in Pretoria, Soweto Oval, Sinovich Park in Pretoria, Saxton Oval in Nelson, New Zealand and Sir Lionel Phillips Park, Johannesburg on my esoteric list of venues that I watched some of the inaugural first-class match to be played there. Middlesex, trying desperately to keep in contention for the title, attempt to make a game of it by setting Somerset a target of 219 in 40 overs, amidst assorted comments about the old Sunday League in England (will the run ups be restricted, eight overs for each bowler, etc.?). But Somerset end up on 147-7 as the game fizzles out.

The home run in baseball is one of the most exciting things in sport. It has both great rarity value (roughly one is struck every 60 minutes) and great game-changing potential as you can score up to four runs in one shot. Last night MLB had their annual Home Run Derby. While this is a bit of fun with some of the biggest sluggers in the game getting powder-puff pitches to belt out of the park it must be one of the more boring events in any sport from a competitive point of view. The rare and exciting becomes the norm and mundane. Often players hit more home runs in one night than they do in the whole season. I pay negligible attention as Todd Frazier of the Cincinnati Reds wins, whacking 39 dingers altogether on the night. He is having a good season to date in proper games and will be very happy with the 25 home runs he has hit in 85 games so far.

July 15

I travel down to Deal on the Kent coast to see another old mate. Brian Croudy is one of the unsung heroes of cricket statistics and the Association of Cricket Statisticians and Historians. I had stayed with him on South Africa's first post-apartheid tour in 1994 and it is good to catch up. All things considered it is a quiet day in preparation for the second Test.

July 16

Those of you who are concerned that I am too interested in baseball will be pleased to hear that today trumps Fenway Park as the highlight of the year. It is my first Ashes Test at Lord's. When I arrive at around 8.15 the queue of members to get in is already snaking past the Wellington Hospital. Those of you who have done the walk down from St John's Wood tube station will know how long that is.

Sadly the actual cricket isn't as inspiring (unless you are Australian, that is). There is an unshakeable belief amongst cricket fans that cricket is better when run-rates are higher, but in Test cricket the wicket-rate is far more important than the run-rate. And it is too low today. Australia finish the day on 337-1 on a very flat pitch with the only wicket falling coming from a huge slog by David Warner off the last ball of Moeen Ali's first over after Australia had already taken 10 runs off the over. It is just the second time in the 131 Tests played at the ground that only one wicket fell on the first day of the match emulating England's 334-1 against India in 1974.

Chris Rogers (158*) and Steve Smith (129*) add 259* for the second wicket to confine Bill Woodfull and Don Bradman's 231 run partnership in 1930 to the wasteland of the Second Wicket Partnership Records For Australia At Lord's bin. Smith's record batting in the first innings of the match (not to be confused with batting in the team's first innings, although it inevitably is by some of the twitterati) is extraordinary. It is the ninth time in consecutive matches when Australia have batted first that he has reached 50 and he has gone on to 100 on eight of those occasions. Only Mike Atherton (10) has had a longer sequence of reaching 50 in consecutive innings when batting in the first innings of the match. At the end of the day Smith has career averages of 97.23 when batting in the first innings of the match and 36.41 when batting in the other three innings.

There is quite a bit of discussion about the Australian team containing three Mitchells (Marsh, Johnson and Starc). They are the only three Mitchells to have played Test cricket and this is the second time they have all played together but the first in an Ashes match. I manage to find a few instances of teams with four players of the same name. Australia's record seems to be four Bills which happened a few times in the 1930s with Bill Ponsford, Bill Woodfull, Bill O'Reilly and Bill Brown all playing in the same match. Bill Hunt also played a few matches in that period, but they never got all five Bills in the same team. My favourite four-of-the-same-name-in-one-team is the four Maurices (Leyland, Turnbull, Tate and Allom) who were in the England team against South Africa at Durban in 1931. Someone on Twitter suggests to Jonathan Agnew that we should have a Mitch of the Match award.

July 17

Don Bradman's 254 at Lord's in 1930 is generally regarded as his finest Test innings. Until today, Bill Brown (206* in 1938) was the only other Australian to make a double-century at headquarters. Steve Smith joins them with 215 as Australia continue to pile on the runs and eventually declare on 566-8. Smith had been dismissed twice in the 190s (192 & 199) in the last seven months so it will have been a relief to get his first double.

Rod Marsh kept wicket in 69 of Dennis Lillee's 70 Test matches, so the inevitable quiz question 'Who kept in Lillee's only Test without Marsh?' has been doing the rounds ever since. The answer is Roger Woolley against Sri Lanka at Kandy in 1983. Woolley makes it into the conversation today after Australia's debutante wicket-keeper Peter Nevill catches Adam Lyth off the second ball of England's first innings. There is a list of bowlers who have taken a wicket with their first ball in Test cricket, but nothing similar for wicket-keepers. So, I decide to research what the earliest was that a wicket-keeper had taken a dismissal on Test debut. In that match in Kandy Woolley caught Sidath Wettimuny off the second legal delivery (bowled by Lillee, of course). But, Lillee had bowled a no ball off the first ball of the innings, so I claim Nevill as the earliest. Steven Lynch of Wisden and ESPNCricInfo points out that in 1884 at The Oval when Hon Alfred Lyttelton famously removed the pads and took 4-19 bowling lobs (still the best bowling figures by a designated wicket-keeper in a Test match). WG Grace had a session behind the stumps and caught Billy Midwinter off the first ball that Lyttelton bowled with Grace keeping. So, it adds an interesting footnote to Nevill's record, although it was Grace's fifth Test.

July 18

The Pint-sized Ashes (a three minute highlights package of the TMS commentary complete with photos and animations) is a lovely initiative on the BBC's website. I arrive at Lord's in the morning to hear that I made my debut on it last night. Unfortunately I am saying '... and the partnership (between Rogers and Smith) was 283 ...' when in fact it was 284.

Today is remembered in South Africa as the birthday of Nelson Mandela (born 1918), but in cricket it is WG Grace's that is more noted. He was born 167 years ago on 18 July 1848.

England recover a bit from their overnight 85-4, but are all out for 312. As he had done on his three previous opportunities as captain Michael Clarke declines to enforce the follow on. Mitchell Marsh bowls Ben Stokes to create the first instance of three Mitchells taking a wicket in the same Test innings. Australia stroll to 108-0 by the close with Warner on 60*. Will I be able to use that second innings century stat tomorrow?

July 19

On arrival at the ground, I open my glasses case to discover that I have managed to leave my reading glasses at home. I can't read a thing without them. Fortunately, photographer Philip Brown comes to my rescue and lends me a spare pair. Being in a more visual field of expertise than me Philip's fashion sense is a bit different to mine and instead of my bog standard thin brown arms on my prescription glasses his are black with green stripes giving me an unusually snazzy look for the day.

Chris Rogers retires ill after a dizzy spell. It is a matter of great concern following the tragic death of Phil Hughes last year and Rogers' own bout of concussion on the recent tour to the West Indies. He is on 49* at the time and thus misses the opportunity to became just the fourth man to reach 50 in nine innings out of ten. Geoffrey Boycott, Andy Flower and Shiv Chanderpaul are the only three to have done that. Then David Warner gets out for 83, so the second innings century stat will have to wait.

Australia cruise to their declaration at 254-2 with Steve Smith joining Jack Ryder and Don Bradman as the only players to have scored a double-century and a 50 in an Ashes Test for Australia. Jimmy Anderson finishes the match wicket-less for the first time since January 2010. His 59 consecutive Tests taking at least one wicket is the second longest sequence for England behind Fred Trueman's 67 (his entire career). Muttiah Muralitharan holds the world record with 72.

England then collapse tamely to 103 to lose by 405 runs, their third biggest defeat by runs in a Test against Australia. Mitchell Johnson's 3-27 to go with his 3-53 in the first innings confirms him as 'Mitch of the Match'.

There is good news for the Samson family name as Sanju Samson makes his debut for India in a T20 match in Zimbabwe becoming the first Samson to appear in an international.

In other debuts, Imad Wasim makes his ODI debut for Pakistan and it would be a run-of-the-mill debut (2-28 in 7.1 overs) but for the fact that he is the first player to appear in an international for Pakistan who was born in Wales (Swansea, to be precise).

July 20

I am reminded of Lady Bracknell's famous quote 'To lose one parent, Mr Worthing, may be regarded as a misfortune; to lose both looks like carelessness' in Oscar Wilde's play *The Importance of Being Earnest*. A few days ago I had to bin a pair of cream trousers (yes, they are chinos) due to a hole having developed in the seat of the pants and today I spot a similarly positioned tear in my other pair of cream trousers. Enough studies have shown that a sedentary lifestyle is not good for one's health, but it probably isn't great for trousers either.

Meanwhile at Colwyn Bay Alviro Petersen (286) and Ashwell Prince (261) add 501 for Lancashire v Glamorgan. Apart from the usual records listing where it stands in overall partnerships (it is the 13th highest for any wicket in all first-class cricket) I can quickly confirm that it is the highest by two South Africans. It also turns out to be the highest without either player making a triple-century. Prince was the South African captain when Kumar Sangakkara and Mahela Jayawardene put on the highest partnership for any wicket in all first-class cricket of 624 for Sri Lanka against South Africa at the SSC in Colombo in 2006.

The Open Championship at St Andrew's has been badly disrupted by weather (rain and wind) and has been forced into a fifth day leading to jokes about the five day cricket Test finishing in four days while the four day golf tournament has taken five. Jordan Spieth's grand slam challenge ends as he finishes just one behind the leaders and Zach Johnson takes the title after a play off.

July 21

It is another day of catching up with work on the South African Cricket Annual. I am beginning to stress mildly as to whether I can complete everything on time by the end of August. Test cricket commitments with TMS reduce my time available for the Annual.

South Africa scrape together 248 on the first day of the Test against Bangladesh in Chittagong. Left-arm seamer Mustafizur Rahman who had taken a world record 11 wickets in his first two ODIs last month against India took three wickets in four balls on Test debut. Three players: Maurice Allom (Eng), Peter Petherick (NZ) and Damien Fleming (Aus) have taken a hat-trick on Test debut and Mustafizur joins five others with three wickets in four balls on debut.

In the evening it is back to Heathrow for the flight to Johannesburg. I am going home for a few days because it is my youngest daughter's birthday on the 24th and the Ashes schedule allows a short gap to get home for four nights and then back to England in time for the third Test in Birmingham.

July 22

The highlight on the second day at Chittagong where Bangladesh finish on decent 179-4 in reply to South Africa's 248 is that South Africa's opening batting pair Dean Elgar and Stiaan van Zyl dismiss their opposite numbers Tamim Iqbal and Imrul Kayes, respectively. This causes great excitement in the Arcane Cricket Statistics Fan Club. I restrict the search to opening batsmen in the first innings only as there are a number of cases of non-regular opening batsmen opening in the second innings including some where opening bowlers opened the batting. I can find only one other case where first innings batting openers each dismissed an opponent's opener in a Test innings. Trevor Goddard and Eddie Barlow must be one of the best bowling opening batting pairs in Test cricket (they were certainly better bowlers than Elgar and Van Zyl) and at Port Elizabeth in 1967 they dismissed Australian openers Bobby Simpson and Bill Lawry, respectively.

July 23

Bangladesh continue their steady performance and are all out for 326, a lead of 78. South Africa end the day on 61-0 in a Test match that has been far more competitive than most people expected as Bangladesh extend their significant recent improvement.

After collecting the kids from school, I take the one who is having her last day as a five-year-old to get a birthday present: Her first proper bicycle. Of course, it has to come with a basket, a bell, tassels for the handle bars and lights (front and back). When buying a bike you clearly need to 'Accessorise, Accessorise, Accessorise'.

July 24

The birthday arrives, and so the five-year-old becomes the six-year-old. The school has a 'Birthday Ring' each time a child in the class has a birthday, so it is the first of the parties today, and my first cupcake of the party weekend.

Fortunately I do not miss any cricket while at the school function on account of the monsoon wiping out play for the day in Chittagong.

July 25

To no great surprise there is a soggy end in Chittagong with the last two days being washed out. The two monsoon season Tests in Bangladesh so far (this one and the one against India in June) have seen a combined total of 405.2 overs, the equivalent of four and a half days' play. I wonder what the odds are of a result at Mirpur next week.

The day is spent in birthday parties. There are two of them for family and friends.

July 26

After the fourth birthday party in three days for the six-year-old I am flying back to London. It is my fifth flight between Johannesburg and London in three months and I wonder what movie I am going to watch, as I reckon I have pretty much covered the ones I am likely to be interested in of the current selection, including two hotel movies (*Second Best Exotic Marigold* and *Grand Budapest*) and *Seven Year Itch*. Yes, that is the 1955 Marilyn Monroe film.

Pakistan have postponed their scheduled tour to Zimbabwe in August. The reasons for this are clearly related to ICC Champions Trophy qualification. The ICC has created qualification based on rankings for the Champions Trophy and the World Cup. Pakistan are ranked eighth, just ahead of West Indies, and are naturally reluctant to jeopardise their position by playing games before the 30 September cutoff that they may lose and thus not qualify for the Champions Trophy. It should be fairly obvious, without even the benefit of hindsight that using a rankings system for qualification in a situation where fixtures are the subject of bilateral bargaining will result in fixtures lists becoming a function of ranking positions. If the ICC wants to have qualification processes for major tournaments (and this is actually a Good Thing) there needs to be independent control over the fixtures. In fact the ICC itself does exactly this for Women's cricket. The eight major teams play a three match ODI series against each other over the qualifying period and the four teams with the most points go through to the World Cup with the rest playing the best of the others for the remaining World Cup places. It should surely be possible to do something similar for the men as well. There are 12 teams in the official ICC ODI rankings. Perhaps they should each have to play one match at home and away against each of the other teams. This would be 22 matches overall over a four year period and would not really affect the current tours program as you could still have as many matches in an ODI series as you want. It would just be that the first match in each series would count towards the qualifying log. And the top teams would not have to schedule series of three or more matches against teams like Ireland and Afghanistan. They could play them in one-off matches, which could be reasonably easy to organise as teams touring England could play one game in Ireland and likewise teams playing Pakistan in the UAE could add a match against Afghanistan while they are there. That may, or may not, be the best solution, but it has to be better than leaving it to the vagaries of potentially cynical fixture list manipulation.

July 27

In the end I abandon the entertainment system on the aeroplane and instead read more of a book that I had bought at Miami Airport. It is the biography of Branch Rickey by Lee Lowenfish. Rickey is one of the great characters of baseball. Involved mostly in management roles in the Major Leagues, he was a real pioneer. In his early career in the 1920s he was using Moneyball type statistical analysis long before Billy Beane was a twinkle in Michael Lewis' eye. But his most significant contribution was to break down MLB's race barriers by signing African American player Jackie Robinson to the Brooklyn Dodgers in 1947 in direct contravention of the so-called 'Gentleman's Agreement' to keep baseball white which existed at the time. Not surprisingly the book is not really a book. It is more of a tome. Reading bits on various flights in the past few months, I have reached page 202 of the 598 pages (I am not planning to read the additional 85 pages of notes, bibliography and index) before I fall asleep on the plane. Sort of.

It is a quiet and drizzly day in London.

July 28

When I connect to the Internet on arriving at the hotel in Birmingham it is to the sad news that Clive Rice has died. He has had a long battle with cancer and has died of septicaemia. One of the most competitive cricketers ever, Rice didn't lose many battles. I don't think it is an exaggeration to say that Rice was responsible for a seminal moment in developing the love of cricket in a generation of South Africans (admittedly almost exclusively white and male) like me that was growing up in the 1970s. Mention of the name of Rob Drummond will see our eyes light up. Drummond had a relatively brief first-class career of 29 matches as a wicket-keeper batsman in the days when wicket-keepers were chosen mainly for their keeping abilities and lost his place to Richie Ryall, a better keeper but lesser batsman. The Currie Cup was intensely competitive in the era of apartheid-induced isolation and no match more so than the traditional Western Province v Transvaal New Year's clash. The 1977 match was a classic and a third-day run-chase eventually came down to the final ball with Western Province needing five to win with the last pair in. At 7:02pm on the fourth of January many of us were glued to the radio as the SABC delayed the national news to broadcast the end of the match (there was no TV coverage of cricket in those days). Rob Drummond tried to block the last ball, but was bowled by Rice and Transvaal won by four runs.

I tweet a few Rice stats: He is the oldest man to score a List A limited overs 100 and one of only two captains to declare with himself on 99* in a first-class match. Rice did this in the 1991 New Year's day Western Province v Transvaal match, and, like the other captain to declare with himself on 99* (Miles Howell for Free Foresters v Oxford University in 1934) he was 99* overnight. A measure of his value as an all-rounder is that Rice and Frank Woolley are the only two players to have scored 20 000 first-class runs at an average over 40 and taken 800 wickets at an average of under 23.

Meanwhile I am reminded of Shiv Chanderpaul playing Test cricket as a teenager and over the age of 40 when, back in the US of A, Alex Rodriguez becomes just the fourth player to homer in the Major Leagues as a teenager and over the age of 40. Baseball's stattos are even busier than cricket's.

July 29

There is a new one for me when I get into the shower this morning. The soap in the hotel is not called soap. It is a 'Refreshing Cleansing Bar'.

And there is another new one when I go to breakfast. The breakfast room is on the 25th floor of the hotel and has a massive view over Birmingham. And therefore I can see the cricket ground from the breakfast room of the hotel for the first time in my career.

Then there is yet another new one when I get to the ground. While injuries are quite common amongst players they are fairly rare amongst statisticians. Mostly statto injuries are of the wear and tear nature like mine, but Channel Nine colleague Max Kruger has managed to rupture his Achilles tendon slipping on a step. He will have an operation on the third day of the match and miss the last three days. Ouch.

To general surprise Australia collapse to 136 all out. Jimmy Anderson, who turns 33 tomorrow, takes 6-47. It is the fifth time he has taken a five-for in Test matches containing his birthday and to date he has taken 42 wickets at 19.09 in these matches. I don't bother to check where he ranks in the pantheon of Birthday Bowlers, but he clearly enjoys celebrating annual chronology events by taking wickets.

Jim Maxwell mentions 'Spedagues' on air in reference to lob bowling. I Google this to discover that the reference comes from a short story written by Sir Arthur Conan Doyle about a chap called Spedague who was a village second XI bowler who developed 'droppers' which catapulted him into the England team. Yes, that is the Conan Doyle who wrote the Sherlock Holmes books and whose only first-class wicket in his 10 match career was WG Grace.

July 30

In Mirpur Dale Steyn dismisses Tamim Iqbal early to reach 400 Test wickets. Of the 13 bowlers to reach this milestone he is joint second quickest with Richard Hadlee in 80 Tests (Steyn might have done it in 79 if the weather had been kind enough to permit a second innings in Chittagong), behind only Muttiah Muralitharan (72). More impressively Steyn is way quicker than anyone else to reach 400 in terms of balls bowed with 16 634. This record had been held by Richard Hadlee. It causes some consternation when I say that Hadlee took between 20 316 and 20 394 balls to reach 400 Test wickets. Contrary to some popular belief, cricket statisticians don't actually know everything and the Test match between New Zealand and India at Christchurch in 1990 when Hadlee took his 400th wicket (Sanjay Manjrekar) is one of those that we do not have ball-by-ball details for. (Please contact me if you have a copy of the ball-by-ball scoresheet for this one). So, we don't actually know which ball of the innings he took the wicket off.

Steyn is also the youngest of the nine seamers to reach 400 Test wickets at 32 years, 33 days. There are three spinners: Muralitharan, Shane Warne and Harbhajan Singh, who were younger. I get a small patriotic kick out of letting Glenn McGrath (who was the previous youngest seamer to take 400 wickets at 32 years, 254 days) know on air that his record has been broken, even though he probably didn't know he held that one in the first place.

There are lots more wickets at Edgbaston. When Australia are 111-6 in their second innings, still 34 behind, with nearly two hours of play left there is a real chance of a two-day finish. The last Ashes Test to finish inside two days was at Nottingham in 1921 and you have to go back to 1890 to find the last time Australia lost a Test in two days. But Australia extend the game into tomorrow by reaching 168-7 by stumps. Jimmy Anderson limps off with a side strain and his participation in the rest of the series may be in doubt. Following Glenn McGrath's stepping on the ball injury at the same ground in 2005 could an injury to a team's premier bowler at Edgbaston be the turning point in an Ashes series again?

July 31

'Miserable Monsoon Means Mirpur Match Minimized' might be the headline in the local papers of Dhaka today as there is no play at all. It is hard to imagine that there will be a lot more play in this one.

Although the Australian tail shows quite a bit of resistance there isn't much drama, or statistical excitement for that matter, as England complete an eight wicket victory at Edgbaston.

August 1

It is school concert day back home and I am missing out. For some strange reason the concerts are today rather than the normal schedule which is November. I might have been able to go had they been in November.

I take a leisurely trip back to London. Arthritis has launched a vicious assault on my right index finger and I am looking forward to resting it and doing as little work computing and writing on the two bonus days' off as possible. This is helped by there being very little cricket today including none at all in Mirpur, again.

August 2

A quiet Sunday with no play in either of the Tests (Birmingham is long finished and Mirpur is washed out. How did you guess?) is disturbed by Joe Leach of Worcestershire who takes a hat-trick with the first three balls of a Royal London One-day Cup match against Northamptonshire. He is just the second bowler to take a hat-trick with the first three balls of a List A match after Chaminda Vaas' famous effort for Sri Lanka against Bangladesh in the 2003 World Cup encounter at Pietermaritzburg. The only bowler I know of who has taken a hat-trick with the first three balls of a first-class match is Ravindra Pushpakumara who did it for Nondescripts v Panadura in Sri Lanka in 2003. Leach's hat-trick does not help much as Northamptonshire recover from 0-3 and 19-6 to reach 126 and go on to win by 21 runs. Nineteen is the lowest total ever at the fall of the sixth wicket by a team batting first that went on to win a List A match.

There has been quite a lot of interest in the shortness of the surnames of players in the current England team. I have succeeded in putting off checking for long enough so that when Sky Sports colleague Benedict Bermange tweets, 'If Wood replaces Anderson, England's surnames would total just 53 letters — breaking Australia's record of 55 letters at Faisalabad in 1988' all I have to do is click the retweet button (along with over 300 other people).

August 3

The Test match in Mirpur is abandoned in sunshine. Three days of rain have left the outfield very wet and there is no chance of a result. A total of 309.1 overs has been bowled in the series and it is the second fewest in any Test series of two or more matches behind the 452.2 overs in the 1889 series between South Africa and England in South Africa. Ah, I hear you say that 452.2 overs is more than 309.1. But it is actually less as there were four-ball overs in that series which is equivalent to 301.4 six-ball overs. I dutifully send out the series averages to my Cricket South Africa distribution list, but with so little play in the series I can't imagine I have ever sent out Test series averages that were more meaningless.

Most cricket fans clearly prefer watching the shorter versions of the game and many administrators seem to agree with them. But something like monsoons should, theoretically at least, be impartial in this matter — an equal opportunity splasher, if you like. So, it is disturbing to note that across the two tours to Bangladesh in June and July the monsoons only took out 23 overs in the six ODIs and two T20 (just 6.7%) while wiping out 63.4% of the available overs originally scheduled for the three Tests.

August 4

I bin my third pair of trousers in three weeks (blue this time). I wonder

137

what Lady Bracknell would make of that.

It is a quiet day of Ashes Test preparation and South African Cricket Annual catch-up and very little of significance happens in the cricket world, although Martin Guptill and Tom Latham add an unbroken 236 for New Zealand's first wicket to win the second ODI against Zimbabwe. I would imagine that they both think a world record partnership to win an ODI by 10 wickets (beating Upul Tharanga and Tillakaratne Dilshan's 231 for Sri Lanka v England at the 2011 World Cup) would qualify as being quite significant.

August 5

I quite enjoy visiting the ground the day before a Test match. There is a lot happening as various people prepare for the match. So anticipation builds as TV and radio crews rig their equipment, ground-staff prepare the pitch and outfield, cricketers practise, journalists write articles and attend press conferences and interviews, caterers get ready, spectators collect tickets, etc., etc. I head off to Trent Bridge as soon as I arrive in Nottingham. I meet up with Nottinghamshire's long serving archivist Peter Wynne-Thomas in his base in the library (he informs me that roughly 16 000 books are housed there). Peter is also one of the great men of the Association of Cricket Statisticians and Historians, having been a founder member in 1973 and the secretary for many of the years since then. He is busy looking through Nottinghamshire's scorebook for 1968. So, I can't resist asking to have a look and take photos of the most famous scorecard in that book — Garry Sobers' 6 sixes in an over off Malcolm Nash at Swansea.

Later in the afternoon I am interviewed by phone for an article that the *Radio Times* wants to do on me. This venerable BBC publication which was the first to provide lists of broadcast times has been going since 1923, so it is quite an honour to be interviewed for it.

August 6

England finish the day on 274-4, so it would have been a fairly ordinary day but for the fact that Australia were dismissed for 60 before that. It would have been an extraordinary start to any Test match, but it is even more astonishing in what is potentially an Ashes deciding game.

I start the day with a few stats prepared, such as this is the first time in 17 Ashes Tests in England since Ricky Ponting did it at Edgbaston in 2005 that a toss winning captain has chosen to bowl. This is the kind of thing to throw in early in the day once we have started to settle into the commentary. Then Stuart Broad dismisses Chris Rogers with the third ball of the match. So, I prepare to do a few gentle stats on Broad's 300th wicket and Roger's first duck (Jim Burke's 44 innings career without a duck is restored as the world record) when the first over finishes. But Steve Smith is dismissed off the last ball of the first over. And then before I get a chance to mention any toss, Broad, or Roger's stats and while I am trying to figure out when last there were two wickets in the first over of the Test Mark Wood gets rid of David Warner with the second ball of his first over. The carnage doesn't stop as Broad produces one of the great bowling spells in Test cricket history. His 8-15 in 9.3 overs are the third best ever for England in an Ashes Test behind Jim Laker's 9-37 and 10-53 at Manchester in 1956. He takes his fifth wicket off his 19th ball which is the earliest ever by anyone from the beginning of the match and equals Ernie Toshack (Australia v India at Brisbane in 1947) as the quickest by any bowler from the start of his bowling in an innings.

I barely get a chance to mention any of the stats as the wickets tumble. By the time I confirm that the eighth ball of the match is the second earliest for the third wicket to fall (behind the Irfan Pathan hat-trick led sixth ball of the match between Pakistan and India at Karachi in 2006), the fourth wicket has already fallen earlier than ever before in a Test and so has the fifth. I don't even bother to check the earliest sixth and seventh wickets. But when Australia are bowled out in 18.3 overs (111 balls) it is the earliest a team has been bowled out in the first innings of a Test beating the 113 balls (22.3 5-ball overs) that England took to bowl Australia out at Lord's in 1896. It is a minor aside, but still significant, that extras (14) is the top scorer in Australia's innings, the first time this had happened for either team in an Ashes Test. England are batting before lunch, only the fourth time that the second innings of the match had begun before lunch on the first day of a Test after the 1896 match at Lord's and two Tests in Cape Town (South Africa v Zimbabwe in 2005 and v New Zealand in 2013). I have been present at three of those, but missed 1896 in case you are wondering.

Australia's collapse is a proper Twitter age condensation of the game. So much so that some people note that at 111 balls you can put the Australian innings into one tweet. The BBC IPlayer crashes as it gets more listeners than any other program (cricketing or otherwise) it has ever had. And, another indication of the excitement that is generated is in my Twitter following. At the start of the day I had about 9 750 followers which meant that at current rate of progress I might reasonably have expected to reach 10 000 by the end of the fifth day. In fact, I pass 11 000 before the end of today. Speaking of Twitter, there is an amusing one in the midst of the avalanche of stats tweets today when an England fan suggests that I need to get out more and follows it with '... unlike Joe Root'.

The rest of the day is fairly normal Test cricket as England cruise to the third biggest lead at the end of day one of a Test of 214 (286 by South Africa v Zimbabwe at Cape Town in 2005 is the most). Ian Bell is out for one for the sixth time this year. His career total of 12 dismissals for one is the most by a specialist batsman and only two behind the world record of 14 held by his team-mate Jimmy Anderson. Joe Root is 130* at the close, the first time in an Ashes Test that a batsman had scored a century on day one for the team batting second.

August 7

It is a much quieter day statistically as England finish the day with 1.98 hands on the old urn as Australia are still 90 behind with just three wickets in hand. Alastair Cook makes the earliest declaration ever by an England captain in the second innings of the match as he calls them in at 391-9 in order to get in a three over burst before lunch. Adam Voges finishes the day on 48* which, in an indication of where things have been going wrong for Australia, is the highest score by a batsman between numbers four and six for them in the series. 23 other innings by these batsmen in the series so far have produced 287 runs at 14.35 with a best of 38.

After the record number of listeners yesterday, Test Match Special asks people to let us know where in the world they are listening so we can compile a map. The number of countries comfortably exceeds 150. Not bad numbers for a game that is supposedly dying. But, despite Henry Blofeld's exhortations we don't hear from Tristan da Cunha. Do the 259 inhabitants of those remote islands even have the Internet?

Speaking of Test cricket dying, I watch *Death Of A Gentleman* in the evening. This documentary film has been made by cricket fans/journalists Sam Collins and Jarrod Kimber and was originally intended to be about the demise of Test cricket. In the end it develops to also cover the 'Big Three' takeover at the ICC. It is certainly worth a watch, but being closely involved in the game the film does not tell me anything I didn't already know. Sadly, I strongly suspect that Test cricket will fade away. It can't compete with the shorter formats amongst the more peripheral cricket fans and even the overwhelming majority of Test cricket lovers watch most of the Fifty50 and Twenty20 that make it to their TV screens. So, audiences for the shorter formats will always be bigger than for Test cricket making the traditional game expendable as even most Test cricket fans would continue watching limited overs games, as they do now, even if there was no Test cricket to watch. I find it depressing that the fans and administrators of the game seem so determined to make a great game into an ordinary one.

August 8

English cricket fans are the best in the world. Only three wickets are needed this morning for England to reclaim the Ashes, and yet the ground is packed at the start for the denouement. When I leave the ground an hour and a half after the finish about a third of the spectators are still there. In any other country in the world with the home team on the verge of an historic series win needing just three wickets to clinch it the ground would be mostly empty. For example the Australians clinched the 2013/14 Ashes with 7 201 spectators at the WACA in Perth. And at least half of those were English. Yes, the English have the best cricket fans in the world by a million miles. That's 1.6 million kilometres for those of you who live in the former colonies and couldn't be bothered to get to the ground for historic cricket wins by your team.

Ben Stokes finishes with 6-36 as England become the first team to have four different bowlers to take at least six wickets in an innings in four consecutive innings following Anderson and Finn at Edgbaston and Broad in the first innings of this match. When I produce this stat on air, Jonathan Agnew asks how I even think of these things. It is a good question. I suppose the main thing is that you need to think ahead in the game. So, when a bowler has three or four wickets, for example, I am already looking at what is of significance if he gets five in the innings. How many five-fors does he have? Is there anything special if he gets there? And that is the process in this case. There has been a spate of six-fors by England bowlers in the last two Tests and I therefore check to see if I can find any other instances of four different bowlers taking six wickets in an innings in four consecutive innings. Broad's spell on the first morning had provided an instance where the rhythms of this process were disturbed. At the beginning of the series Broad had 287 Test wickets. So, assuming he stayed fit he was likely to pass Derek Underwood's 297 wickets to become England's sixth highest wicket taker at some stage in the middle of the series. Once he got to 298 he was likely to get to 299 and 300 quite soon after that. Then, you would think, Broad Wicket Watch could relax for a bit as the odds suggest that his next target, Fred Trueman's 307, would only occur in the next match following the one in which he reached 300. So, it was quite a shock to the system when he caught Trueman just an hour and a half after getting to 300.

Alastair Cook joins WG Grace and Mike Brearley as the only England captains to have won two Ashes series at home, which seems like pretty good company. This is also the first time since the 19th century that England have won four consecutive Ashes series at home. They won six in a row between 1884 and 1896. And as the last stat of the match, Joe Root has continued his record of being top-scorer in the match — nine times in his 31 Tests to date. He will jump to number one in the ICC's Test batting rankings when the update is announced today.

The match finishes at 11:40 which is an hour and five minutes before the start of the English Premier League football season. At least the Ashes win will get some attention from the broader sporting public, if only for 65 minutes.

For the second Test in a row we have about two and a half days off. It is nice work if you can get it, but it certainly feels like we have crammed five days' worth of work into two and a bit. I use school exercise books to score in. It is not very elegant, I know, but I can fit two Test matches into one book. So, for this tour I have brought three exercise books to cover the five Tests. But the short third and fourth Tests have used up just half a book so I will be able to cram all five Tests into two books leaving the third one redundant.

August 9

A quiet day recovering from all that work is in order and I manage to get that. On my walk in the nearest park I see the pleasing sight of a dad playing cricket with his young son. You don't see much of that kind of informal fun cricket outside of the sub-continent these days and the cricket world is poorer for it.

Michael Clarke has announced that The Oval Test will be his last. He has had a disappointing run of form lately and his body has kept letting him down, so, sad that it may be, retirement had a feeling of being rather inevitable.

Meanwhile there has been more excitement for Twirler Spotters in the shires following Matthew Carter's sensational debut (see June 15). Catching up with county action I notice that leg-spinner Mason Crane has become the youngest bowler to take five wickets in an innings in the County Championship for Hampshire with 5-35 against Warwickshire at the age of 18 years, 171 days. Australian Jackson Bird is also playing for Hampshire. 'Bird' and 'Crane' in the same team? Henry Blofeld would have a field day doing Hampshire games these days.

The South Africa A team have managed to have 10 of their 16-man squad hospitalised due to food poisoning in Chennai so it is no great surprise that they lose their one-day triangular series match (Australia A are the other team) against India A today.

August 10

It is another quiet day off. I contemplate heading down to Lord's for Middlesex v Sussex, but settle for the lazy option of listening to the commentary of what turns out to be a very good game with the home team winning by 21 runs: Middlesex 234 and 331, Sussex 300 and 245. These are pretty much ideal scores for a good game of first-class cricket.

My brother, John, does a blog on South African music charts. He is working through from the beginning and is pleased to announce today that the week he has reached (sometime in the late 1960s) is the first time that the top twenty hits contain all 26 letters of the alphabet between them. And you thought cricket statisticians are mad.

August 11

The family arrive today. So I get up early to meet them at Heathrow. I can greet the seven-year-old with the news that the Toronto Blue Jays (which are her team having worn one of their caps ever since she witnessed a game in Toronto when aged eighteen months) have gone to the top of the American League East. Given that the Red Sox have continued their dismal year, I have adopted the Blue Jays as my 2015 team. It would be good if they could get into the playoffs for the first time since they won back-to-back World Series in 1992 and 1993.

Meanwhile a Women's Test match starts in Canterbury. In the Twenty20 era Women's Tests have tended towards extinction. This one, between England and Australia is just the ninth played worldwide in the last nine years. The Twenty20 era has brought more TV coverage and money into the Women's game which is becoming increasingly professional. As a result the game has improved significantly and has had a big profile jump. With the additional finance and time available to Women's players now that more of them are professional you would think that more Women's Tests could be organised. Australia finish day one on 268-8 with Jess Jonassen (95*) leading a recovery from 99-5. With so few games played career stats are not substantial enough to really tell you how good, or otherwise, a player is.

Over the past few weeks TV viewing has included many of the world's great crime fighters: James Bond, Hercule Poirot, Sherlock Holmes, Colombo, even Jim Rockford. I add another one today: Rastamouse. Yes, the kids have arrived and I am not going to be winning the TV remote fight any time soon. By the way David Suchet who plays Poirot in the TV series is currently appearing as Lady Bracknell in a theatre production of *The Importance of Being Earnest*. What would Poirot think of my trouser situation?

August 12

There are 30 teams in Major League Baseball. So, a full round is 15 games. Last night, for the first time ever, all 15 games were won by the home team. Now there's a proper stat.

It is tourist time for the family as we head into central London and spend time at the Science Museum. It is very busy as most of the kids in London for whom it is also school holidays seem to be there. As a result I am disappointed that I hardly get any chance to play with any of the gadgets. The most interesting exhibit is the actual Apollo 10 command capsule. This was the one that orbited the moon, but, unlike Apollo 11, did not land. So, I suppose it must be the Rahul Dravid of Apollos. Eugene Cernan was one of the crew members of Apollo 10 and in 1972 went on to become the answer to a great quiz question: 'Who was the last man on the moon?'

England are bowled out for 168 in replying to Australia's 274 in the Women's Test with Jonassen becoming just the third player to be out for 99 in a Women's Test.

In Galle, Kumar Sangakkara starts his penultimate Test by scoring five as Sri Lanka are dismissed for 183 by India who finish the day on 128-2 in reply. Perhaps the great man has gone on for too long.

Tomorrow is a travel day.

August 13

The trip up north begins. The kids have always enjoyed watching *Balamory*, the CBeebies show. So, we are taking them up to Tobermory on the Isle of Mull, the real town where the fictional story is based. We start a new game in the car. The six-year-old is incorrigible with the 'Are we there yet?' So the new game is that the seven-year-old has to count how many times the six-year-old says it. We all get bored with the game when the number gets well into the 40s and we are still only halfway there, yet.

Mrs S likes to collect old churches. The older, the better. We break the trip up to Bolton, our stop for the night, with a visit to All Saints' Church in Brixworth. It has been going since 675 AD, so they don't get much older than that and parts from the 10th century are still in the current building.

In the city centre of Bolton there is a statue of Fred Dibnah who managed to achieve celebrity status as a steeplejack (someone who does maintenance scaling buildings, chimneys and church steeples). In 1978 he was filmed making repairs to Bolton Town Hall and as a result of the documentary on BBC he became a TV presenter.

India have taken command in Galle by scoring 375 in reply to Sri Lanka's 183 and then dismissing both openers for ducks as the hosts end the day on 5-2. Kumar is still there however.

A proper rainstorm means that there are only 38 overs at Canterbury, but Australia finish the day on 90-4 and there may be enough time for them to push for victory in the Women's Test tomorrow.

August 14

I do enjoy driving around as it is the best way to see any country. Today it rains all the way up to Scotland from Bolton making the actual driving part of the drive a bit more stressful than usual. We spend most of the day on the road up to Oban.

We take a break at the bonnie, bonnie banks of Loch Lomond where I try to teach the kids to skim stones in a vain attempt to recreate my own youth having done that on a trip to Scotland when I was a teenager. Sadly, my shoulders, arms and technique are not what they were all those years ago and I cannot persuade any of the stones to bounce on the water. We took the M6 to get into Scotland. I have no idea, and have not bothered to find out, whether this is the High Road or the Low Road.

The drive to Milford Sound in New Zealand is my favourite for spectacular scenery, but driving up the west coast of Scotland is comparable to anything in the world. There is the classic combination of mountains and water (lochs) and it is very pleasing on the eye, especially as the sun actually makes a bit of an effort to come out in the afternoon.

Oban is a pleasant little seaside town whose main purpose seems to be a base for the ferries heading off to the Hebrides. There is a decent selection of Chinese, Indian and Italian restaurants, but there does not seem to be any point in having anything other than fish and chips in this part of the world. When in Oban, etc. At the restaurant I notice a drink called Irn Bru on the menu. I enquire of the waitress what this is and am informed in a thick East European accent that 'It is a kind of Scottish lemonade. You only get it in Scotland. It is horrible, but you must try it'. So I did. And she was right: it was horrible, a bit like drinking bubblegum.

Billboards in the town alert me that shinty's MacAulay Cup Final is taking place on the 22nd in Oban. I have heard of shinty, but need to Google it to find that it is a Scottish version of hockey and I actually watch a bit of a game on the local TV.

Galle seems further away than ever, but there has been a significant world record there as Ajinkya Rahane has become the first fielder (not including keepers) to take eight catches in a Test. The record used to be held by five players and always reminds me of Yajurvindra Singh who played four Tests for India between 1977 and 1979 and on his debut (v England at Bangalore in 1977) became the second fielder to take seven catches in a Test match. He is still the only one to take seven on debut.

When Dinesh Chandimal made his Test debut in 2011 in South Africa, his captain Tillakaratne Dilshan predicted that he would score 10 000 Test runs. Things haven't quite gone according to plan since then (1 167 runs at 41.67 in 18 Tests before this one in the nearly four years since his debut). Today he rescues Sri Lanka from 95-5 (Kumar 40) with a spectacular 162* off 169 balls. Having been 97 behind at the fall of their fifth wicket Sri Lanka make 367 setting India 176 to win and nip out KL Rahul before the close leaving India 23-1 at stumps. I will definitely be keeping an eye on that game before and after our ferry trip to the Isle of Mull tomorrow.

The remarkable Ellyse Perry (who also plays international football) bowls Australia to a comprehensive 161 run victory in the Women's Test with 6-32.

August 15

When I wake up I immediately check the score at Galle. By the time we go to breakfast, India are 63-5 and they are 78-7 when we get back to the room. But we have to leave straight away, so it will be a while before I can see what finally happened as we are on our way to the Isle of Mull. Before we leave I send out a stats pack for the Twenty20 International back home between South Africa and New Zealand and it does seem rather strange to be doing this in faraway Oban.

We arrive at our hotel in Tobermory after the 45 minute ferry from Oban and a drive from Craignure to discover we are in Josie Jump's house. The hotel was used to film the *Balamory* character's house. So, there is much excitement among the younger members of the family.

I am more interested in what is happening in Galle, however, and as soon as I get the chance I check the Internet to see that India were all out for 112. So, Sri Lanka complete the great turnaround with a 63 run win. Only one team has been in a worse position at the fall of their fifth wicket in the third innings of the game than Sri Lanka in this match and gone on to win, and that was in the greatest turnaround of all Test matches: England were still 122 runs adrift in their follow-on innings at the loss of their fifth wicket against Australia at Leeds in 1981 before winning by 18 runs. Rangana Herath is a remarkable cricketer and his 7-48 seals victory. All told it has been an amazing game. Test cricket is the best cricket.

There is a lot of discussion on the future of Women's Tests following the match in Canterbury. England scored at less than two runs per over throughout the match so it was not quite the spectacle the organisers and Sky TV would have hoped. There are suggestions that Women's Tests should be done away with completely. But we are still regularly reminded that cricket is a sport with *three* formats. As such I think we should be trying as much as possible to give all players opportunities in all formats. With the increased funding and professionalism in the women's game it should surely be possible to schedule more Tests. Nobody has ever got better at anything by *not* doing it.

August 16

We take a drive across the Isle of Mull and a short ferry trip to the island of Iona. The island has historical importance as it was a base for St Columba who arrived there in 563 and created a monastery which he used as a base for spreading Christianity in Britain. Iona Abbey is the most prominent structure on the island. It is my third visit here and it remains beautiful and the most tranquil place I know.

It is a gloriously sunny day and the temperature gauge on the car got up to at least 15 degrees centigrade. I was amazed to see a teenage girl going for a swim in the sea at the beach in Iona. The water temperature has to be a lot lower than that usually associated with swimming beaches.

August 17

We bid sad adieus to the lovely Isle of Mull and head inland to Edinburgh, our resting place for the night. On the way, I collect another first-class cricket ground. New Williamfield in Stirling hosted its inaugural first-class match in June this year when Scotland played Afghanistan in the ICup. So, as our route passed through Stirling we stopped to visit the ground. It is a pleasant ground with a view of the National Wallace Memorial which commemorates William Wallace (*Braveheart*) in the hills in the background. Mel Gibson is nowhere to be seen.

We arrive in Edinburgh in the evening and take a walk around town. It is certainly a dramatic view of the city looking up from Princes Street Gardens, with the Castle prominent along with a number of grand old buildings. It does seem odd, however, to be in town at Festival and Tattoo time and not take in a show. Having children around is wonderful, but it can hamstring some of the more obvious tourist activities.

Warwickshire play Sussex today in a Royal London One-day Cup match at Rugby school. Fortunately no-one picks up the ball and runs with it over the boundary line. Otherwise we may have had to add another format to cricket and three seems like too many as it is.

August 18

We drive through the sea today. Yes, I now know the answer to the question 'What is a causeway?' It is an elevated road through a body of water. We head towards Lindisfarne, an island accessible by road, but only when the tide is out. You have to check the tide timetables to know when you need to be off the island if you don't want to be stuck there for the night.

Lindisfarne has ruins of an ancient Priory as well as a castle. But the day is ruined by water; not the water on the ground that we drove through, but water from the sky. It rains steadily throughout our stay. So, we abandon the day earlier than anticipated and head grumpily and wet to our overnight destination of Newcastle. The 'upon Tyne' version.

August 19

We stop at Jesmond Park briefly on our way to the museum. It becomes number 219 on my list of first-class grounds visited. Newcastle is in a Minor County, Northumberland, for cricketing purposes and the ground hosted the 1965 South Africans and 1974 Pakistanis for first-class tour matches against the Minor Counties. In the 1965 match, Ali Bacher made 121, his highest first-class score for South Africa as the tourists won comfortably by 203 runs.

On our way down to London, we stop off at Corbridge, just outside Newcastle to see more Roman ruins. I told you Mrs S likes old things (cue jokes about her choice in husbands. Ha, ha, ha. Ho, ho, ho. Ho hum).

It is back to work tomorrow as the final Test at The Oval begins.

August 20

The day starts slowly as Australia take 14.4 overs to hit their first four. I get a bit of stick on Twitter for saying this is the longest wait for the first four of the match in an Ashes Test since December 1979 at Perth. It is correctly pointed out that the 1979/80 England tour of Australia (the one immediately after the Packer upheaval) was not officially played for the Ashes. While my instincts tend towards being pedantic, I generally use the term 'Ashes' as a generic term for all England v Australia matches.

Having been put in, Australia bat serenely through the day to finish on 287-3 with Steve Smith becoming the third youngest Australian to reach 3 000 Test runs behind Don Bradman and Neil Harvey.

In Colombo, Kumar Sangakkara begins his final Test and spends the day in the field as India reach 319-6 in a day of limited statistical excitement.

In the evening the sponsors of the Test series in England, Investec, have a Pub Quiz function for the media with Al Murray ('The Pub Landlord') as quiz master. I am on the TMS team and expectations are unreasonably high. Questions are general knowledge as well as cricket. Although I manage to knock a couple of cricket questions on the head, we go for Dennis Lillee as the leading wicket-taker in Ashes matches as I couldn't remember whether Shane Warne had passed him. It was an elementary error – of course Warne (195) had the most, well ahead of Lillee's 167. I was quite pleased to be able to answer which city was the capital of Burkino Faso, although I was not sure at all of the spelling of 'Ouagadougou'. We finish in a disappointing fourth place.

August 21

Cricket themed tube stations become the talking point on TMS. Someone suggests one based on Richie Benaud's famous greeting 'Morning Everyone' for Mornington Crescent. As any good listener to *I'm Sorry I Haven't A Clue* can tell you, that should be the end of the game. 'Mornington Crescent' is one of the best known of the silly games played on the celebrated BBC Radio show and involves the panellists going through London Underground stations with the winner being the first to get to Mornington Crescent. There are no actual rules, but they pretend there are all sorts of clever strategies in getting there. All good fun.

In the cricket Steve Smith goes on to get 143, his 11th Test century. Amazingly all 11 have been in the first innings. He joins Tom Graveney and Ashwell Prince as the players with the most first innings centuries without one in the second innings as Australia finish on 481 all out.

Since the introduction of the Umpires Decision Review System (DRS) the percentage of reviews turned down has been consistently around 75%. When England successfully review an lbw shout against Mitchell Starc that was given not out by the on-field umpire it is, remarkably, just the second decision overturned in 33 reviews in the series to date and the first since the first Test. Well done, the umpires.

Australia have replaced Josh Hazlewood for this match with Peter Siddle, so Mitchell Johnson opens the bowling for the first time in the series. He and Mitchell Starc bowling to Alastair Cook and Adam Lyth provide the first time in Ashes' history that two left-handed opening batsmen have faced two left-handed opening bowlers. It does not help England as they put in an awful performance and finish the day on 107-8. The number of injudicious shots played, especially against bowlers just beginning a spell and considering the match situation leads Jonathan Agnew to say, 'They say it is the modern way. It is the wrong way.'

The end is very nigh for Kumar. He does better than Bradman in his final Test with 32 as Sri Lanka end the day on 140-3 in reply to India's 393. But there is now only the second innings as a chance for a tremendous end to his career.

August 22

I don't do well on bananas, and I am only a bit better on Roman Emperors. When the conversation on TMS turns to Peter Siddle's vegan diet which involves, amongst other things, eating lots of bananas, Phil Tufnell mentions that banana trees move. An astonished Jonathan Agnew turns to me for help. But, apart from how to eat them, I unfortunately know very little about bananas and can't assist. Things improve a little, but not enough, when the discussion turns to Roman Emperors who have played Test cricket. I immediately name Constantine (Learie Constantine was a wonderful player in the early days of West Indies Test cricket before going on to become Lord Constantine). But it is a bit of a struggle after that. The name Nero comes up and I say there is currently a West Indies umpire Peter Nero, but I was pretty sure no Nero had played Test cricket. Wrong. The question turns out to be quite clever, because one automatically thinks of male Test cricketers. Juliana Nero played a Women's Test in 2004. The other thing that tends to happen is that you think of surnames, so it takes a while to come up with Gus Logie (Augustine Logie to his parents). Even when given a clue that one is South African I still struggle, but immediately get it when told that the Emperor was Augustus. Bernard Tancred (Augustus Bernard Tancred to be more comprehensive) was the first man to carry his bat through a Test innings. Dick Lilley, England's famous wicket-keeper of the late 19th and early 20th century also turned out to be an Augustus (Arthur Frederick Augustus Lilley).

Of course, Julius Caesar would have played Test cricket had it been around in the 1850s. The Surrey man was one of the leading players of that era and went on the first ever English cricket tour: George Parr's XI to North America. Yes, Julius Caesar did play first-class cricket. If you don't believe me click the disambiguation for the cricketer under Julius Caesar on Wiki and you will find all you need to know about him. Oh, and 15.78 was actually a pretty good batting average in those very low-scoring days.

England put up a better performance but end the day on the verge of a massive defeat. Mark Wood makes 24 with 6 fours as nightwatchman, the highest Ashes score consisting entirely of boundaries, but Michael Clarke enforces the follow-on for the first time in his captaincy career in his last Test. In four other opportunities in Tests and six overall in first-class cricket, he had declined to enforce each time.

Alastair Cook has played some of his best innings when England have batted in the third innings of a Test after a first innings deficit, including making centuries both times he has batted after England have followed on. All told he has made seven centuries from this match situation and for most of the day he looks likely to add another one and join Martin Crowe and Sachin Tendulkar as the only ones with eight (as well as rectifying a hole on his CV — it would have been his first century in an Ashes Test at home). But he gets out in Steve Smith's first over of the day for 85 and with only two overs remaining. Apart from virtually certainly condemning England to an innings defeat, he also ruined all the stats that I was going to pull out. Suffice to say that on his dismissal today he has scored 1 544 runs at an average of 64.33 with 7 centuries and 5 fifties when he has batted in the third innings facing a deficit.

Cook's dismissal means that he still hasn't batted with Stuart Broad in 84 Tests they have now played together although it was looking possible today until he was sixth out. If the pair play another seven Tests together without being at the crease at the same time they will pass Sanath Jayasuriya and Muttiah Muralitharan's 90 Tests without batting together. I wait with bated breath for my opportunity to enlighten the listeners to this proper arcane stat when it happens.

It is a quiet day statistically in Colombo as India establish a good position being 157 ahead with 9 wickets in hand at stumps.

August 23

While walking through the ground to the broadcasting positions, I notice something interesting on a mural which gives a timeline of The Oval and

Surrey history. Jack Hobbs is the leading run-scorer in first-class cricket, as everyone knows. But there is a dispute as to how many runs and centuries he made. On retirement Wisden published his numbers as 61 237 runs and 197 centuries. The Association of Cricket Statisticians and Historians on the other hand has compiled a full list of first-class matches and while researching this included a tour to India and Sri Lanka in 1930/31 that had not previously been included. As a result the ACS has Hobbs on 61 760 runs and 199 hundreds, while Wisden has steadfastly maintained the original figures that they published. The mural at The Oval says Hobbs retired in 1934, having scored 61 237 runs and 199 hundreds, so they have hedged their bets.

England hang around a bit with the help of a rain delay of nearly three hours but they are all out for 286 to lose by an innings and 46 runs. This provides just the fifth instance in all Tests and the second in the Ashes (after 1965/66) where a team has won a match by an innings and lost the next by an innings within a series. There were only 18 playing days in the series and it is thus one of the shortest ever, but we need to be careful in framing the stat. It only makes sense to include series of five or more matches with all matches being scheduled for five or more days. (I suspect a lot of modern followers are not aware of the differing lengths that Test matches have had historically, given that five days has been used for all Tests for a long time now). Within that definition 18 days equals the record of the England v West Indies series in 2000 and beats the record for the shortest Ashes series of 19 days way back in 1884/85 (that series consisted of five timeless Tests).

Kumar's gone! He is dismissed for 18 in his final Test innings as Sri Lanka end the day on 72-2 needing a further 341 to win. Sangakkara has finished as the fifth highest run-scorer Tests with 12 400 runs. His average of 57.40 is the best of the 11 players with 10 000 Test runs and fifth best of all batsmen with 5 000 Test runs. He could play a bit.

Actually, Retirement Watch turns out to be the theme of the day. Michael Clarke's recent dip in form means that he has fallen short of a career average over 50, ending with 8 643 at 49.10 with 28 hundreds. The average might not be over 50, but it is still a highly impressive career.

Someone tweets that Chris Rogers has retired in the year 2015 with 2 015 Test runs. I can't resist checking this and find one other player who scored as many Test runs as the year in which he played his last Test: India's Anshuman Gaekwad played his last Test in 1985 having scored 1 985 runs.

It is the end of the series so we all do the customary tearful goodbyes, but it is also 'See you in Dubai' for quite a few as we will be there in six weeks' time for England's series against Pakistan. Such is the way of the cricket world.

August 24

It is a day in London spent mostly at the Transport Museum (lots for the kids to play on) and Foyle's bookshop. Cricket has always claimed to have produced the best literature of all sports but it is clear where the focus is these days when the shop has one bookshelf of cricket books compared to five for football.

August 25

It is another day trawling around various museums in London. Sir Henry Wellcome was a pharmaceutical man who collected medical artefacts and some of these are on display at The Wellcome Collection. My Squeam-Ometer ramps up rapidly while looking at some of the exhibits, although it's interesting to see Napoleon's toothbrush and Florence Nightingale's moccasins on display. Nightingale is probably the most famous nurse of all-time, but she was also a pioneering statistician and popularised the use of pie charts.

I retreat queasily from the exhibit and browse through the highbrow books in the shop at the museum. There is stuff like *Plato at the Googleplex* by Rebecca Goldstein. Regretfully and, I suppose, shamefully, my knowledge of the world's great philosophers doesn't extend much beyond Monty Python's drinking song. Assuming that I exist, that is. And that you exist. I watch cricket, therefore I am? Anyway, I find myself gloomily contemplating my intellectual inadequacy and it is at the lowest point of contemplation that a lady attempts to push the revolving doors at the exit in the wrong direction. And suddenly, all is well with my world.

We get home and check the computer to find that nothing of great consequence has happened in the cricket world. If I am not on the Internet, does cricket exist?

August 26

We visit the Royal Air Force Museum and I discover my useless bit of information for the day: The first air stewardess was a Miss Ellen Church on 15 May 1930. So there is a bit of knowledge you can impress your friends with. And then tell them you read it in a cricket book.

In Durban, South Africa clinch the ODI series against New Zealand with a 62 run win: 283-7 plays 221. In the interview afterwards, Hashim Amla is quoted as saying, 'This is the way ODI cricket should be played' as there was quite a lot in the pitch for the bowlers. I concur whole-heartedly, although the average '400+ is good' fan might not. By the way, I have been monitoring ODI scoring rates since the implementation of the new playing conditions and early evidence (18 matches) suggests that they are coming down to more sensible levels at an overall average of 5.34 compared with 5.67 in the first six months of the year.

August 27

Unlike the punny entries to the cricket-related London Underground stations on the commentary the other day, we head off to a station that is an actual cricketer's name: Forest Hill, to go to the Horniman Museum and Gardens. Yes, Forest Hill played 31 first-class matches as a wicket-keeper/batsman for Natal and Natal B (mostly Natal B) between 1975 and 1981.

The Horniman is quite pleasant and mostly keeps the kids entertained with activities such as Nature Notebooks and Pond Dipping.

August 28

Christopher Robin, and Alice for that matter, would have been disappointed if they had gone down to Buckingham Palace today for the Changing of the Guard. As it was, it was just me, my two daughters, and a few thousand other people who did not get to see the famous royal event. There was no Changing of the Guard today. I later discovered that for August this year the Changing of the Guard is only on odd numbered days. The moral of this modern story: Always Google before you go.

Sri Lanka begin their PSE (that is Post Sangakkara Era) at the Sinhalese Sports Club (SSC) in Colombo but rain is the winner of the day as India are 50-2 in the 15 overs possible.

At what looks from photos to be lovely new ground, the Krishnagiri Stadium at Wayanad, South Africa A slump to an innings defeat against India A with a disastrous 76 all out in their second innings. The truly observant may have noticed that this could be seen as some form of revenge for the national Indian team as this is exactly the same score South Africa bowled India out for in a Test at Ahmedabad in 2008. India A left-arm spinner, Axar Patel had taken a five-for in the first innings and produces the astonishing figures of 6-6-0-4 in South Africa's second innings. In first-class cricket only 13 bowlers have taken four or more wickets in an innings without conceding a run and Patel is just the fifth of those to bowl as many as six overs doing so.

August 29

In Colombo, Cheteshwar Pujara is on the verge of carrying his bat. The former Number Three is back in the team as an opener after a slump in form and selection policy (five bowlers where possible) had seen him out for a while. He ends the day 135* with India on 292-8.

Los Angeles Dodger broadcaster Vin Scully has announced that he will return for a 67th and final season in 2016. Now that is a long career.

It is a rainy evening, but the weather will be clear in the morning. How do I know this? Well the rain was falling steadily at Heathrow as we waited for our plane, but Johannesburg will be clear tomorrow.

August 30

To pass time on the flight back home, I count my flights for the year to date. This is number 17. I then try to work out how many hours I have spent on an aeroplane during the year. My calculations suggest that by the end of the year I will probably not quite have spent a full week (168 hours) of the year on aeroplanes, but it will be over six days. It has been a busy year. My passport receives its final stamp when we arrive at OR Tambo International Airport in the morning, as I will be using the new one for the next trip.

When the home computer finally wakes up from a few weeks' hibernation the first thing I check, naturally, is whether Pujara has carried his bat. And he has: 145* out of 312. It is an impressive and relatively rare event (this is the 49th time it has happened in the 2 179 Tests to date), but I fail to come up with any particularly special stat for it.

August 31

It is time to get back to the real world and the news this morning is of possibly the finest performance by a Test cricketer in Beijing. Yes, a Test cricketer has won a bronze medal in the javelin at the IAAF World Athletics Championship in Beijing. Sunette Viljoen played one Women's Test and 17 ODIs for South Africa between 2000 and 2002 before setting out on an impressive athletics career.

Cheteshwar Pujara's carried bat becomes interesting as he makes a duck in the second innings, making him the first player to be dismissed for a second innings duck after carrying his bat in the first innings. Three players: Bill Woodfull, Geoff Boycott and Saeed Anwar have all carried their bat in the second innings after a first innings duck. It has been a good competitive series and Sri Lanka recover from 47-6 in reply to India's 312 and reach 201 before reducing India to 21-3.

But, perhaps the highlight of the day is when I take the kids to school and see one of the younger boys wearing a tee-shirt that says, 'If Mummy says No, I'll SMS Granny'.

September 1

At 7:31am I send my last two files for the South African Cricket Annual to editor Colin Bryden. They are the Limited Overs International records and the Who's Who, which is easily the biggest section of the Annual for me. So, I have completed my part of the 21st Annual that I have done with Colin. It seems like a good time for a rest. But, the Africa Cup Twenty20 starts in Benoni next weekend, and I need to produce stats packs for that. It really never ends.

I watch a fair amount of the play at the SSC on the TV and Sri Lanka create some possibilities of a remarkable win (it would have been one of the greatest of all time), or at least an excellent save with a partnership of

135 between Angelo Mathews and Kushal Perera which rescued them from 107-5, chasing 386 to win. But with 10 minutes before tea and with the new ball due immediately after tea, Perera gets out playing a reverse sweep to R Ashwin and Sri Lanka's last four wickets clatter shortly after the break. As Aggers may have said, 'They say it is the modern way. It is the wrong way'. Perera had had an excellent debut with scores of 56 and 70 making him just the third wicket-keeper to reach 50 in both innings on Test debut after India's Dilwar Hussain in 1934 and his own current team-mate Dinesh Chandimal in 2011.

September 2

My hand therapist tells me to pull finger. Apparently it helps with arthritis to pull the various bones apart briefly. So that is another exercise I will be doing on my swollen right index finger in days to come. I will be having the operation on my left ulnar nerve on Friday as it is a rare opportunity when both the doctor and I are in the country at the same time. I just realised that I have not put the days of the week into the diary entries. Friday is the fourth of September, two days' time in case you need to know.

September 3

The County Chairmen have voted in favour of a reduction in the County Championship from 16 games to 14 from next season, despite the County Chief Executives voting to stay with 16 matches, which they did despite the apparent determination of the ECB to reduce the number of games to 14 or even 12. The structures of English cricket administration, in particular, are labyrinthine, but it is the business of cricket that interests me here. A reduction in County Championship fixtures will make it easier to add more Twenty20 games to the fixture list. There seems to be an eternal conflict between financial and cricketing interests, or as leading writer Gideon Haigh succinctly puts it: 'Does cricket make money to exist or does it exist to make money?' For the sake of argument, let's assume that cricket exists to make money, i.e. it is run purely from a business point of view. Clearly the shorter formats have bigger spectator numbers, so it would seem at first glance that the best way to make money is to play mostly, even exclusively, limited overs games. However, it is also true that while good businesses need to attract new customers they must also make sure of maintaining their best customers. Who are cricket's best customers? I suspect that outside of county cricket there are very few people anywhere in the world who attend more than 10 days' cricket a year. County members diligently pay their annual subscription and many of them watch a lot of county cricket. A 16-match program gives them 32 days of first-class cricket at their home ground as well as the numerous Fifty50 and Twenty20 matches. Many of these good people watch 20 or more days in a season. These are cricket's best customers, no matter if they are a small proportion of the overall number of cricket watchers. In general I don't think that there is any doubt that fans who love the long game watch more cricket and provide far greater Customer Lifetime Value to cricket (not least because many of them also watch lots of short format games) than the fan who only watches a few Twenty20 games a year and doesn't pay much attention to anything else. Sometimes cricket seems to be the only sport in the world to be played primarily for the benefit of people who aren't really interested in it. Good businesses look after good customers, and a reduction in County Championship games will undoubtedly upset county members.

September 4

It is another day in hospital under the knife. Things seem to have gone well and it proves to be the first (and probably only) computer-free day of the year for me. Typing one-handed right-handed is easier than one-handed left-handed, but only marginally.

September 5

Surrey clinch promotion to Division One of the County Championship for next season when they beat Derbyshire by an innings. Captain Gareth Batty takes the last three wickets with a hat-trick. Game-ending hat-tricks are a bit more common than you might expect, which I know from a previous attempt to research it. But what about game-ending hat-tricks by captains? That should narrow it down quite a lot. So, I will check this up. It might take a bit longer to do than usual as I will be doing it one-handed in between bouts of pain-killer induced sleep.

With computing limited I spend most of the day reading an actual book. This is not something I do often enough. Today I read *Welcome to Just a Minute*, Nicholas Parsons' history of the greatest radio show of all-time (Er, what's that you say? Oh yes, er, after cricket commentaries, of course). The remarkable Parsons has been ever present on every episode since 1967 and is still going strong at the age of 92.

Bryce Harper played a starring role for the Washington Nationals against the Atlanta Braves the night before last. He had four walks, four runs and an RBI (run batted in), something without parallel in at least 100 years in Major League Baseball. He saw 20 pitches in the game and did not swing at a single one of them, yet helped his team to win. Try explaining that to a cricket fan, especially one who thinks Twenty20 is the only way to play the game. Twenty consecutive leaves? Imagine that.

In other baseball news, Tony Zych made his MLB debut for the Seattle Mariners last night and has replaced Dutch Zwilling at the end of the alphabetical listing of Major League players. David Aardsma is the first name on that list. Test cricket's alphabetical list ranges from Aamer Malik to Zulqarnain Haider. Or, using the Anglo-Saxon 'first name, surname' construct it ranges from India's Varun Aaron to South Africa's Billy Zulch.

September 6

I finish reading the book on *Just a Minute* in Just a Weekend. It may be a personal record for me — 450 pages in one weekend.

You probably shouldn't tell anyone this, but I am quite happy when matches are completely rained out. Fewer scorecards to process means less work. And, in the case of the two Africa Cup matches that were rained out in Benoni yesterday it also ensures I do not need to bother with net run-rate calculations as the winner of the Northerns v Easterns match will advance to the semi-finals — a most welcome situation especially in my current one-armed state.

September 7

World Cricket League Division Six, the notional starting point for World Cup qualification begins at club grounds around Essex today. Botswana, Cayman Islands, Fiji, Guernsey, Norway, Suriname and Vanuatu are the competing teams. Saudi Arabia were also supposed to be there, but don't seem to have sorted out their visas in time.

September 8

Recuperation is again the main objective of the day but I sneak out in the evening for a short while to attend the launch of Ali Bacher and David Williams' new book *South Africa's Greatest Batsman*. I have already read most of it in my role of proof-reading and stats checking and it is a good read.

There is another ICup game starting today. Or at least there is supposed to be. There is no play at Voorburg between Netherlands and Scotland although it doesn't appear to have actually rained much. Associate games are generally played at club grounds and the quality of drainage is not what you would expect to get at a first-class or international ground in a Full Member country.

September 9

Yorkshire clinch the County Championship, their 33rd in history (including ones that they shared). Only New South Wales (46) and Mumbai (40) have won more domestic first-class titles than Yorkshire. I can only imagine the excitement when, in the year 2132 Delhi Daredevils become the first team to win 50 IPLs. Yorkshire's game against Middlesex at Lord's has a dramatic start, as Ryan Sidebottom begins the match with a triple wicket maiden in the first over. It takes a bit of research to find a similar start to a County Championship match, but I manage to find one: Playing for Nottinghamshire in 1957, Arthur Jepson reduced Essex to 0-3 within the first five balls of the match. Jepson went on to be one of the leading umpires in the game in England, officiating in 528 first-class matches up to 1984 to go with the 392 first-class matches that he played. That's a lot of cricket.

I finally complete the task of finding captains with match-ending hat-tricks in first-class cricket and there is only one other apart from Batty: Mahinda Halangoda did it for Sinhalese Sports Club against Singha Sports Club in 1990.

So, it is another busy day researching arcane cricket statistics. But Royal statisticians are busier than their cricketing counterparts today as Queen Elizabeth becomes Britain's longest serving monarch. Her 23 226 days has knocked her great-great-grandmother Victoria into second place on that list. She is a remarkable lady, but will have to go on for at least four more years to pass Vin Scully's 67 in the same job.

The game in Voorburg finally starts today and it moves ahead, as they say. 'Moves ahead' is basically cricket-speak for 'there were lots of wickets'. Sixteen, to be precise as Scotland finish the day on a precarious 35-6 in reply to Netherlands' 210.

It is the anniversary of the first computer bug. And, in case you didn't know this, it was a real bug. A moth was found to have caused a malfunction in a US Navy computer on 9 September 1947.

September 10

At Taunton, 21-year-old Tom Abell scores his maiden first-class century with 131 for Somerset against Hampshire. Opening partner, Marcus Trescothick who will be 40 on Christmas day this year also collects a century (153). So, I feel compelled to research biggest age gaps between opening batsmen who both made centuries in the same innings. There were a fair number of cases in earlier days when players played on well into their 40s, so I revise the search to find when last there was a bigger age gap than the 18 years, 70 days of these two and it turned out to be Geoffrey Boycott and Martyn Moxon back in 1985 with 19 years, 196 days. Geoffrey was the older of the two in that one, in case you were wondering.

September 11

It is a happy day for Oliver Twist, the one who appears on March 7 of this diary, as Ireland announces a three match ODI tour to Zimbabwe. It is good to see that these kind of fixtures can actually be arranged despite the fact that they will cost money rather than generate it. An added bonus is that there will also be a four-day game against Zimbabwe A, a much needed fixture if Ireland's Test ambitions are to be advanced.

Netherlands are generally one of the more consistently competitive Associate teams, so it is a bit of a surprise to discover their win over Scotland today is their first in 16 ICup matches spread over seven years.

The game threatens to have a really close finish when Scotland are 150-6 chasing 201, but Netherlands captain Peter Borren produces an Axar Patel-esque spell of 3.2-2-1-4 to win it for his team by 44 runs.

Long serving Nottinghamshire wicket-keeper Chris Read reaches 1 000 first-class dismissals when he catches Durham's Paul Collingwood off the bowling of Brett Hutton. He is the 23rd to make 1 000 wicket-keeping dismissals (all 23 are English) and will most likely be the last as the number of first-class fixtures will inevitably decline in the Twenty20 era. He should pass Roger Tolchard this year and if he plays another season he will probably pass Walter Latter Cornford on the list. At five foot tall Cornford is Test cricket's shortest player and was commonly and, not terribly surprisingly, known as 'Tich'.

September 12

Yorkshire suffer a notable case of 'Post Series Triumph Relaxation Syndrome' that surpasses even England's effort in the fifth Ashes Test. Having begun their match at Lord's with the famous triple wicket maiden, dismissed Middlesex for 106, collected the Championship, and made 299 in reply they end up losing the match by 246 runs. It is the fourth biggest losing runs margin by a team with a first innings lead over 190 in the history of first-class cricket.

September 13

Last night, Red Sox designated hitter David Ortiz became the 27th player to hit 500 Major League home runs to much excitement in Boston and for that matter my house in Johannesburg when I wake up to see the news.

CricketArchive proudly provides scorecards for as many cricket matches at all levels as they can get hold of. So, I am delighted to see this headline on their website today: 'Continental Star Second XI win Warwickshire Cricket League Division Nine West'. I eagerly await news of the winners of the Warwickshire Cricket League Division Nine East.

The evening's entertainment is a precious piece of video that has appeared on YouTube courtesy of Australian statto Lawrie Colliver. It is the last 26 minutes of play in the Sheffield Shield match at Perth on 20 November 1970 which, as any scholar of the game can tell you is the famous day that Barry Richards scored 325 for South Australia in the day on his way to 356 (off 381 balls with 48 fours and a six). In the 26 video minutes Richards scores 47 runs to go from 278 to 325.

September 14

It is a sad day as the seemingly indestructible Brian Close has died. Close had a 22 match Test career spread over 27 years and the abiding image today (all over YouTube for the remaining few of you who haven't seen it) is of him surviving a brutal assault from Michael Holding as a 45-year-old for England at Old Trafford in 1976 in the days before helmets. *I Don't Bruise Easily* was the title of his autobiography, but he collected a few that day as photos show. A less well known statistic of that famous evening was that Close closed the day on 1 not out off 56 balls as England finished on 21-0 off 17 overs. Tell that to a Twenty20 fan and they will assure you that it must have been the most boring cricket of all time.

Among many other interesting events in Close's career was the time he lost the England captaincy in 1967 because he used what was considered the terribly unsporting tactic of slowing the over-rate down in order to defend a target as captain of Yorkshire in a County Championship match against Warwickshire. Here is the interesting part: In implementing these time-wasting tactics, Yorkshire bowled 24 overs in 100 minutes, which at 14.4 overs per hour would be considered quite good in 2015.

I started following cricket in 1972 and the players of that era are now all reaching their 70s, so sadly more of them are no longer with us. Another death announced today is that of Neil Rosendorff who was a stalwart for Orange Free State (as they were in those days). His 4 914 first-class runs for the province stood as their record aggregate for over 20 years.

September 15

The Lancashire League is finished for the season, so I sneak a look at Daryn Smit's final figures and they are still hugely impressive: 1 248 runs at 113.45 and 74 wickets at 8.18. His all-rounders' ratio is 13.85. While the Lancashire League is clearly not first-class, I decide to see how this compares to first-class cricket. The best ratio in a season of first-class cricket by a player scoring 1 000 or more runs and taking 50 or more wickets is quite a long way short of Smit's at 4.95 by WG Grace back in 1873. Grace scored 1 805 runs at 72.20 and took 72 wickets at 14.57 in that season. With a slightly lower qualification of 500 runs and 25 wickets it will be hard to beat Mike Procter's famous season for the then Rhodesia in 1970/71 when he scored 956 runs including centuries in six consecutive innings at 119.50 and took 27 wickets at 16.11, a ratio of 7.41.

Surrey's opening batsman and left-arm spinner Zafar Ansari has an interesting day. In the morning he is selected for the England Test squad for the series against Pakistan in the UAE next month. In the afternoon he dislocates a finger while fielding and is unlikely to make the tour. One has to hope that his turn will come again.

September 16

I have been diligently writing this diary all year without having a publisher confirmed. The brick wall continues to win as I get another rejection today. I fully understand the publishers' view that this book will have a fairly limited niche appeal, but today's rejection is interesting in that they let me know, in very kindly written email, that they did not think that the 'abbreviated' format of a diary would work. In an era of Twitter and Twenty20 I have been rejected for being 'abbreviated'. Oh, the irony!

Kumar Sangakkara is not quite as gone as I may have suggested earlier following his Test retirement. Like most modern players he is retiring in stages and is still playing county cricket for Surrey. Today he scores 118 against Lancashire, his 54th first-class century. Looking at Charles Davis' wonderful *Z-score's Cricket Stats Blog* the other day, I was reminded that Sangakkara took quite a while to get his maiden first-class century — 76 innings in fact. So, I decide to check where he rates in terms of most hundreds scored by players who waited a long time for their first. It turns out that he is well behind the leader in this obscure stats category. Only Jack Hobbs (199) has scored more first-class centuries than Patsy Hendren, the great Middlesex and England player between the wars. Hendren collected 170 first-class 100s, but only scored his first in his 90th innings.

September 17

Good news for those of us who love the County Championship is that the 16-match program has had a stay of execution. Next year will still be 16, but it will almost certainly diminish after that. Ostensibly the reduction in matches is to allow for more time for rest and preparation but this won't happen in practise as the extra time available will inevitably be filled with more Twenty20 and Fifty50 games. One interesting aspect of keeping the program at 16 matches for now is that there are proposals to lengthen the season and play matches in March at overseas venues. Of the options for places mentioned, Spain would be my favourite. It is about time they had some first-class cricket there.

September 18

Fortunately I am only mildly famous, so am not inundated with interview requests. Today, I am interviewed for the second time this year. It is for *The Times* (The Johannesburg version, not London's or indeed New York's). Apparently the concept of cricket statisticians with injuries is of interest to newspaper readers.

The season known in England as 'overseas' first-class cricket begins today with the first round of matches in Bangladesh in the Walton LED TV National Cricket League. What will Rony Talukdar do this season, I wonder?

September 19

The seven-year-old turns eight today, so there is the first of the weekend's three parties. This one is at the school. My cupcake intake for the weekend will disturb my dietician, no doubt.

The Rugby World Cup has started. The Union version, that is. Today, I watch Japan pull off what is probably the biggest upset in rugby history when they beat South Africa. Don't tell anyone this, but patriot fervour dissipates and I join most of the rugby world, and indeed, sporting world in cheering as Japan score the last minute try to win. Sport really doesn't get much better than that. Comparisons with cricket are inevitable. Japan are ranked 13th in rugby, so if the ICC ran that sport they would not even be at the World Cup as there would only be 10 teams. Initially I thought I would find myself using Japan's win to bang on about cricket's 10 team World Cup folly, but a different thought occurred to me. When I discover Japan's ranking in rugby, I realise that cricket doesn't even have a 13th ranked team. ODI rankings stop at 12. Only 10 teams play Tests. Yes, there are 15 in the T20 International rankings, thanks for asking. Sports like rugby and soccer seem to be able to rank all their members. Did you know, for instance, that Trinidad and Tobago, home of cricketing greats such as Brian Lara, is ranked 45th in the world in rugby union. As someone who knows a little bit about numbers, I can assure you that it would not be beyond the realms of mathematics to come up with a system that would rank all 106 of the ICC's members. You really are going to struggle to achieve your ambition of becoming the World's Favourite Sport if you think you only have 12 teams worth bothering about, especially when sports that will want to compete for that title have their 13th ranked team beating one of the great teams at a World Cup.

An email pops into my inbox announcing that Griqualand West has rebranded as Northern Cape. This makes a lot of sense as it aligns them with the geopolitical province that they represent and not just the region of Griqualand West. It is however sad to say goodbye to one of the old evocative team names in the sport. Griqualand West hosted the first Currie Cup match in 1890 and won the tournament the following year. Admittedly they were known as Kimberley in those years, but they rebranded as Griqualand West by 1892 and have been known as that since then.

September 20

I spend the day blissfully unaware of cricket as the now eight-year-old is having her big party. Aeroplanes are the theme (kids' birthday parties have to have a theme) as we head off to the Grand Central Airport just outside Johannesburg for the event.

September 21

There is not a lot happening in the cricket world at the moment. The most interesting news is that Richie Richardson has become an ICC Match Referee. Told you there is not much happening.

September 22

Glamorgan start a County Championship game without wicket-keeper Mark Wallace in the XI for the first time since 6 June 2001. Wallace was injured in the previous match and this has ended an extraordinary modern sequence of 230 consecutive County Championship matches without missing one. Ken Suttle's record of 423 consecutive Championship appearances for Sussex between 1954 and 1969 will never be broken. Even in the unlikely event of the 16-match Championship program being maintained it would take 27 seasons to do that many these days. Wallace's sequence is the longest since Gloucestershire wicket-keeper Ron Nicholls' 276 which ended in 1972.

September 23

Zak Chappell scores 96 on his first-class debut batting at number 10 for Leicestershire against Derbyshire and I manage to establish that this is the third highest score by anyone batting at number 10 on their County Championship debut, but I can't dredge up any enthusiasm to check best scores on debut by players with first names beginning with 'Z'.

Sad news from the baseball world is that Yogi Berra is no longer with us having passed away at the age of 90. Apart from winning more World Series than anyone else (13) as player or manager, he was well-known for his malapropisms, such as 'It's like déjà vu all over again' and 'Baseball is 90 percent mental. The other half is physical.'

September 24

At The Oval, brothers Tom (7-35) and Sam Curran (3-46) take all 10 wickets as Surrey dismiss Northamptonshire. Sons of the late Kevin Curran (poignantly a Northamptonshire player for nine years) these two have lit up the season for Surrey. Twenty-year-old Tom is one of the leading wicket-takers in first-class cricket for the season while Sam has been described by Alec Stewart, no less, as the best 17-year-old cricketer he has seen. Naturally the challenge for me is to find a list of pairs of brothers who have combined to take all 10 wickets in an innings. I do not have a proper record of brothers and other related players in the database, so the trick is to find all cases where 10 wickets were shared by two bowlers with the same surname (to confuse the matter, there are a few cases of brothers with different surnames, e.g. Fidel Edwards and Pedro Collins) and then check through manually to find which were cases of brothers. WG Grace features prominently having done it three times with EM and four times with GF, but the most recent in a County Championship match was back in 1950 when Charles and Jack Oakes did it for Sussex against Somerset at Taunton.

September 25

It is the last day of the season in England. County cricket, unlike any other cricket, feels like an old friend. So it is goodbye for now, and winter well. See you in April.

I notice a little jump in my number of Twitter followers (is there anything more conducive to narcissism than Twitter?) for no apparent reason, so I check who the new followers are. I am amused to see that I appear to have collected a few followers in Japan, presumably as a result of tweeting about the rugby result the other day. In the somewhat unlikely event that these new followers are actually humans I suspect that they will be disappointed in me only tweeting the strange sport of cricket. On the other hand in the more likely event that my new followers are machines ('bots') it is pleasing to know that machines are just blindly following me because I mentioned Japan despite the fact that I am extremely unlikely to tweet much about Japan ever (or at least until they play their first cricket Test) and therefore we can take comfort that humans are still cleverer than machines. Until the Singularity in 2045, presumably.

On Twitter I notice that Qiktionary has kindly informed us that 'Americans eat nine times more broccoli than they did in 1970'. Not bad for a land noted for an obesity problem, although George Bush senior might not be too impressed with his countrymen, having been famous for not eating the green vegetable. He is still going strong, by the way, having been born before both Yogi Berra and Queen Elizabeth.

September 26

My apologies to the Cubs for suggesting back on 22 June that they would not be using their ballpark in October. They clinched a playoff spot last night for the first time since 2008. So there will be much joy on the north side of Chicago. Baseball enjoys its 'curses'. The Red Sox were supposedly under the 'Curse of the Bambino' when they did not win the World Series between 1918 and 2004. Curse theorists attributed this to the fact that the Red Sox sold Babe Ruth to the Yankees in 1919. At that point the Red Sox had won the World Series five times and the Yankees had not won it at all. Between 1919 and 2003 the Yankees won 26 World Series titles and the Red Sox none. Theo Epstein was the Red Sox general manager in 2004 when the curse was ended. Epstein is now performing a similar role at the Chicago Cubs, a team also apparently under a curse. In 1945 the owner of Billy Goat Tavern was evicted from a World Series game at the Cubs' Wrigley Field when fellow spectators complained about the goat he had brought into stadium with him. He then 'cursed' the Cubs and they haven't been to the World Series since then. So the question is can Theo Epstein go two-for-two in curse-beating?

September 27

For some reason when I wake up I have Kris Kristofferson's *Sunday Morning Coming Down* in my head especially as it is a long way down the list of my favourite songs. I suspect the main reason is that it is actually Sunday morning. But for me it is more of a case, far less musical, of 'Sunday Morning — Africa Cup stats'. The competition has been played between the 13 South African provincial sides as well as Namibia, Kenya and a Zimbabwe President's XI in four pools spread over the past four weekends. The prospect at the beginning of the tournament was that I would be doing net run-rate scenario calculations in between mouthfuls of Sunday roast for the four weeks. But, amazingly, I have not had to do a single net run-rate calculation for the whole tournament. I am always positively disposed to the idea having less work to do rather than more.

September 28

It is an early start as there is a rare simultaneous lunar eclipse and 'Super' Moon. So, it is a 04:30 wake-up call. And it is a spectacular sight. We wake the kids up. The eight-year-old says, 'It looks like someone has toasted it' and goes back to sleep. The six-year-old just goes back to sleep.

September 29

I need to continue in 'Apologies to American Cities' mode. On May 7 I hinted that Hartford, Connecticut was not a particularly special place, albeit based on a half-hour stop at the central bus station there. An article by New Zealander Dave Roberts in CricInfo's *Cricket Monthly* magazine about his search for cricket on America's East Coast alerts me to the fact that America's Cricket Hall of Fame is based in Hartford, Connecticut. So, good on them. I must visit it next time I am in the neighbourhood.

September 30

It is a very quiet day in cricket. The English season has finished and most of the other countries have not started their season. A Women's Twenty20 between Pakistan and Bangladesh is the only entertainment for the day.

October 1

The Ranji Trophy starts today in India with 27 teams all hoping to win the tournament. There are often debates in all cricket playing countries about what is the ideal number of teams to have in the premier competitions. India either has the most or the fewest first-class teams of any country depending on how you look at it. In absolute terms 27 is more than any other country but everything is relative and India currently has a population of 1 276 267 000 and the ratio of 47 269 148 people per first-class team actually makes them the most under-represented of all Test playing countries in relative terms.

I check the long-term weather forecast for Dubai as I will be heading there on the 11th. The general public does like to mock weather forecasters for getting it wrong 'all the time'. However, they really are not that bad and modern weather forecasts are pretty good especially in the short-term. Dubai weather forecasting is probably easier than most and today's 10-day forecast shows nine big yellow balls with maximums of about 36 and minimums of about 28 every day. The 10th day of the forecast – the day that I land – has a few clouds as variety. It is going to be hot.

October 2

There is news of another death as Australian Lindsay Kline passes away. He is the first of the four men involved in the final ball of the greatest of all cricket matches to depart from this earth. With one run needed to win and two balls remaining at Brisbane in 1960 Kline faced great West Indies' fast bowler Wes Hall, hit the ball to Joe Solomon and set off for a single. A direct hit from Solomon ran out Ian Meckiff for cricket's first tied Test. In that same series Kline was also involved in by far the longest match-saving 10th wicket partnership in the fourth innings of a Test when he and Ken 'Slasher' Mackay defied the West Indies for 109 minutes at Adelaide facing 35.3 8-ball overs (the equivalent of 47.1 six-ball overs).

Australia cancel their tour of Bangladesh which was supposed to have started already. This is due to security concerns. While it is obviously important to take security issues very seriously, it is sad to see two more Tests disappearing from the calendar, especially as this series between an improving and increasingly confident Bangladesh team and a new look Australian team following all the retirements around the Ashes was shaping up as a particularly intriguing one.

A few days ago the Red Sox arrived in New York for a four game series against the Yankees with the Yankees sitting on 9 999 total wins in their history. The Red Sox defiantly won the first three games of the series in an attempt to avoid being the losers in the Yankees' famous 10 000th win, but stumble at the final hurdle last night. The Yankees are the first in the American League to reach this milestone, but amazingly there are five National League teams that have already reached 10 000 wins (admittedly they did have a 25 year start). It will be a very long time before any cricket team wins that many games. Yorkshire have won more first-class matches than anyone else with 1 525. So, just the 8 475 to go to catch up with the Yankees then.

October 3

I notice that progress is being made with the demolition of the Warner Stand at Lord's. It is a sad day to see the demise of my famous toilet there. The toilet is famous as I have always enjoyed telling the story of how I scored for the Afrikaans commentators, Kotie Grove and Omar Henry, in the toilet at Lord's during South Africa's historic first match there after unity in 1994. Of course, it wasn't actually in the toilet, but a very small storage room right next to the toilet. I had to sit on one of the boxes that technical producer Gawie Swart used to carry his equipment around in, scoring on my lap behind the two commentators who were squeezed in at the front of the box. Needless to say that, apart from the business end (i.e. the pitch), I could hardly see any of the ground. The weather that week was as hot and humid as any I have experienced (yes, it was in London) made worse by my ridiculous dedication to wearing a jacket and tie because it was Lord's. And of course, the toilet next door was fully functional and busy, so by mid-afternoon the smell was not pleasant, to say the least.

October 4

The Rugby World Cup is heating up: Last night South Africa stayed alive by beating Scotland while England went home, or would have gone home if they weren't there already. Defeat to Australia eliminates them. But the sporting performance of the day was in baseball when the remarkable Max Scherzer completed his second no-hitter of the season, this time against the New York Mets and again he does not give up a walk and is denied a perfect game when the only base-runner reaches on a fielding error. He is just the sixth pitcher to toss two no-hitters in one season and his 17 strike-outs equals the most in any no-hitter. He really is a man at the top of his game. All of which is much more interesting than anything that may be happening in the cricket world today.

October 5

My service provider's email servers are down for most of the day. As a result I spend the time vacillating between unremitted frustration and overwhelming bliss with nary an emotion in between. It is a truly modern type of day.

October 6

I had noticed a headline yesterday to the effect that Travis Head had scored a double-century for South Australia against Western Australia in a Matador BBQ's One-Day Cup match, but I must admit I did not pay much attention. After all, one-day double-centuries are almost two-a-penny these days. Or one-a-penny at least, whatever a penny is at 2015 inflation-adjusted rates. But when processing the score into my database this morning I notice this one is actually a bit different: Head's is the first of the 20 List A limited overs 200s to have been scored for a team batting second.

A Cricket Australia XI has been added to the normal Sheffield Shield teams for the Matador BBQ's One-Day Cup ostensibly to give 'fringe' players more opportunities. These kind of initiatives, well-intentioned as they may be, seldom work as far as I have seen. The teams invariably look and feel as though they have been invented and designed by a committee, which is exactly what they are. Yesterday the Cricket Australia XI made 59 in reply to New South Wales' 338-3.

As I was saying the other day, everything is relative. A short video on the BBC website compares relative sizes of buildings. The tallest building made by humans is the Burj Khalifa which I will be seeing in five days' time in Dubai. But relative to the size of the average human it has nothing on a termite heap in Democratic Republic of Congo which at 12.8 metres is far bigger relative to the size of the average termite.

October 7

The dates and venues for the exhibition T20s involving former stars in teams captained by Shane Warne and Sachin Tendulkar have been announced and fortunately the long johns will not be needed in Chicago.

The three venues will be the New York Mets ballpark at Citi Field which could get very cold and then Minute Maid Park, home of the Houston Astros and Dodger Stadium in Los Angeles which should both be a bit warmer. Interestingly, all three hosts have their teams in the baseball playoffs.

October 8

The Cricket Australia XI has shown some improvement. Yesterday they made 79 against Victoria and took a wicket in the 11.1 overs that they bowled as their opponents knocked off the runs.

Generally on a hot day in Johannesburg temperatures get into the low 30s — 32 is about the highest. But there is currently a heatwave here with the mercury (do they still use mercury to measure temperatures?) hitting 34 for a few days in a row. As a result, sporting events at the kids' school are being cancelled. I am, of course, acutely aware of the irony that I will be watching professionals play cricket in 37 degrees centigrade next week.

October 9

Zimbabwe and Ireland produce yet another close match with the hosts sneaking home by two wickets with an over to spare to the approval of my friend Master Twist. The discrepancy in the financing these two countries get from the ICC is way out of proportion to their relative playing strengths, just because one is a Full Member and the other isn't.

The challenge of the day is set by *The Independent*'s cricket correspondent Stephen Brenkley. It has become most likely that Moeen Ali will open the batting for England in the first Test against Pakistan in Abu Dhabi. Moeen has had great success in this role in ODIs, but interestingly, he has never opened in a first-class innings. So the challenge is to find how many players have opened the batting in a Test for England without having opened in first-class cricket. It is actually fairly simple to program. First, I find all the players who have opened the batting for England in a Test with the date that they first opened (MinStartDate for the technically minded). Then I search each of those players' first-class careers up to that date and find the lowest batting position numerically that they batted in that time, i.e. one is the lowest numerically although it is the top of the batting order (MinBatPos for the technically minded). Anyone whose lowest batting position is three or more had not opened in first-class cricket. The answer is interesting as I find five cases, but all were lower order batsmen in dead match situations or on 'sticky wickets' when batting orders were often reversed. So, the list includes the like of Ken Farnes and 'Big Jim' Smith. Moeen will thus be the first to do so in an 'authentic' match situation and, more importantly for me I have my first stat of the series ready four days before it starts.

October 10

I seem to have been apologising quite often recently and another one is in order today as the Cricket Australia XI beat Tasmania by three runs. Clearly, composite teams are a brilliant initiative and all countries should have one in their domestic competitions.

Meanwhile there is another milestone for my database. I have been maintaining a ball-by-ball table for a while now and today this table passed 10 000 000 records.

October 11

It is time for the next adventure: Pakistan v England in the United Arab Emirates. So, it is a day on the plane to Dubai. I leave at 09:30 and arrive eight hours later at 19:30 local time. There are a number of choices for flight times between Johannesburg and Dubai and all-day flights are generally less popular than overnight ones. I deliberately chose the all-day one for this and am rewarded with three seats to myself which is a great bonus for those of us who only travel in what is colloquially known as 'cattle-class'. In a very rare event for me I spend time on the laptop while 30 000 feet up, mostly checking and typing up this diary actually, as well as doing a bit of prep for the upcoming series.

I try to keep as little of the currency of the country I am leaving as possible on the way out, including my own country. So, I am quite pleased to set a personal record (for South Africa) when I leave with just 10 rand in my pocket.

I arrive in Dubai and meet up with TMS colleagues Charles Dagnall and Ed Smith. The three of us have arrived on three different planes within half an hour of each other and we collect our transfer (travel-speak for 'catch a minibus') to Abu Dhabi which is about an hour and a half drive from Dubai Airport. Jonathan Agnew is taking a rare break and missing this Test series and Charles Dagnall will be doing his first Test series outside of England. Yes, that's right: Daggers has replaced Aggers for this one.

October 12

It is always a reassuring sight at the beginning of a tour to see TMS producer Adam Mountford smiling and bearing gifts. Well, bearing media passes, anyway. And today is no exception. We head off to the ground in Abu Dhabi to check the place out and get ready for the Test starting tomorrow.

I quite like the Sheikh Zayed Stadium in Abu Dhabi. The setting probably wouldn't be regarded as particularly beautiful. But it is certainly different from the standard circle of bucket seats that most stadiums are these days. From our vantage point we look out across ground with its grass banks on either side to a vast expanse of desert which stretches out towards the housing estates in the background. So, it is an interesting and contrasting view. There won't be many spectators at the match except for Friday which is the day off in this part of the world. And when the fans do come in it will be quite a sight to see them literally walking through the desert to come to the cricket. It will also be interesting to see various matches taking place on concrete pitches in the sand fields surrounding the stadium.

October 13

The pitch looks depressingly flat as Pakistan calmly compile 286-4 although England don't help themselves by dropping two relatively simple catches (I Bell x two) and taking a wicket with a no-ball (S Broad). Shoaib Malik scores 124* in his first Test for five years, having missed 42 in that time. I dredge my memory to try and recall any great performances by players in comeback matches after a long break and can't remember anything spectacular. So, I dredge the database and it confirms my brain's suspicions. Shoaib Malik is just the fifth player to score a century in a comeback Test having missed 40 or more Tests and his 124* is the highest of these scores beating Australian Andrew Hilditch who scored 113 against West Indies at Melbourne in 1984 having missed Australia's previous 53 Tests.

October 14

Pakistan pile on the agony and the runs before declaring at 523-8 (Shoaib Malik 245). The worst of the agony is reserved for England's debutante leg-spinner Adil Rashid who finishes with 0-163 in 34 overs which is the worst nought-for on Test debut. I was at Cape Town when fellow member of the leg-spinner's fraternity, Australian Bryce McGain, set the record with 0-149 (in just 18 overs) against South Africa in 2009. Leg-spin is cricket's most difficult art and has always been my favourite of the game's range of skills ever since I tried it out myself in my brief playing career at school, and I can only wish Rashid more success in the second innings and the rest of his Test career than McGain, who never appeared again.

Over the past 12 months Pakistan have played Australia, New Zealand and England at Abu Dhabi. In each game Pakistan have batted first and compiled 500–and–something–for–not–many–declared. The opposition spinners in those three innings have combined bowling figures of (Age-restriction warning before you read this) three for 882, including one over of speculative off-spin from Ben Stokes for five runs.

England finish on 56-0 by close of play with Moeen Ali opening as suspected, so I can bring out the stat mentioned earlier.

Meanwhile, overnight the Chicago Cubs have ensured more baseball at Wrigley Field in October by dispatching the St Louis Cardinals and advancing to the National League Championship Series. What was I saying about them always losing? It comes to light that the 1989 Michael J Fox movie *Back to the Future II* had a scene with him arriving in the year 2015 to hologram headlines about the Cubs winning the World Series for the first time since 1908. Will the Cubs' prediction prove more accurate than the prediction of holograms being ubiquitous by our current year?

October 15

Alastair Cook bats through the day for 168* as England reply strongly with 290-3. This match is beginning to look like a long hard slog. Will the authorities ever act against pitches which are too flat? Cricket, as I may have mentioned before, is clearly much better when wickets are falling than when they are not.

The Cricket Australia XI are knocked over for 101 in reply to Western Australia's 347-5. See, I told you composite teams are not a good idea.

On my only visit to Namibia in 2011 I discovered that a new ground was being built in Walvis Bay. So I am pleased to see that ground is hosting its inaugural first-class match today with Namibia taking on South Western Districts in the Sunfoil Provincial Three-day competition. Of course, the venue did not exist when I visited so I could not collect it, but now that it is a first-class ground I will need to pay a visit. I find it is always good to have an excuse to come back to places I have seen on my travels.

October 16

The game continues on its merry way with only the very occasional interruption by a wicket falling. We have had 16 wickets in total over the four days. The most significant of these is the demise of Alastair Cook for 263. Cook is dismissed by the match's other double-centurion Shoaib Malik. So, I have to check whether this has happened before. It is a relatively simple query. I extract the database player number for each double-centurion in each game and then match that against the field containing the bowler's name for each wicket in those games and list these wickets where the opposing batsman's score is 200 or more. It turns out that the only other occasion was when Mohammad Hafeez scored 224 and then dismissed Tamim Iqbal for 206 at Khulna earlier this year. #Busses.

Cook's 263 took him 836 minutes to compile and is the third longest innings in Test history behind Hanif Mohammad's 337 in 970 minutes for Pakistan v West Indies at Bridgetown in 1958 and Gary Kirsten's 878 minute effort for his 275 for South Africa against England at Durban in 1999. Many cricket fans dismiss really big scores and marathon innings as being too easy given that they are inevitably played on flat pitches and often against ordinary or demoralised bowling attacks. While I agree that this can diminish some of the batting in these circumstances, I have only the greatest admiration for the really big scores and really marathon innings. To my mind Cook's 836 minute effort makes it a genuinely great innings. Even allowing for the flatness of the pitch, to bat for that long without getting out requires levels of concentration, stamina and sheer bloody-mindedness not normally found in even elite sportsmen. Cook had split the webbing in his fingers on the second day, so that would have added to the discomfort of batting in perpetual 36-37 degrees heat having fielded in the same heat for almost two days before embarking on the innings. Yes, it was great innings.

I have not been paying much attention to the Sri Lanka v West Indies Test in Galle, but a headline catches my eye today. Shai Hope has been in the West Indies team for recent Test matches, and with a surname like his, he will inevitably light up the eyes of headline writers around the world. Indeed, you may recall me shamelessly abusing his name for punning purposes earlier in this diary. When he is dismissed early in West Indies' follow-on at Galle the headline appears 'West Indies lose Hope'. That seems appropriate on so many levels as they begin subsiding to what will most likely be an innings defeat tomorrow.

October 17

After seeing just 16 wickets in four days 15 wickets fall on the fifth. Eleven of these tumble after tea as Pakistan squander a comfortable position and leave England 99 to chase in a nominal 19 overs. There were never going to be 19 overs as bad light was always going to intervene and England finish on 74-4 in 11 overs. The regulation that the ICC brought in a few years ago leaving bad light decisions purely in the hands of the umpires has created an imbalance in this type of situation. When a batting team is chasing a target and is unlikely to be bowled out and bad light is pending the bowling team has always slowed down the over-rate in attempting to secure the draw. Prior to the current regulation when the umpires would offer the light to the batting team rather than decreeing it to be too dark, the batting team could counter such tactics by continuing to bat in the dark. They can't do that anymore and this seems unfair to me.

The 11 wickets after tea are the second most ever after tea in the final possible session of a Test match. I was a little surprised to find a game with more: 12 in the Ashes Test at Manchester in 1953. On that occasion England were 209-6 in reply to Australia's 318 at tea on the final day in a rain-affected match (rain in Manchester, surely not?). After their final brew and cake for the match, they lost their last four wickets for 67 and then reduced Australia to 35-8 at the close.

Shoaib Malik collects a duck in Pakistan's second innings, making his 245 the highest score by a player who also made a duck in the same Test beating Ricky Ponting's 242 v India at Adelaide in 2003. But, the statistical and indeed cricketing and human excitement for the day was reserved for Adil Rashid. He ran through the tail to finish with 5-64 thus becoming the first player to concede 100 runs without taking a wicket in the first innings on Test debut and then take a five-for in the second innings. He was also the first leg-spinner to take five wickets in an innings for England since Tommy Greenhough's 5-35 against India at Lord's way back in 1959. For me it was reminiscent of another debut that I was at: Lance Klusener at Kolkata in 1996. Klusener got smashed all over the place, particularly by Mohammad Azharuddin who made a 74-ball 100 in the first innings, finishing with 0-75 in 14 overs, but returned with 8-64 in the second innings. My favourite of the Rashid stats, however, was that he was the first English bowler to take a five-for on Test debut having also taken a five-for on first-class debut (6-67 Yorkshire v Warwickshire at Scarborough in 2006) since 'Big Jim' Smith in 1935.

In the stats pack that I send out for the various domestic competitions in South Africa I include each team's averages for the season to date sorted alphabetically. Glancing through the pack for tomorrow's Momentum One-day Cup matches I see the name RE Levi listed first for the Cape Cobras averages. Thinking that my trusty laptop must have let me down, I check thoroughly and am surprised to find that Levi *is* actually first alphabetically for the Cobras this season. (It is not called my 'trusty' laptop for nothing). It must be some sort of a record for a team to have no players before 'L' in the alphabet, but I manage to persuade myself to have the good sense not to check this.

October 18

It is back to the bus again as we head off to Dubai and our hotel on the Marina of this remarkable city. Fifty years ago fewer than 60 000 people lived here, but today it has well over 2 000 000 inhabitants and its neck-straining collection of thoroughly modern skyscrapers rivals that of New York.

Performances in domestic one-day competitions provide the cricketing stats highlights of the day. In South Africa Alviro Petersen scores his third century in three innings at the start of the season, joining Doug Watson (in 2005) as the only players to have done this in South African one-day competitions. Even more impressively, Mitchell Starc has now taken at least four wickets in an innings in each of his five matches in Australia's competition. He has 23 wickets at 7.47 in these matches and joins

Pakistan's Fazl-e-Akbar (in 1999) as the only players to have taken four or more wickets in five consecutive List A games.

October 19

Things get interesting at Harare in the four-day match between Zimbabwe A and Ireland. On the first day, Regis Chakabva (104) and Malcolm Waller (138) had both made centuries for Zimbabwe A. In the second innings today they both collect centuries again (Chakabva 101, Waller 118). Not many teams will have had two players scoring a century in each innings in a match. So I check and there are not many — this is only the seventh time in all first-class cricket that this has happened.

Laundry is always an interesting challenge on tour. In most hotels it costs almost as much to wash a shirt as it would to buy a new one. So, I always look for somewhere that I can get it done a bit cheaper. I take a stroll around the Dubai Marina and manage to find a laundrette that will wash and iron an entire week's worth of laundry for about the price of a new shirt.

October 20

There was an election in Canada yesterday and the Blue Jays won last night (although they still trail 2-1 in the American League Championship Series against the Kansas City Royals), so it feels like a Canadian sort of day and I visit the Tim Horton's coffee shop next door to the hotel for my afternoon tea. Tim Horton's, for those who don't know, is the definitive Canadian brand. Anyway, as I sat there knocking off my cappuccino and chocolate muffin, I found myself contemplating cricket and the Olympics. Headlines that I saw yesterday suggested that the ICC was looking at 'all formats' for the Olympics. 'All' formats? Really? Your chances of seeing 'Test cricket' and 'Olympic Games' in any sentence other than this one are more remote than seeing 'Aviation Activities' and 'Pigs' in the same sentence. The thought does occur to me, however, that the now ditched proposals for a Test Championship (four teams, two semi-finals and a final) would actually work within the two-week timeframe of the Olympics. And imagine an Olympic Gold medal being the prize for a Test Championship. But returning from the extremes of the extremely hypothetical and back to the real world, one of the many formats being considered for the Olympics is indoor cricket. Canada, with its long and freezing winters would be an ideal candidate for indoor cricket — would they be favourites for cricket's first Olympics medal since Devon and Somerset Wanderers won it for what is now known as Team GB by beating France (actually France Athletic Club Union) in Paris in 1900?

In the evening we attend a function at the British Embassy along with the England team. It is an outdoor event, and although it is evening there are still a few sweaty shirts to be seen as the temperature only cools down to about 28 degrees centigrade. One interesting thing about the weather here is that it can be very comfortable when there is a bit of a breeze. Who would have thought that the wind chill factor would be significant in Dubai weather?

October 21

Today's newspaper is full of news of technological advancement being implemented in the country: Smart immigration procedures (you may even be able to be processed on board), smart street lights that only brighten up when vehicles approach, and chairs that can do a basic health check (six minutes from sitting down to print out). The United Arab Emirates is a thoroughly modern country.

I am not really a shopping mall type of person. And the mall is the most noticeable effect of globalisation. Once you get inside a shopping mall you could be anywhere in the world as local flavours and cultures disappear into the air-conditioned sameness of retail. Having said that (and I probably shouldn't admit this in public), I actually quite enjoy the Dubai Mall. The reason for this is that it is, simply, the World In One Mall. Major retail chains, fashion stores and various other shops from all over the world have outlets in this mall, the biggest on the planet in terms of shopping space. So, a walk around it (which will also provide exercise above the Daily Recommended Allowance) will give you a feeling of a mini world tour. I enjoy my visit today and the highlight is the Dubai Fountain display. In the evenings the fountains do a show choreographed to classical music (Arabic and Western) with the magnificent Burj Khalifa (at 829.8m, the world's tallest building) as the backdrop — all quite blissful.

October 22

The first day of the Test match at Dubai International Cricket Stadium proves to be fairly quiet, until the last over. Misbah-ul-Haq is 87* when Moeen Ali starts the last over, so I am fairly relaxed knowing that I will be able to save the slew of Misbah 100 stats that I have prepared for tomorrow. However Misbah hits the first and third balls for six and reaches the 100 off the fourth ball of the over. (What ever happened to playing quietly for the interval?) So, it is a bit of a rush to get the stats in as the commentators prepare for the end of day winding down and summaries. Misbah is the oldest player to score a Test century since Bobby Simpson in 1978, he now has four centuries after the age of 40 which puts him second behind Jack Hobbs' eight, and he equals Inzamam-ul-Haq's record of seven Test centuries as Pakistan captain. But my favourite is that he has now hit 25 sixes after the age of 40. Clive Lloyd is second with six and Wally Hammond is third with four.

Last year Afghanistan played a four-match ODI series in Zimbabwe which was split 2-2. They are back there this year for a five-match series and Afghanistan win the fourth ODI today to level up this series 2-2. So the final game looks like it is the decider of the nine-match series. It is good to see teams like Ireland and Afghanistan playing against Zimbabwe and hopefully more fixtures between these sorts of evenly matched and competitive teams can be arranged.

The Chinese restaurant where I have my dinner reassuringly informs us on the billboard outside that it belongs to a chain that is 'America's Number One Chinese Restaurant'. It would, of course, have been even more reassuring if it had been China's Number One Chinese Restaurant.

October 23

It is a varied day on TMS. Diversions include the hole in one that Charles Dagnall managed to hit yesterday, the centenary of WG Grace's death (he died on 23 October 1915) and even who should play Andrew Samson in a movie! Daggers has to confirm to the sceptics that it was actually a proper seven iron and it wasn't one of those that went under the windmill and through the crocodile's teeth.

Discussions about WG Grace allow me the opportunity to talk about his stats. I find it unfortunate that the modern image of him seems to be mostly of a fat old man with a grey beard who cheated all the time, and a Test average of 32 from 22 matches with two centuries is hardly impressive looking through a purely 2015 prism. There is not much doubt that he was prone to occasional bouts of gamesmanship, but he was further ahead of any cricketers of his day than anyone else (including Bradman) has ever been. In his youth (pre-photographs and very pre-video) he was a fine athlete and I try to illustrate his greatness by looking at his stats for the 1870s when he was at his peak (aged 22 to 32). In that decade he scored 17 126 first-class runs at 50.22. The next best average by anyone in that period was 28.45. Included in that were 50 centuries. Nobody else made more than eight. Oh, and in his spare time he was the third highest wicket-taker in the decade with 1 157. He was truly one of the very greatest cricketers ever.

With regard to the Samson Movie, I am flattered by suggestions of Dustin Hoffman (good with numbers in *Rain Man*) and Robert de Niro, but perhaps the winner was Al Pacino with the movie being called *ScoreFace*.

In the actual cricket England do well to restrict Pakistan to 378 from their overnight 282-4 and reply with 182-3. The statistical highlight was Moeen Ali taking 3-108 which is the first time that an England opening batsman (first innings only disclaimer) had taken three wickets in a Test innings since Graham Gooch's 3-39 against Pakistan at Old Trafford in 1992.

Ravindra Jadeja, scorer of three first-class triple centuries by the way, has had an extraordinary start to the Ranji Trophy. His 7-60 for Saurashtra in Hyderabad's second innings today means that he has taken at least five wickets in each of the six innings he has bowled this season. Tich Freeman holds the world record for consecutive five-fors with 10 for Kent back in 1930, while CS Nayudu has the Ranji Trophy record with a sequence of nine for Holkar between 1943 and 1944.

Northern Cape play their first first-class match with their new name and beat Free State by three wickets: Free State 58 and 134, Northern Cape 107 and 86-7. Now that is what I call a proper game.

October 24

It is a busy sporting day. I wake up a little earlier than I would have liked, but it enables me to watch the live streaming of Game Six of the American League Championship Series where sadly the Blue Jays lose the game 4-3 and thus the series to the Kansas City Royals. So, it will be a Royals v New York Mets World Series. The Royals last won in 1985 and the Mets in 1986 so there will be much joy for whichever team wins this time. Then it is a day at the cricket and in the evening it is World Cup rugby semi-final time in the sports bar at the hotel. And it is another sad result as the Springboks lose to New Zealand. Fortunately, expectations were low as New Zealand are clearly the better team at the moment. So, a 20-18 score-line represents at least a respectable loss.

England collapse spectacularly from 206-3 to 242 all out, which effectively seals the Test match. Pakistan confirm their dominance of the day by adding 222-3 to their first innings lead of 136. Their two older statesmen, Younis Khan and Misbah-ul-Haq, have added an unbroken 139 for the fourth wicket so far. They have an extraordinary record batting together — currently 3 134 runs at 80.35 in Tests. Of their last nine partnerships together in the UAE they have reached 50 eight times and gone over 100 on five of those occasions for an average of 157.71. But their 14 conversions of 20 fifty partnerships to 100 partnerships is perhaps the most impressive stat. At 70% this is the highest of all pairs with at least 15 partnerships over 50, ahead of Jacques Kallis and AB de Villiers who converted 13 out of 20. Misbah joins Jack Hobbs, Patsy Hendren and Tom Graveney as the only players to have scored 1 000 Test runs after the age of 40, although Geoffrey Boycott got as close as you can with 999.

In faraway Bulawayo, Afghanistan beat Zimbabwe by 73 runs to become the first Associate team to win a bilateral series against a Full Member as their extraordinary rise up cricket's ladder continues. More strength to them, I say.

But the most extraordinary cricketing feat of the day was in Colombo. Coming into the second Test against West Indies Kraigg Brathwaite had taken one wicket for 137 in 23 Tests with his very part-time off-spin and just three in total in 81 first-class matches. Today he takes 6-29 as Sri Lanka are all out for 206 in their second innings. It has been a good game so far (Sri Lanka 200 and 206, West Indies 163 and 20-1) so I will be keeping a close eye on it tomorrow as West Indies try to achieve a rare away win chasing 244.

I am amused to see an interview with an NFL executive on the TV. They are announcing an extended program of NFL games at Wembley and in the interview he compares NFL with football (or soccer depending which side of the Atlantic you are). A game of soccer he points out is a few hours' entertainment, while an NFL game is a day out. Imagine if cricket was to regard a 'day out' as a Good Thing. Sadly, cricket is mostly embarrassed by its epic length and is trying its best to be as short as most other sports.

October 25

Pakistan duly stroll on to a declaration at 354-6 setting England 491 to win and England muddle their way to 130-3 at the close. I was aware that Younis Khan was not a '90s' man and when checking his scores in the 90s I found that his only one was 91 in 2001. Which is a long time ago. So the next thing to check is consecutive conversions from 90 to 100. Thus, when he reached 100, I could announce that his 29 consecutive conversions equalled the world record. As the man he equalled was Don Bradman the retweets inevitably stack up quite quickly.

I do keep a close eye on proceedings in Colombo. But there were not very many proceedings, apart from the occasional trip to the middle by the groundsmen and umpires as rain prevented any play. I hope it clears for what could be a tremendous denouement tomorrow.

Alviro Petersen continues his extraordinary form in the Momentum One-day Cup as he makes his fourth century for the Lions in the four innings he has played this season. He joins Kumar Sangakkara (who did it in the World Cup this year) as the only players with centuries in four consecutive List A innings. #Busses, again. As you may have noticed near the beginning of this diary, Petersen retired from international cricket earlier in the year so he is enjoying prime post-international-retirement form. Don't go, Alviro!

South Africa make 438. Again. They clinch the ODI series in India by walloping 438-4 (the same total they made in the famous world record run chase against Australia at The Wanderers in 2006) and winning by 214 runs. They repeated the feat of earlier this year when three batsmen made centuries in an innings, the only occasions that this has happened in ODIs. Yet more #Busses. This time it was Quinton de Kock, Faf du Plessis and AB de Villiers who plundered the tons. De Villiers reached his 100 off 57 balls, fairly ordinary by his standards as it was only his third quickest this year. He now has eight ODI 100s off 75 or fewer balls with power to add. Virender Sehwag is second on this list with six.

October 26

The first thing to check in the morning is how many teams have saved a match by batting through the final day having started the day with three wickets down. Defining the parameters is again important for this one.

Matches where rain helped save the team on the final day were excluded (these are fairly easily found by checking the number of overs bowled in the day) and matches where the batting team had a reasonable chance of winning were also left out. I found 32 cases where the team batting last went into the final day with three wickets down and needing at least 250 to win, i.e. a save situation. Of these I was a little surprised to find that as many as eight had batted through the day to draw. Thus England have an empirical 25% chance of saving the game.

They came within 6.3 overs of doing it despite slumping to 193-7 ten minutes after lunch. As in the first Test Adil Rashid again came to life late in the match. In the first Test his five wickets after tea had turned the game and today he batted four hours for 61 before slapping one to cover with the finish line in sight. Apart from these two performances his record in the first four days and one hour of the two Tests he has played is 12 runs for twice out and two wickets for 354 runs. Rashid's partnership with Mark Wood turned out to be the longest for the ninth wicket in the fourth innings of a Test at 29.2 overs, beating the effort by Frank Woolley and Tich Freeman whose 21.5 eight-ball over effort at Sydney in 1924 is the equivalent of 28.5 six-ball overs.

Earlier in the day, Joe Root had reached 3 000 Test runs. There were various numbers floating about in terms of the innings it had taken him to reach this milestone (pretty impressive at 62), but I prefer that he is the second youngest for England behind Alastair Cook. Those kind of 'age' stats give a sense of what he may be expected to do over his career.

I don't generally pay much attention to Man of the Match awards, but I was pleased when Wahab Riaz got it this time. His match haul of 5-144 (4-66 & 1-78) was not the statistically outstanding return (Yasir Shah took eight wickets and Misbah-ul-Haq and Younis Khan both made a century and a fifty) but his spell of 9-3-15-3 on the third morning effectively won the game. So the award meant the adjudicator was actually paying attention to the match and not just glancing through the scorecard.

Looking at Zulfiqar Babar's record in the fourth innings of Tests provided another stat with a different angle. He now has 18 wickets in the fourth innings at 20.22 compared to 30 at over 50 in the first three innings of Tests. It occurs to me that his percentage of wickets in the fourth innings must be quite high. Checking this, I can confirm that at 37.50 (18 out of 48) it is the second highest percentage of anyone with 40 or more Test wickets. The record is held by Australia's Jack Saunders at 40.50%. He took 32 of his 79 Test wickets in the fourth innings, including one of the most famous fourth innings wickets of all time. He bowled England's number 11, Fred Tate, at Manchester in 1902 with just four needed to win.

Rain relents in Colombo, so I can keep an eye on that match. Sadly another Calypso Collapso (80-1 to 138-9) snuffs out the chance of a rare away win for the West Indies and indeed the prospect of a classic finish. The remarkable Rangana Herath continues his march towards 300 Test wickets — his 4-56 leaves him on 293 at the end of the match.

October 27

Ireland take the last three wickets they need to complete an innings and 107 run demolition of Namibia and continue their dominant start to the ICup. Ed Joyce had made 205 in Ireland's first innings, his second double-century in two innings in the competition. Otherwise it is a quiet day off. There aren't many of them. Goodnight.

October 28

It is an early start as I wake up at 4am to watch Game One of the World Series. And it is a proper classic, featuring an inside-the-park home run by the Royals' Alcides Escobar (the first in a World Series game since Mule Haas — don't baseball players have wonderful names? — did it in 1929), a starting pitcher (Edinson Volquez of the Royals) whose dad had died earlier in the day, but he wasn't told until after he finished pitching, a stoppage in play due to a power failure at the broadcaster meaning that no TV reviews would be available, a potentially disastrous fielding error at first base by the Royals' Eric Hosmer (the first to allow the go-ahead run to score in the eighth innings or later of a World Series game since the most famous of all fielding errors in baseball: the one by Boston Red Sox first baseman Bill Buckner against the Mets in 1986), a game tying ninth innings homer by Alex Gordon and a redemptive 14th innings walk-off sacrifice fly by Eric Hosmer. A true epic at five hours nine minutes — even longer than it took for me to type that previous sentence.

A shopping expedition results in the purchase of a 3D Burj Khalifa puzzle which should keep the kids happy and entertained when I get home.

There must have been something happening in the cricket world, but I was not paying much attention today.

October 29

New Zealand have a pretty ordinary day at the Blacktown Olympic Park Oval in Sydney as the Cricket Australia XI clock up 376-0 on day one of their first-class fixture. Good team, that Cricket Australia XI. I check on most runs in a day by a team not losing a wicket and am not surprised to discover it is one of the really big first wicket partnerships that wins this stat. Jack Brown and John Tunnicliffe set a world first wicket partnership record in first-class cricket with 554 for Yorkshire against Derbyshire at Chesterfield (lovely ground in Queens Park, by the way, with views of a church with a crooked spire) in 1898. Another 'by the way' is that Yorkshire were all out for 662 in that innings, a pretty decent collapse. But, back to the point: Yorkshire made 503-0 on the first day of that match.

October 30

We move hotels to be nearer to the ground at Sharjah, venue for the third Test. The new hotel overlooks Dubai Creek and comes with the added bonus that I can see the Burj Khalifa from my room. The word 'creek' conjures up images of small bodies of water gently bubbling down a mountainside. However, Dubai Creek is a proper waterway and pretty busy — more Thames than quiet stream.

A wicket falls in Sydney and then the game is abandoned due to a pitch that is not fit for first-class cricket. 503-1 and the pitch is not playable. Huh? Photos on social media confirm that chunks have come out the pitch, so the decision seems reasonable, but there are inevitable comments along the lines of '503-1 on unplayable pitch. What would they have scored if the pitch had been decent?' Aaron Finch has had an interesting career. He is the holder of the world record T20 International score of 156 and has made six ODI centuries and yet coming into this game he had a first-class career average of 29.92 from 49 games. In fact, the reason he is in the Cricket Australia XI game is that he is not needed by Victoria in their Sheffield Shield game happening at the same time. The end of the game leaves him stranded on 288* and thus he misses out on what may be his only chance to score a triple-century.

There are games in first-class cricket where fall of wickets are not known. When I am upgrading old scorecards and come across such games I enter '999' for partnerships that are unknown and then I have a programming procedure that replaces 999 with a blank. Unfortunately for one game I had entered 888 instead of 999 which was thus not replaced by a blank. In the excitement surrounding the 503 run first wicket partnership in Sydney, the 888 (allegedly by MS Shapcott and EG Northway for Royal Air Force v Royal Navy in 1928) surfaces on Twitter as the best for the first wicket in first-class cricket — not from me of course, but from one of the users of my database. So, I need to correct that as soon as possible and snuff out Messrs Shapcott and Northway's undeserved social media fame 87 years after their unknown first wicket partnership.

October 31

Victoria's new red-ball opening batsman, replacing Aaron Finch, is a youngster named Travis Dean and today he collects his second century of the match on first-class debut. He has made 154* and 109* against Queensland at the MCG and is just the seventh player to score two centuries in the match on first-class debut. The first player to do this, and the only other Australian, was Arthur Morris in 1940.

Pictures have appeared on social media of the Afghanistan team being garlanded and paraded on their journey home after winning both the ODI and T20 series in Zimbabwe. So it is good to see the joy that their rise in cricket is creating. When South Africa became the number one ranked Test country by beating England in 2012 there were no ticker-tape parades or masses of people greeting them at the airport. All they got on their welcome home was an email from Cricket South Africa saying 'Well done chaps'. Test cricket, with its much greater range of challenges and situations than the shorter formats, is supposed to be the pinnacle of the game. But, it isn't.

There was much joy in New Zealand at 06:48 on a Sunday morning as the All Blacks beat Australia to become the first team to defend a Rugby World Cup title in a reversal of the Cricket World Cup final result.

Japan beat China easily in the East Asia Men's T20 Championship in Hong Kong. China make 56 and Japan lose one wicket in the seven overs it takes them to chase it down.

I discover an article by 'Undercover Economist' and presenter of BBC's program on numbers *More or Less* Tim Harford suggesting that the Singularity may be further away than we think. Which is good news for humans. I have no idea how that affects cricket's Singularity.

November 1

England go into the Test in Sharjah with three spinners, Samit Patel having replaced Mark Wood. But the seamers once again out-bowl the spinners as England dismiss Pakistan for 234. Jimmy Anderson and Stuart Broad produce magnificent combined figures of 28.1-15-30-6. Third seamer, Ben Stokes injures his shoulder badly trying to take a catch. So, the spinners have to do even more work than they would have done and will have to do even more in the second innings. Interesting counter-intuitive theories are starting to develop that perhaps England should rather have played five seamers. Spin is always the first consideration in Asia, but England don't have an established frontline Test spinner these days so instead of selecting three ordinary spinners who are inevitably ineffective perhaps they should rather have packed the team with seamers. Five may seem a bit excessive, but in the heat of this part of the world you couldn't really expect four to bowl 90 overs between them in the day. Five would have allowed England to rotate them all day in short spells to keep them relatively fresh. As it is, Pakistan have successfully adopted the tactics of blocking the seamers and hitting the spinners in this series. This is best exemplified by the captain. In the series to date Misbah-ul-Haq has scored 86 runs off 345 balls off seam at a strike-rate of just 24.92 and been dismissed four times while he has whacked 228 runs off 287 balls off spin at a strike rate of 79.44 and only lost his wicket once to the twirlers.

The Sharjah Ground proudly displays billboards indicating that it is in the *Guinness Book of World Records*, having hosted more ODIs than any other ground in the world — 218 to be precise, and counting.

Internet based opinion polls are often quoted despite being very far removed from the kind of rigour that would make them scientifically meaningful. There is a classic example of this today. Stephen Harper, the long serving Canadian Prime Minister was recently defeated in an election. Some people are suggesting that Calgary International Airport should be named after him in recognition of his service as Prime Minister. An opinion poll has appeared on the Internet with the question 'Where do you stand on the Stephen Harper/Calgary International Airport renaming debate?' The options are:

1. The Calgary International Airport should be renamed after Stephen Harper.
2. Stephen Harper should be renamed after the Calgary International

Airport.

3. Both names are fine as they are.

Shamefully, my click is one of the 58.74% who have chosen the second option.

November 2

It is a steady day for England as they reach 222-4. James Taylor, having replaced Jos Buttler in the team is 74* in just his third Test and first for over three years leading to inevitable 'Where has he been?' type questions. There is little to get statistically excited about and it is a tweet-free day for me.

I woke up early to watch Game 5 of the World Series. The Mets, 3-1 down in the series, lead 2-0 going into the ninth innings with starting pitcher Matt Harvey tossing a gem. Then things get interesting as there is a classic clash between heart and head. The head and indeed the original intention of Mets' manager Terry Collins said that Harvey should be taken out of the game at that stage and the normal closing pitcher should come in and close the game off. Harvey, however, insisted on continuing and with the crowd baying 'We want Harvey', Collins' heart took over and he left Harvey in the game. The Royals duly tied the game up 2-2 in the ninth innings. I must admit that I was with the idea of leaving Harvey in the game as 'Starting Pitcher Keeps Mets Alive In World Series With Complete Game Shutout' is a much better story than the colder 'Correct Application Of Data Analytics Keeps Mets Alive In World Series'. With the game extending into extra innings, I miss the ending as I have to get on the TMS bus to the ground and when I get there I discover that the Royals have won 7-2 in 12 innings to collect their second World Series and their first since 1985. It is a bit of redemption for losing last year's World Series to the San Francisco Giants. Those of you who aren't interested in baseball will no doubt be pleased to know that this is probably the last baseball entry in this diary.

November 3

England are dismissed for 306 and a 72 run lead. I check the history of matches in Asia and find that teams going into the third innings of a Test with a deficit of 72 or more have won 12, lost 186 and drawn 72 times. So theoretically at least, England should be clear favourites at this stage. Pakistan reply with a solid 146-3. This includes a first ball duck for Shoaib Malik, who had started the series with 245 in the first innings in Abu Dhabi. To general surprise Malik announces his retirement from Test cricket, which seems like a fairly extreme reaction to a first ball duck, especially from someone who had just returned to Test cricket after a five year break. He has always been more of a short format player, however (35 Tests compared to 229 ODIs and 65 T20 Internationals), and wants to play in the 2019 World Cup. I decide to check how his one-innings-dominated series compares to others in history. And, his 245 out of a series total of 292 is, at 83.90%, the second highest such percentage by anyone with 250 or more runs in at least six innings in a series behind the 84.48% of Alastair Cook (294 out of 348) against India in 2011. Earlier in the day Malik had taken a career best of 4-33, so I feel compelled to research players who had made their highest score and taken their best bowling in their final series. I can find only one other who did so having played at least 30 Tests in their career and that is Sri Lanka's Lasith Malinga. Malinga is still plying his trade in the various T20 leagues as well as purveying the white ball with a high level of success for his country, but sadly it is very unlikely he will play another Test.

November 4

England miss what could be another crucial stumping as Jonny Bairstow fluffs one off Mohammad Hafeez from the third ball of the day from Adil Rashid. Hafeez goes on from 97 to 151 as Pakistan bat solidly to set England what looks like a very tough target of 284. England lose two wickets for 46 before the close. The last time England actually took a stumping was back in 2012 in Mumbai, 37 Tests ago.

Speculation on Misbah-ul-Haq's retirement is rife, as is inevitable for a man well into his 42nd year. I hope that he gets to 50 (runs that is, I don't expect even him to still be playing Test cricket at the age of 50), as if he was retiring it would mean that he would be the first player to scores 50s in each of his last five Test innings. So, I am disappointed when he is dismissed for 38 although Australia's Ian Redpath would no doubt have been highly relieved as he still holds the record of having reached 50 in each of his last four Test innings.

The contrast in this series between England's seamers who were truly admirable and their spinners who were rather ordinary is stark, so I do the calculation. The seamers took 31 wickets at 24.58 and an economy rate of just 2.29 per over, while the spinners' 20 wickets cost 59.85 each and they were whacked for 4.06 runs per over. Spin has become a major worry for England.

Michael Vaughan leaves the TMS team after today's play to head off to the US of A to play in the Warne/Tendulkar All-Star Series. Fellow TMS pundit, Graeme Swann had left after the second Test for a few days' break at home before also heading off to that series. I hope they have packed their long johns.

November 5

Spirits are high, as they usually are on the rare occasions when there are three Test matches going on at the same time. In addition to the one in Sharjah, Australia and New Zealand begin their series at Brisbane in the early hours of the morning UAE time and India and South Africa start their series in Mohali.

To no great surprise, Pakistan win in Sharjah, although England's collapse seems unnecessarily dramatic as they lose four wickets in the first seven overs of the day and find themselves 59-6 from which they never really recover. There is great excitement for me, and probably no one else on the planet, when the seventh wicket falls and Stuart Broad walks out to bat to join Alastair Cook who has managed to avoid all of the carnage at the other end and is still there. As you may have noticed from earlier entries in this diary I have been waiting for this for a while and can happily let everyone know that this is the first time that these two shared the crease in the 87 Tests they have played together. In Colombo, I suspect that Sanath Jayasuriya took a brief break from his parliamentary, or perhaps Sri Lanka cricket selector, duties to give a fist pump in the knowledge that his 90 Tests with Muttiah Muralitharan without ever batting together will remain the record for a while.

In Brisbane, Australia pile up 389-2 on day one in 88 overs. I don't want to bang on about it, but even though the run-rate is 4.42, the wicket-rate is far more important in Test cricket and two in a day makes it difficult to get terribly excited. A stat appears suggesting that David Warner has got his new (and junior) opening partner Joe Burns to face the new ball because he (Warner) has a better record when he faces second rather than first — he averages 24.50 when he takes the first ball and 55.91 when he doesn't. While this is interesting it is hard to imagine that there is a genuine causal effect here given that 99.9% of his actual batting is not spent facing the first ball of an innings.

South Africa go into the Test in Mohali with a proud record at stake: They have not lost an away series since 2006 in Sri Lanka. And they start reasonably well dismissing India for 201 although they lose two wickets in reply for 28 by the close. There is an extraordinary spell by part-time left-arm spinner Dean Elgar who finishes with 4-22 leading to comments (mostly by me, well probably exclusively by me) to the effect that England should check whether he has a British passport as he is clearly more effective than England's current spinning options. Kagiso Rabada makes his Test debut following an injury to Morne Morkel. Somewhat appropriately he is, at the age of 20, the first 'born-free' (i.e. someone born after the 27 April 1994 elections) to play Test cricket for South Africa.

It is naturally obligatory for Twenty20 tournaments to have names that project the image of excitement and power hitting: Big Bash, NatWest Blast, RAM SLAM, etc. But New Zealand's has the best name of the lot. The Georgie Pie Super Smash starts there today.

November 6

It is another day on the plane as I fly home and therefore miss most of what is happening in Brisbane and Mohali.

I get home to discover that Australia have piled up 556-4* and New Zealand are struggling in reply on 157-5 with only the admirable Kane Williamson (55*) showing much resistance. Usman Khawaja, who had made just 377 runs at 25.13 in nine previous Tests for Australia with a best of 65 made 174 in his first Test for over two years.

The news from Mohali is not good for South African fans. They were bowled out for 184. Conceding a first innings lead on a spinning pitch is generally a bad idea. R Ashwin leads India's bowlers and his 5-51 includes his 150th Test wicket. Amongst spinners, only Clarrie Grimmett (28) has reached this milestone in fewer Tests, although Hugh Tayfield and Saeed Ajmal also took 29. India are comfortable at 125-2 by the end of the day.

I check the weather forecast in New York and am pleased to see that temperatures there are the highest they have ever been for 6 November. No long johns tomorrow after all.

It is always amusing when a sports administrator has to defend something by saying 'It is not a silly idea'. It's Cricket Australia's CEO

James Sutherland's turn to do this. He is defending the idea of having beach cricket at the Olympics. While there is a lot of general enthusiasm around trying to get the game into the Olympics there is one fundamental problem. Cricket is not the 'World's Favourite Sport' and as such the overwhelming majority of countries including most of those where the Olympics are likely to be held have no internationally acceptable facilities for cricket and no good reason to construct them. As such, the lateral thinking to deal with this has produced indoor and beach cricket as options. Will Brazil win the first Olympics cricket gold medal since 1900 on the beach in 2028?

November 7

Australia knock over New Zealand for 317 and a 239 run first innings lead and naturally decline to enforce the follow-on. They end the day on 264-4. Having added 161 in the first innings the new Australian opening pair of Joe Burns and David Warner put on 237 in the second innings to become the first pair in Test history to add over 150 in both innings for the first wicket. Warner's first innings 100s had taken a rare lead over his second innings 100s (seven to six) after his 163 in the first innings, but he ties them up again with 116 in the second dig and joins Sunil Gavaskar and Ricky Ponting as the only players to have made two centuries in a Test on three occasions.

South Africa do well to take India's last eight wickets for 39 reducing them from 161-2 to 200 all out. Even though this means the final target is just 218 it inevitably proves too much and South Africa only get halfway there. In 245 Tests played in India only one team: India 387-4 v England in Chennai in 2008 has ever made the highest total of the match in the fourth innings to win. No fewer than 34 wickets fall to spin in the match. Only three Tests have had more with the India v New Zealand match at Nagpur in 1969 the most with 37. South Africa's 15 wickets by spinners is easily their most in the post-unity era, the previous best having been 12.

In the afternoon it is Dance Mouse concert time for the six-year-old, so various family members gather for the event. Around 700 dancers aged mostly between about four and 12 are on display in five events across the day. They seem to have enough energy between them that they could probably be used to power a small town for a week.

After putting the kids to sleep, I switch on the TV to find out what is happening in New York. The game at the Mets' Citi Field between Sachin's

Blasters and Warne's Warriors All-Stars teams is a daytime affair, so an 8pm start South Africa time is quite accessible. As the screen stumbles into life I am greeted by a caption letting me know that Courtney Walsh is bowling from the Dwight Gooden End. Beautiful! Courtney is even older than me (and Dwight Gooden for that matter) and is purveying some right-arm slow off a run up of about eight paces at probably no quicker than what Mr Warne will be doing in a few overs' time. Which is not quite the same as he was in his pomp. It looks like a pretty decent crowd has turned up although the ballpark is obviously not quite as full as it was for the World Series last week. Kumar is also playing, of course. So, I am not sure when he will actually stop playing at all. But I suspect that when he is embarrassing himself in Masters games in 10 years' time there will be a few of us saying 'Please go, Kumar'. His Beijing Ultra All Stars Masters Series debut in 2025 may also be his swansong. Enthusiasm levels for actually watching the game dissipate quickly after the initial curiosity and I change channels after about 15 minutes. I prefer to remember the great players as they were in their prime.

November 8

I briefly contemplate capturing the All Stars game into the database. Certainly the thrill of adding 'Citi Field, New York' to my list of venues in the database makes it quite tempting. But my rational side wins out, as the game has no real status and I have not included any other exhibition matches in the database in the past, so there is no good reason to start now.

A bit of rain at the Gabba gives New Zealand some hope and they end the day on 142-3 chasing a mere 504 to win. As we know from research during the Dubai Test this means that they have an eight out of 33 chance to save the game tomorrow.

England warm up for their ODI series against Pakistan with a 13-a-side affair against Hong Kong at one of Abu Dhabi's Nursery grounds. As Hong Kong has official ODI status there are suggestions that the match should have been played as a full ODI. While one can understand that purpose of the game was more 'practice' than 'match' it would have been a small gesture for a game that is so orally committed to expansion and becoming the world's favourite sport to have played it as a proper ODI. Reasons that it is not played as such apparently include that England would have had to pay their players full ODI rates (really?) and are not terribly compelling. While it is good that England have actually made the effort to play against

Hong Hong, cricket's oral commitment to expansion remains disproportionate to actual efforts in that regard.

November 9

Australia duly complete a 208 run win over New Zealand. Their record in Brisbane at what is known locally as the 'Gabbattoir' is quite extraordinary. They last lost a Test at the ground in 1988 when West Indies beat them by nine wickets and have won 20 of the 27 Tests there since. I decide to tweet about this. All well and good, except that I make a typo doing it. I correctly note that Pakistan were unbeaten in 34 Tests at Karachi and West Indies in 27 at Bridgetown, but the finger slips and I let the world know that Australia have 26 Tests without defeat in Brisbane. So, it is the delete button when I realise that and I make the correction and repost. All of which is not particularly auspicious from me for what is my 1 000th tweet.

November 10

It is hard work doing this diary, trying to think of something to say every day for 365 days in the year. At least the end is in sight — just 51 entries to go. I am not going to do one next year (2016). It is hard enough for 365 days, I can only imagine how much worse it will be to have to do it for 366 days.

November 11

Babar Hayat scores Hong Kong's first first-class century when he makes 113 against United Arab Emirates at the ICC Academy ground in Dubai on the first day of the ICup clash between these teams.

November 12

First-class cricket is second class in everything but name these days. And provincial cricket which has first-class status despite being the second tier of domestic cricket in South Africa, after the franchises, has an even lower profile. Nonetheless I make my way down to The Wanderers for a few hours to watch Gauteng play North West. Dominic Hendricks, who was Man of the Tournament at the 2010 Under-19 World Cup has spent most of the five years since then treading water playing primarily in the backwaters of the provincial competition having never established a place in the Lions franchise team. Today he carries his bat for Gauteng with 142*.

At Minute Maid Park in Houston last night Warne's Warriors smashed 262-5 in 20 overs. Clearly batting skills decline less sharply with age than bowling ones (especially for bowlers of the quicker variety), although having boundaries which Bob Beamon (or whoever the current world long jump champion is) would probably be able to jump to from the 30-yard circle no doubt also helps. Baseball park dimensions don't seem particularly conducive to cricket.

November 13

Another Test starts today. This time it is at Perth and close of play is remarkably similar to the Gabba as Australia wallop 416-2 in the day. Joe Burns and David Warner add 101 for the first wicket to join countrymen Matthew Hayden and Justin Langer as the only opening pairs to put on 100 plus stands in their first three partnerships together. Warner goes on to finish the day on 244*. Only Don Bradman (309 at Leeds in 1930) has scored more runs on the first day of a Test match, and Warner joins Bradman (again — 244 at The Oval in 1934) in second place. It is not too far-fetched to suggest that Brian Lara's Test record 400* could be in danger of being beaten tomorrow.

November 14

It is back to the SABC studios for India v South Africa at Bengaluru, which means a 4:20 wake-up call for a 6am start. Dale Steyn and Vernon

Philander are both injured so South Africa have a new look bowling attack. Surprisingly, Virat Kohli sends South Africa in after winning the toss. The only other occasion this had happened in 21 Tests at the Chinnaswamy Stadium was back in the very first Test at the venue in 1974. And it is only the 21st time in 246 Tests in India that a toss winner has sent the opposition in to bat in the traditionally spin-friendly country.

In Perth New Zealand finally start taking some wickets. Until the end of yesterday they had taken 11 wickets in the three first-class matches on tour and conceded 1 739 runs. Your calculator will (or should) reveal that to be an average of 158.09 runs per wicket. But today Australia 'collapse' from 416-2 to 559-9 declared. If Brian Lara had been watching the early play from his hotel in Los Angeles he would no doubt have been happy to see that his record remains safe after David Warner is dismissed for 253. New Zealand reply solidly with 140-2 by the close.

Travis Dean has a first-class average at last. Following his 154* and 109* on first-class debut a couple of weeks ago he threatens to join West Indies' Joe Solomon (he of the Tied Test run out fame) as the only players to have made centuries in each of their first three first-class innings, but is dismissed for 84 by Western Australia at Melbourne leaving his career average at a fairly healthy 347.00. It is the most runs before being dismissed in first-class cricket history passing the 310 by Raymond Watson-Smith who made 310 runs before losing his wicket for the first time for Border in 1969/70. That season proved to be Watson-Smith's only one and he ended with a career record of 444 runs at 88.80. Let's hope Dean has a longer career.

November 15

It is raining in Bengaluru meaning that I got up early for no good reason and more is forecast over the remaining days of this Test suggesting that I could be getting up early for no good reason rather more than I would like over the next three days.

With no play in Bengaluru and a lot of waiting around time, I get to see a fair amount of the play in Perth. Not a great deal happens as the pitch is clearly too flat. Ross Taylor may disagree that not much has happened as he finishes the day on 235* and becomes the first touring player to score a double-century at the WACA. New Zealand finish on 510-6 so I suspect there is no need for Brian Lara to press the remote on his hotel TV with trepidation as even if Taylor does start to get close to 400 he will probably run out of partners.

November 16

Yes, it is still raining in Bengaluru, but at least it is raining properly and we get to go home earlier today as it is called off around lunch time. It looks very much as though South Africa are going to be saved by the rain.

In Perth Ross Taylor misses out on a triple-century as he is last out for 290. At least he has the consolation of making the highest Test score ever by a touring batsman in Australia passing the 287 by England's RE 'Tip' Foster at Sydney in 1903. And Foster has the consolation that his score is still the highest by anyone on Test debut. After New Zealand are all out for 624 Australia pile on 258-2 at over four runs per over with Steve Smith ending the day on 131*. He has finally made a second innings century and his 11 first innings century before making a second innings century is the second most behind Virender Sehwag's 12. Which I am sure Sehwag would have been pleased to hear on his flight home from Los Angeles when someone interrupted his contemplation of the 27 he made off 15 balls for Sachin's Blasters at Dodger Stadium the other night to let him know. Did Vin Scully 'announce' that game, I wonder. I suspect not.

November 17

I can ditto first sentence from yesterday regarding today at Bengaluru.

But the news is more interesting from Perth where batsmen all over the world will have been relieved to hear that Mitchell Johnson has announced his immediate retirement. He had snuck into fourth place on Australia's top wicket-takers list in the first innings when he passed Brett Lee's 310 and adds another two in his final bowl in the afternoon to finish on a pretty tidy 313. In between the occasions when 'he bowled to the left, he bowled to the right' (only Jacques Kallis, with 103 has bowled more wides in Test cricket than Johnson's 90) he was also spectacularly effective and, indeed, terrifying when at his best. Not least when he took 37 wickets at 13.97 in the Ashes whitewash in 2013/14 and followed it with 22 at 17.36 in the next series helping Australia to beat number one ranked team South Africa in South Africa. The game itself inevitably ends in a tame draw, but there is a bit of statistical interest as there have been six scores over 100 and none between 50 and 99 in the match. It seems worth checking and I am a bit disappointed to discover that there was a match with more: India v South Africa at Kolkata in 2010 had seven centuries without any scores between 50 and 99.

November 18

Although there doesn't appear to be much rain in Bengaluru it remains quite overcast and general lack of enthusiasm (there is now no chance of a result) means that there is once again no play. So, for the second time in three Tests, South Africa have seen only one day's play. In fact over their last four Tests combined between the Bangladesh and India tours there have only been the equivalent in overs of marginally over seven days' play. The two Tests with only one day's play each have been interspersed with two matches that have had only three days' play each: the rain-induced one in Chittigong and the result-induced one in Mohali. So, better weather in Nagpur next week would be greatly appreciated by all.

I did say that I would not mention baseball again, but it is a sad day for Red Sox fans. David Ortiz (or Big Papi as he is affectionately known) turned 40 today. That is not the sad part. After all, there isn't much he could do to stop turning 40. The sad part is that he has announced that next season will be his last in the Major Leagues. He has led the Red Sox to three World Series titles so it will be sad to see him go.

November 19

England announce their squad for the Test series in South Africa. The most interesting selection is a recall for Nick Compton. Since Andrew Strauss retired in 2012 they have been searching without success for a partner for Alastair Cook at the top of the order. Seven different players have been tried and none has lasted. Compton was the first one and his pairing with Cook was easily the most successful — their first wicket partnerships averaged 57.93 while none of the others averaged more than 36.60. Perhaps Compton was discarded too quickly?

November 20

It is back to ball-bashing mode in the ODI in Dubai as Jos Buttler breaks his own record for the fastest century for England with one off just 46 balls. He joins AB de Villiers (see 18 January) as the only players to have made an ODI century having come in to bat after the 35th over (in a 50-over match, that is). Buttler now has the three fastest ODI 100s for England and these are his only three centuries. At 46, 61 and 66 balls I decide it is worthwhile to compare his average balls per hundred to others. Not terribly surprisingly his average of 57.66 is the best of players who have hit three or more hundreds. I get a bit of abuse on Twitter with comments along the lines of this being a convenient cut-off, but the point was to compare Buttler to everyone else and it had to be three as a minimum as Buttler only has three centuries. So there was no real choice in this case, but generally finding an appropriate minimum is part of the art of doing cricket statistics.

November 21

It is a dark day for the game as Namibia's Raymond van Schoor died last night after suffering a stroke while batting against Free State in a CSA (Cricket South Africa) Provincial One-day game five days' ago. Van Schoor was only 25 but had been a mainstay in the Namibian team ever since he made his debut in 2007 as a 17-year-old. He had played more first-class matches for his country than anyone else (92) and he was the second highest scorer in first-class cricket, third highest in List A and highest in T20 for Namibia. Had he been able to play another eight to ten years he would no doubt have been way ahead of any other Namibians in all formats. Apart from his batting he was also a useful wicket-keeper and off-spinner as well as having captained the team on numerous occasions. In such a small cricket-playing community as Namibia's he will be sorely missed. Coming just a few days before the anniversary of Philip Hughes' death it is another reminder of the fragility of life even within the relatively safe environment of cricket.

In Roseau yesterday Leeward Islands declared their first innings on 24-7 in their match against Windward Islands. There seems to have been excessive movement so in a tactic reminiscent of 'sticky wicket' matches in the days of uncovered pitches they were hoping to get their opponents in to take advantage of the bowling conditions while they were most favourable. Windward Islands finished on 104-5 so it remains to be seen how successful they would be. In a CSA Provincial Three-day match in 2011 KwaZulu-Natal had successfully used this strategy in similar conditions against Boland at Paarl. On that occasion KwaZulu-Natal declared on 29-6, bowled Boland out for 160, made 390 in their second innings and went on to win by 80 runs. Even if the Leewards aren't as successful they will at least have the honour of making the lowest ever total in first-class cricket that has been declared on with seven wickets down.

November 22

Windwards go on to win by eight wickets — so much for that idea. I don't pay much attention to cricket today. It is ballet time as we take the family off to go and watch *The Nutcracker* at the State Theatre. The six-year-old has done ballet at school, but she is most disappointed with the show as the performers don't talk to each other. She will learn.

November 23

On the way home from dropping the kids off at school I generally listen to the *Breakfast Quiz* on Classic FM. Today there is a cricket question which elicits a wonderful quote from a caller. The question is 'Who holds the record for the highest score by an overseas batsman in Australia?' I assume the answer is Ross Taylor, but as there is no indication of whether they are referring to Test cricket I might have been tempted to argue that it was Barry Richards' 356. But the caller says 'I am not interested in cricket and don't know when or why they play'. Why indeed?

Where they play cricket is about to be expanded as it is announced that Hong Kong will host their first ODI and first-class match in January when Scotland visit for World Cricket League fixtures and an ICup game at the Tin Kwong Road Recreation Ground has been approved by the ICC as an ODI venue. So, it will be good to add a new country to the list of places where first-class cricket has been played. One day, hopefully, I will be able to add the ground to my first-class venues visited list.

November 24

I nail the Grip-O-Meter at my session with the hand therapist. Measurements are up to 25. This may still be a bit off what one would like, but it is a lot better than the 12 I started with. Hey Mom, I may be ready for that arm-wrestle soon.

One of the great things about Afghanistan cricket is that they never, ever, give up. In their ICup game against Papua New Guinea at Sharjah (their de facto home ground) that began on the 21st they were bowled out for 144 on the first day and Papua New Guinea were 205-6 by the close of that day. Today Afghanistan complete a 201 run win. A second innings score of 540 went a long way to securing the win. There were three centuries in that innings, including Hashmatullah Shaidi (remember him) who made 112. His form in this year's four-day competition in Afghanistan was not quite as impressive as last year, but 389 runs at 64.83 are not to be sneezed at, or even indefinitely ignored by selectors for that matter. Whether it leads to a longer run in the national team remains to be seen.

November 25

It is back to the studios for the third Test between India and South Africa. The studios are two floors below ground level so are affectionately known as the 'dungeons'. Anyway it looks like another raging turner at Nagpur and South Africa pick just two specialist seamers for the first time in 22 years. In 1993 at Moratuwa they picked only Allan Donald and Brett Schultz. India only bother to pick one seamer (Ishant Sharma) and it doesn't look like he will do much bowling. India win the toss again (three for three in the series to date) which is always useful on a spinners pitch. On a day of minimal statistical excitement, India meander to 215 which already seems like a decent total and not terribly surprisingly South Africa are two down (for 11) by the close.

Cricket Australia announces that it is going to recognise World Series Cricket. Matches played during the World Series organised by Kerry Packer between 1977 and 1979 have never had any official status. Although the standard of the games was exceptionally high (many players will tell you it was the hardest cricket they ever played), the matches were not organised by an official governing body and thus have never had first-class or List A status. A first glance at the headline suggests that Cricket

Australia's statement means that they have granted first-class status to the games, but it turns out that it is a far less radical change. Essentially what it appears to mean is that stats from those matches will be included as separate lines on the players' career records in any official Cricket Australia documents. Which does not actually change very much.

November 26

11-2 quickly looks quite good as South Africa lose ('throw away' might be a more accurate description) three quick wickets before most of their countrymen back home have woken up (India Tests start at 06:00 South Africa time). So I am diving into the record books early in the day. Or at least I would have been had we still kept all cricket statistics in books. Instead the computer's hard drive whirrs away and I can find that 12 is the lowest total that South Africa had lost their fifth wicket in a Test innings. It is the joint fourth lowest for any team. The lowest is six by India against England in 1952. I was a little surprised to see that this was at The Oval rather than Leeds, as they famously lost their first four wickets for 0 to a Trueman-inspired opening attack from England at Leeds. But on that occasion they managed to 'recover' to 26-5 only to lose their first five wickets for six at The Oval three Tests later.

One of those wickets to fall was AB de Villiers for a duck. De Villiers famously holds the world record for most innings before first Test duck with 78 and he hasn't got many since, so it seems worthwhile to contextualise this. In fact it was just the fourth time De Villiers had been dismissed for a duck in 150 dismissals (2.66%) and I can find only one player with a lower percentage of ducks having been dismissed at least 150 times and that is Clive Lloyd who made only four ducks in 161 dismissals (2.48%).

South Africa end up all out for 79 which means a slew of lowest total stats. It is their lowest total since unity in 1991 beating the 84 that India dismissed them for at the rather less likely venue of Johannesburg in 2006. But most remarkably it is the lowest total by anyone in a Test against India. Ever.

South Africa manage to bowl India out for 173 and are 32-2 by the close. Altogether 20 wickets fall in the day and we are clearly in line for a rare Test match without a 50 (the best in this match so far is 40 by Murali Vijay in the first innings). So that is a stat that I will need to keep an eye on tomorrow. Imran Tahir joins West Indies' Pedro Collins as the only players to have gone in as nightwatchmen and been dismissed before close of play in both innings of a Test.

Discussion on Radio 2000 turns to Abdul Qadir as Aslam Khota relates that Imran Khan always wanted the great leg-spinner in his team when he was captain while Javed Miandad tended not to want to use him when he was captain. I reveal that Qadir took 116 wickets at 37.56 in the 35 Tests that he played under Imran's captaincy but actually had a much better record (64 at 24.75) in the 15 times he played for Miandad. Aslam seems a bit flabbergasted that I can do this, but players' records under each captain is a standard query in my database.

There is a remarkable international debut in the T20 between Pakistan and England in Dubai. Rafatullah Mohmand plays his first international for Pakistan at the age of 39. He made his first-class debut on 28 October 1996. His 6 968 days' wait from first-class debut to international debut is the 17th longest overall, but the most for a Pakistani debutante. Most of those on the list, including the leader, Namibia's Lennie Louw, were for countries that were not playing international cricket at the time of their first-class debut for various reasons, e.g. International cricket did not exist at the time (pre 1877 in other words), their country was banned from international cricket (see CEB Rice) or they were an Associate team at the time. Lennie Louw made his first-class debut for Griqualand West in 1977 and played, at the age of 43, for Namibia in a World Cup game in 2003, 9 508 days after his first-class debut. Of players whose countries were playing international cricket for the duration of their first-class careers England's ER (Rockley) Wilson had the longest wait from first-class to international debut at 7 960 days from his first-class debut in 1899 to his only Test appearance in 1921.

Meanwhile in a bit of a surprise it has been announced that there will be no mandatory toss in the County Championship next season. Instead the visiting team will have the choice of whether to bowl or to have a toss if they prefer. The move is clearly designed to create a disincentive for teams to prepare excessively home-friendly pitches and especially to create more opportunities for spinners within the English system. If you want to promote spinners it would, of course, have been simpler to revert to playing the County Championship during cricket season as the drier pitches in July and August traditionally provide more assistance to the twirlymen. But of course high summer is now given over to the more lucrative shorter formats and the four-day matches confined mostly to the bookends of the season. It is difficult however, if not impossible, to argue with money. It will be interesting to see how the Law Of Unintended Consequences plays out in the toss-less environment next season. For example, will home teams take the low-risk option of preparing the flattest pitches in the history of cricket to offset any advantages the visiting team will have?

November 27

South Africa put up a bit of a fight but eventually succumb to 185 all out and a comfortable 124 run win for India. The feature is a long partnership (certainly by the standard of this series to date) of 46.2 overs between Hashim Amla and Faf du Plessis which yields just 72 runs in that time. Du Plessis maintains his reputation as a fourth innings fighter making 39 off 152 balls. It is the fourth time in the 10 fourth innings that he has played that he has batted for more than 100 balls. I feel sure that his career average of 142.37 balls per dismissal in the fourth innings must be pretty high on the list, but even restricting it just to 21st century players (we don't always have balls faced information for earlier matches) he is only in a slightly disappointing third place behind Angelo Mathews (171.14) and Misbah-ul-Haq (143.18).

Along with Du Plessis' 39, Amla also makes 39 and this is the highest score in the innings meaning that Murali Vijay's 40 is the top score in the match. So, we have just the third completed test without a 50 since 1935. But as these were a bit more common in earlier, lower scoring times, the fact that the highest score in the match was just 40 is probably more interesting. It turns out to be the sixth lowest highest score in a match. This is a record that WG Grace still has a part in as his 24 against Australia at Lord's in 1888 is still the lowest highest score in a completed Test match.

I manage to 'miss' a stat. When Ravichandran Ashwin dismisses AB de Villiers it is his 20th wicket in the series. This is the most by an Indian bowler in a Test series against South Africa beating Harbhajan Singh's 19 in the 2008 series in India. I should, of course, have let the listeners know immediately but I only noticed about an hour later.

And so, South Africa loses its proud record of not having lost an away series since 2006 (in Sri Lanka). It is the second longest such run in Test cricket behind the great West Indies team of the 1980s and early 1990s. Some sources report West Indies as having an 18-series streak and South Africa 15, but I prefer to report the streaks as 17 and 14 respectively as I have excluded one-off Tests from the sequences.

The match ends in a bit of a hurry with Ashwin completing a match haul of 12-98. It occurs to me right at the end of the game that not many spinners would have had better match figures opening the bowling in each innings, not least because spinners have not opened the bowling all that often in the past 100 years of Test cricket. So, while the presentation ceremony is going on and the commentators are doing their match summaries I dive into the laptop and write a program to check this. And it turns out that Ashwin's are the best match figures by a spinner opening in both innings since England's great left-armer Colin Blythe managed 15-99 against South Africa at Leeds in 1907.

The downside of South Africa's resistance is that I miss the six-year-old's graduation from pre-primary school. If South Africa had collapsed properly and quickly I would have been able to get there in time to see the full-on graduation ceremony complete with the black gowns and mortar boards that you only used to get at university in my days.

But of greater overall importance to cricket the day/night Test has started in Adelaide. Bring on the pink ball! It is a much better day for the bowlers (but probably not for statisticians) than the previous two Tests in this series as Australia end on 54-2 in reply to New Zealand's 202. Such was the day for the bowlers that when asked on air by Natalie Germanos what was happening in the 'Pink Ball Test' I couldn't resist replying 'Well, the pink ball is winning.' In honour of the day I wear the pink shirt that I bought when I was in Sydney in 2014 for the Pink Day of that match in honour of Jane McGrath and raising breast cancer awareness and funds. The most important number of the day was undoubtedly 47 441 which was the attendance at the Adelaide Oval, far higher than anything else seen on this tour.

Cricket Australia announces that it is looking at playing international matches in America given that America is their third biggest overseas audience behind India and England. I suspect that one of the reasons for this is that matches in the Australian day time are played at ideal evening viewing hours in America. So there is a bit of an irony in this announcement being made during the day/night Test in Australia which will be the middle of the night in America, thereby no doubt knocking a significant chunk off their US of A viewing figures.

November 28

Today is the eight-year-old's music concert. I was going to miss the cricket to attend it anyway, but at least with the game having ended yesterday I have the added bonus of not actually missing any cricket. She plays various instruments but the highlight is her rendition of baseball's famous ditty *Take Me Out To The Ballgame* (sung during the seventh innings stretch at all Major League Baseball games) on the keyboard.

I notice for the first time on Twitter that there is a link to 'Analytics' so natural curiosity leads me to click on the link. There are a lot of details about my activity and followers. It is mostly pretty predictable — my following is 95% male, 66% are in the UK, 13% in South Africa and most of the rest are in cricket playing countries. The one surprise is that 96% of my followers are interested in cricket. Only 96%? What are the other 4% thinking?

Australia's coach Darren Lehmann is no doubt very busy with the pink ball Test, but he must have been keeping an eye on proceedings in Hobart. His son, Jake, completes his maiden first-class double-century with 205 for South Australia against Tasmania. This makes the Lehmanns the first father and son to have both scored 200s in the Sheffield Shield. Australia has a great cricketing history, but they have surprisingly few famous father-son combinations.

In that pink ball Test TV umpire Nigel Llong gives Nathan Lyon a reprieve on a decision that looked out to everyone else including the batsman who had started to walk. Had the correct decision been made Australia would have been 118-9 in reply to New Zealand's 202 with just the injured Mitchell Starc to bat. As it is Lyon went on to make 34 and a one-legged Starc 24* (3 x 4, 2 x 6 — no need to run much) and Australia finish with a 22 run lead. The decision could thus prove crucial in a low-scoring affair. New Zealand finish the day on 116-5. So, although it has yet to produce anything to cause frissons of excitement amongst stattos it has been a close and riveting match.

November 29

A glance at the averages in the Sunfoil Provincial Three-day Cup following the games completed yesterday reveals that Daryn Smit is once more in the stats. After his 156* for KwaZulu-Natal v North West that was completed yesterday he now has an average of 418.00 for the season to date having been dismissed only once. It seems worthwhile to check what the highest average obtained in a first-class season is (without any qualifications for minimum number of innings, minimum number of times out or minimum number of runs for that matter). And the winner is ... Subramaniam Badrinath. There are of course various complications in defining what constitutes a season, but in 2007 Badrinath scored 458 runs and was dismissed only once on India A's tour of Zimbabwe and Kenya. So, I am happy to claim that as the record. Smit will need to stay not out for the rest of the season and score at least 41 more runs to better Badrinath. So, it is quite precarious for him as one more dismissal will most likely put the record out of reach.

At Adelaide Australia wobble a bit at the beginning (66-3) and again at the end (161-4 to 185-7) but they still get home by three wickets chasing 187. Peter Nevill's 66 in Australia's first innings will remain the highest score in a day/night Test until the next one is played. But by far the most important stat of the match is 123 736 which is the total attendance over the three days. It is a fairly basic statistical principle that you should compare like with like, or apples with apples as they say. This does not always happen and an example in cricket would be someone looking at a small crowd for a Test match at 11:00 on a Thursday morning and bemoaning how bad that looks compared to the full house there was the previous Friday night for a T20 match. Of course more fans will watch on a Friday night (which is leisure time for most people) than during working hours on a Thursday. But there is an opportunity here to make a decent comparison because the previous two Tests played by New Zealand at Adelaide were also both played on the last weekend in November (in 2004 and 2008). So we have the same opponent playing at the same venue at the same time of the year and this can thus give us a decent idea of the effect of playing the Test at night. The combined attendance over the nine days' play at the two previous New Zealand Tests at Adelaide was 117 466 or 13 051 per day. This one had 41 245 per day — more than triple that for the day time games. While there is clearly great novelty value for this particular match those kinds of attendance numbers will have everyone else investigating the possibilities of more day/night Tests. I suspect that Peter Neville's record 66 will not last all that long.

With Mitchell Johnson having retired and Mitchell Starc getting injured early in the match you would have thought that Mitchell Marsh would have fancied his chances for Mitch of the Match. But the fourth Mitchell in the history of Test cricket has made his debut in the match: New Zealand's left-arm spinning all-rounder Mitchell Santner. And pretty impressive he is too with scores of 31 and 45 and two wickets with some tidy bowling in the match.

November 30

I notice on Twitter that there is great excitement in the UK as Great Britain has won the Davis Cup. It is the first time they have collected the famous tennis trophy since 1936, the days of Fred Perry. I confess that I have to Google who their opponents were on this occasion and was a bit surprised to see that it was Belgium. Andy Murray led Team GB to the win with victories in both his singles matches as well as a doubles win with his brother, Jamie. Jamie is not only less famous than Andy, but he might also well be less famous than their mother, Judy.

December 1

There is a bit of a milestone on the database today. In February 2013 Dwaine Pretorius scored 177 for North West v South Western Districts at Potchefstroom. His 33 fours and 4 sixes represented 88.13% of his runs. At the time I had details of boundaries for a little over 40% of all scores over 150, so it was with a bit of trepidation (and appropriate disclaimers) that I claimed this to be the highest percentage of boundaries in a first-class innings over 150 (excluding contrived innings). Given that most innings for which details are available occurred in recent times and this coincides with a period of the highest percentage of boundaries in cricket history I felt it was unlikely that there would be any higher. Since that time one of my projects in the database is to add boundaries and timings to as many big innings as it is possible to find. As of today I now have boundary details for over 70% of all scores over 150 and pleasingly Pretorius is still the leader.

December 2

It is a quiet day with not much happening in the cricket world and I pass a little bit of time checking Twitter Analytics. You can compare your followers' profiles with the overall profile of all Twitter users. I was a little concerned to find that the overall percentage of Twitter followers who are interested in cricket is … 1%. Although I did cheer up a bit when I realised that 'all' Twitter followers seems to be restricted to one country: America.

Still, 1% is a very small number in what is the world's largest market measured by money and third largest measured by people. The game has a lot of work to push that figure up to the kinds of numbers that you might expect from the World's Favourite Sport.

Meanwhile in the Quaid-e-Azam tournament in Pakistan, Federally Administered Tribal Areas have beaten Rawalpindi by four wickets. Which would have been quite unremarkable except for the fact that they lost their first four wickets in their first innings before they scored a run. The only other team to win a first-class match having been 0-4 was Mumbai v Baroda at Vadodara in 2007.

December 3

Virat Kohli wins the toss. Again. He joins Nawab of Pataudi jr as the only Indian captains to have won the toss in all Tests of a series of four or more matches. In the most predictable decision in Test cricket history he chooses to bat. As had all the other captains who had won the toss in each of the 32 previous Tests played at the Feroz Shah Kotla Stadium in Delhi.

Dane Piedt has had an interesting career. In the Sunfoil Series of 2013/14 he was the best bowler in the competition. I repeat 'best bowler'. Not just 'best spinner'. It is very rare for the best bowler in a South African season to be a spinner. This led to his selection to the Test team and he made a good debut against Zimbabwe taking a wicket with his first ball and eight in the match. Then he suffered a bad shoulder injury and struggled to come back as is reflected in his Sunfoil Series performance in 2014/15: four wickets in five matches at an average of 140.00. Rehabilitation has gone better since then with two five-fors in A-Tests on the August tour of India. So, today he gets his second Test cap. And he picks up four more wickets, becoming just the second South African to take at least four wickets in each of the first three Test innings that he has bowled in after Alf Hall back in 1923. John Ferris of Australia (at the time — he later played a Test for England) in 1887 and Sri Lanka's Ajantha Mendis in 2008 both managed to take at least four wickets in each of the first five innings that they bowled in. The thought occurred to me that there can't be many spinners who had taken at least four wickets on the first day of each of their first two Tests. After all, spinners traditionally take wickets later in the match. I manage to confirm that Piedt is in fact the first to do this. It is a fairly complex process using the various queries in my database and merging them to get the results. The process went as follows:

1. Run the query 'Most wickets in a day' and then extract those that were at least four and on Day One of the Test.
2. Merge this with the players' file to extract the spinners.
3. Run the 'Youngest on debut' query and match the player numbers in the Wickets in a Day file. This gives me a list of spinners who took four wickets on Day One of their debut Test.
4. Use this list and merge back with the Wickets in a Day file and use this to extract which of the spinners who took four wickets on the first day of their debut Tests had also taken four wickets on the first day of any other Test.
5. Fortunately this process produced just one possible candidate: West Indies Neil McGarrell. Then the simple process of listing McGarrell's match-by-match returns reveals that he did not take four wickets on Day One of his second Test leaving Piedt standing alone and my mouse clicking on Twitter to reveal this stat.

By the way, India finished on 231-7 having been 139-6 at tea. Ajinkya Rahane is 89*, the highest individual score of the series. Will he get a century tomorrow and prevent this from becoming the first Test series of four or more matches to go century-less?

Namibia start their first game since the death of Raymond van Schoor. They are playing a Sunfoil Provincial Three-day Cup against Border in East London and are promptly bowled out for 68. The hosts are 103-2 at the close. It must be hard to play when you are so overwhelmed by sadness.

In the Ranji Trophy, Rajasthan have put in a Federally Administered Tribal Areas-esque performance. They beat Odisha by two wickets having been bowled out for 51 in their first innings. Winning having made such a low total is not quite as rare as winning from 0-4 but it is a fine comeback effort nonetheless.

December 4

Cricket boards these days employ communications departments and one of their jobs is to write match reports each time the national team plays. Inevitably these reports tend to 'take the positives' as they say. So, after today's play in which South Africa let India add a further 103 runs for the last three wickets to be 334 all out and then collapse to 121 all out in reply you would expect the match report to say something along the lines of '... a fighting 11 from Dane Vilas and useful contributions of 9* by Morne Morkel and 5 from Dane Piedt supported AB de Villiers (42) as South

Africa managed to keep their hopes alive ...' Instead when the beep from my email box alerts me to Cricket South Africa's report on the days' play, I notice that the subject line is 'Horrendous Proteas collapse puts India well ahead'. Which pretty much tells you exactly how bad it is.

December 5

We finally have this first century partnership of the series in India as Virat Kohli and Ajinkya Rahane add 154 for India's fifth wicket. ESPNCricInfo quickly put up a stat that there were 115 partnerships before the first century partnership in the series. So, I inevitably have to check whether this is a record or not. And it turns out that 115 partnerships in a series before the first one over 100 is actually the most in a Test series beating the 112 in the England v South Africa series in 1965 before Ken Barrington and Colin Cowdrey added 135 for England's fourth wicket in the penultimate partnership of the series.

The West Indies have narrowly averted an innings defeat to the Cricket Australia XI (fine team, that) but still get clobbered by 10 wickets in a very poor warm-up to the Test series. Perhaps viewing of that forthcoming Test series may need to come with an age restriction.

December 6

The eight-year-old is 3 000 days old today. She seems suitably impressed and there are now just the 5 344 days to go until the younger one reaches 21. In years, that is. Parenting makes a best of 15 Timeless Test series seem like the height of instant gratification.

Unfortunately I don't get much of a chance to celebrate the 3 000 day-a-versary as I need to go to watch South Africa block. It is hashtag time with #blockathon trending as South Africa, facing an impossible 481 to win, go on a proper block. They finish the day on 72-3. Off 72 overs. At least the run-rate, irrelevant as it is, is an easy one to calculate. Earlier in the day Ajinkya Rahane completed his second century of the match just before the declaration in the morning. Apart from making what will almost certainly be the only two scores over 100 in the series, Rahane has put to rest the rather laughable suggestions that he struggles at home. Sure he was averaging just 7.83 with a best of 15 in Tests in India but a sample of only six previous innings is clearly too few to draw any meaningful inferences. As it is he will most likely finish as the series' leading run-scorer.

Hashim Amla proves to be an adept blocker and threatens the South African record for most balls to get off the mark, but falls just short as he scores a two, though not really on purpose off the 46th ball he faced. The South African record is slightly complicated as the most balls faced on nought is by Harry Bromfield who made a 49 ball duck against New Zealand at Port Elizabeth in 1962. Of players who actually did get off the mark Clive Eksteen holds the South African record having got off the mark off the 47th ball he faced against New Zealand at Auckland in 1995. Amla ends the day on 23 ... off 207 balls.

With the blockathon in full flow I suspect that tomorrow is going to be a busy day for me, but perhaps not for anyone else in the commentary team.

During the 1992 World Cup Harrup Park in the town of Mackay, nearly 1 000 km north of Brisbane saw its only international match with India meeting Sri Lanka. Disappointingly for the local fans only 2 balls were bowled (India were 1-0) before rain set in. Today sees the start of the first Sheffield Shield game at the ground with Queensland taking on New South Wales.

December 7

The blockathon continues on its merry way and is still on course for a famous draw at tea with only five wickets down as they headed into the pavilion for their cuppa and cakes on 136-5 off 138 overs. Will runs or overs come out higher at the end of the innings? But Dane Vilas is out in the first over after tea and the rest collapse. South Africa are all out for 143 runs and the overs just win at 143.1. Which is easily the highest Test total made at less than one run per over.

Faf du Plessis consolidates the South African 'balls to get off the mark/balls for duck' as he passes both Harry Bromfield and Clive Eksteen by taking 53 balls to get off the mark. The bowlers are also cashing in by taking the opportunity to improve their economy rates and Ravindra Jadeja threatens some of the records that seem to have fallen into the 'will never be broken' category. Great South African off-spinner Hugh Tayfield bowled a world record 137 consecutive dot balls to England at Durban in 1957 spread across two innings. In an epic match-up between the Unhittable bowler and the Non-Hitting batsman, Trevor Bailey faced 88 of those dot balls. He wasn't known as Barnacle Bailey for nothing. But Tayfield bowled eight-ball overs so he didn't bowl a record number of consecutive maidens. That record belongs to India's Bapu Nadkarni who bowled 21 consecutive six-ball over maidens to England at Madras in 1964 on his way to figures of 32-27-5-0. Nadkarni had a 130 ball dot sequence in that spell. Today Jadeja bowled 108 consecutive dot balls. There was a brief moment of concern on ball number 70 of that sequence, but I breathed a sigh of relief when the umpire signalled leg-byes. The sequence ended with a straight drive for four by Faf du Plessis, but Jadeja had bowled the third longest known sequence of consecutive balls without conceding a run in Test cricket history.

As AB de Villiers starts to threaten the slowest Test 50s' record (he was out for 43 off 297 balls) the TV puts up a graphic of slowest 50s in terms of balls faced. These kind of stats irritate me a bit, as they tend to glibly ignore the reality that there are 50s for which we don't have details of balls faced. So, while the overall record of 350 balls by Trevor Bailey (not known as Barnacle for nothing, in case you missed the last paragraph) for England against Australia at Brisbane in 1958 is almost certainly the record, the second name on the list on the TV, Allan Border 262 balls v West Indies at Sydney in 1989, most definitely is not the second slowest Test 40. The commentators reading the list would no doubt have been saying that Border's was the second slowest ever even though I know of four other cases of slower ones as well as a number of other ones where we don't have balls faced but we do know minutes and the minutes are such that the balls faced are almost certainly higher than 262. Told you it irritates me.

When the fixtures for South Africa's tour to India were announced a lot was made of the fact that it was a 72-day tour. Although this hardly registers in historical terms of long tours the simple fact that the number of days for the tour was given as part of the press release has had people harping on about its supposedly epic length. With rain and result-shortened Test matches there have been only 23 actual playing days on the tour. It seems to me like it must have been a bit of a holiday.

It is Travis Dean-Watch again. When players make a dramatic entry into first-class cricket as Dean has done this season it is natural to keep an eye on their scores as their career progresses. Dean is out for 33 today against South Australia and this means that he has now been dismissed six times for 71 runs since he reached 347 without getting out. So his career average has tumbled to 69.66 as he has quickly and not terribly surprisingly discovered that it is not such an easy game after all.

December 8

It is school holidays so naturally the kids, who we normally have to wake at about 06:30 on a school day, are wide awake by 05:30 today. Which isn't that great for me after five consecutive 04:20 wake-up alarms.

It is a fairly quiet day, interrupted by an interview with Tim Harford for the BBC Radio's numbers show *More or Less*. They have asked a few people for their favourite numbers of the year and I am honoured to have been selected for this. I choose 111 as my one. Apart from being a significant cricketing number (Nelson and all that) it was the number of balls England needed to bowl Australia out at Trent Bridge to effectively clinch the Ashes. In the discussion I was asked to read out the whole innings ball-by-ball (as per the tweets to that effect). It didn't take long.

Graeme Smith is apparently considering un-retiring. His retirement in 2014 did seem a bit premature, but it is hard to think of successful comebacks after retiring in international cricket. The one that comes to mind is Bobby Simpson who returned to captain the official Australian team in 1977/78 (most of the top players had been signed to play World Series Cricket that year) nine years after retiring and did so fairly successfully, scoring two centuries amongst his 738 runs at 38.84 in 10 Tests that season as well as adding 11 wickets to his career tally. He was one of the great slip fielders, but his 11 catches in the 10 Tests meant his catches per match ratio slipped from 1.90 to 1.77 although it remains the best ever. Offhand I can't really think of any other notable returns from retirement, so it should suffice to say, 'Don't come back, Graeme'.

December 9

News from India is that Arman Jaffer of Mumbai, nephew of Wasim Jaffer who recently became the first player to reach 10 000 Ranji Trophy runs, has become the first player to score double-centuries in three consecutive matches in the Under-19 Cooch Behar Trophy. In 2010 he had made a score of 498 in a schools match for Rizvi Springfield School. So, he definitely joins the 'One To Watch' list.

I catch up with a bit of recent news and discover that there has been yet another cricket auction. These auctions for the various T20 leagues seem to attract more attention than the actual play these days and this one is for the Masters Champions League that will take place in the United Arab

Emirates early next year. At US$ 175 000 Jacques Kallis has won the auction, er, has the highest price tag. To no surprise, Kumar Sangakkara is high up on the list being signed by the Gemini Arabians. In years gone by when players retired, they used to move into coaching, commentating or, occasionally, administration. Clearly there is a new option for the modern player on retirement: Continue playing.

December 10

Daryn Smit gets out today. Which as you may recall is a rare event this season. He is dismissed for 87 in KwaZulu-Natal's Sunfoil Three-day Cup game against Northern Cape (The Team Formerly Known As Griqualand West And Even More Formerly Known As Kimberley Even Though No One Remembers That Far Back). So his first-class average for the season tumbles to just 252.50. Which is all good news for Subramaniam Badrinath.

Meanwhile two more Test matches get underway today and they should be good viewing because even if the actual cricket isn't particularly good the backdrops at the University Oval in Dunedin and Blundstone Arena in Hobart will be pleasing on the eye. It is a good day for the batsmen as New Zealand pile on 409-8 against Sri Lanka and Australia bludgeon 438-3 against West Indies, which turns out to be the first time in Test cricket history that two Tests starting on the same day have both had 400 or more runs on the first day.

December 11

I have a good sleep and wake up late enough that I am too late to see any cricket from Dunedin. Fortunately there has not been much excitement or even earth-shattering statistics so I am pleased to discover that I haven't missed much. Sri Lanka are 197-4 in reply to 431.

In Hobart, Adam Voges has made 269* as Australia declare on 583-4. He scored it off 285 balls making it the fourth fastest score over 250 in Test cricket history. Only Virender Sehwag (three times) has made a faster such score. Coming into the match Voges had a first-class career strike-rate of 51.18 which is pretty much average these days. So the fact that he could score so freely is an indication of just how poor the West Indies have been. West Indies then slump, predictably, to 116-6 before restoring a vague sense of respectability to end at 207-6. Another massive defeat awaits. It is a desperate state of affairs to see how rapidly and how far they have declined since the days that they dominated the cricket world through the 1980s. It is hard to see how they will turn it around, however much one might hope they will. Everyone who loves the game knows how much it needs a strong West Indies team.

December 12

Australia win in Hobart by an innings and 212 runs. Darren Bravo has provided first innings resistance with 108, his seventh Test century and sixth away from home, and Kraigg Brathwaite provides the only second innings resistance as the West Indies are all out for 148. Brathwaite makes 94 out of these and threatens the oldest of all Test records. Charles Bannerman's 67.34% (165*/245) made in the very first Test match way back in 1877 remains the highest percentage of an all out total in Test history. Brathwaite falls just short of this and his 63.51% slots in to fourth place on the list.

Wicket-keeping and fielding records don't get anywhere near as much attention as those for batting and bowling and teams. So, I am delighted to note that BJ Watling has become the first New Zealand wicket-keeper to take six dismissals in an innings twice, adding today to the occasion in 2014 when he did it against India at Auckland, on an otherwise unobtrusive day in lovely Dunedin. New Zealand end the day well on top — 308 ahead for the loss of just one second innings wicket. Kane Williamson is in the runs. Again. He will be looking to add to his 48* tomorrow.

December 13

I wake up earlier, but still don't get to see any play from Dunedin as a hailstorm has brought a premature end to proceedings. But I soon discover that those proceedings included Brendon McCullum lashing 2 sixes off Rangana Herath in his 17* off six balls as New Zealand chased a declaration. These are quite significant as he has equalled Adam Gilchrist as Test cricket's leading six-hitter on a round 100. After play McCullum says that it is the only record he cares about, noting that Ross Taylor and Kane Williamson are bound to break all other records he might hold, but neither are likely to ping the ball out the park quite so often. I use the opportunity to tweet a list of the chronological leading six-hitter in Tests. For most of Test history no one would have bothered with such a list partly because ball-bashing wasn't so incessant as it is today and partly because the information wasn't available in the scorecards of the day. But we now have pretty much a comprehensive list of sixes hit thanks to the researches of the likes of Ross Smith who published a full list of sixes hit in Test cricket and Charles Davis who has re-scored numerous old Test matches into ball-by-ball format from existing scorebooks.

By the end of the day Sri Lanka are 109-3 chasing 405 to win. Intriguingly all three wickets have been caught by BJ Watling taking him to nine dismissals in the match. The world record is 11 and there must be a chance of that being equalled or even broken tomorrow. He has already equalled the New Zealand record.

December 14

Sri Lanka slide quietly to a 122 runs defeat. With no one scoring more than 58 by Dinesh Chandimal and the best bowling figures being 3-52. The stats men on duty would have struggled to come up with much especially as BJ Watling does not add to his dismissal count. So, I am not surprised to see that 'six wicket-keepers have now scored a 50 in both innings of a Test in New Zealand' is featured amongst the highlights. Ah, but how many on a Monday in December you may well ask.

Back home England have arrived for a four-Test series plus the usual splattering of ODIs and T20s at the end. So, I am resting up a bit in anticipation of a busy few months ahead. Their first warm-up game starts tomorrow.

December 15

There is not much happening in the cricket world today, although there will be many watching the final of the Bangladesh Premier League. I presume Kumar Sangakkara must have been playing in the tournament, but couldn't be bothered to check.

December 16

Society is constantly changing. Is change always 'progression'? I am not going to bother with trying to answer these sorts of philosophical questions. But one thing that has undoubtedly changed in recent times in cricket is the tour match. With the need to play so many ODIs and T20s on tour these days there are far fewer warm-up matches and increasingly these matches are shorter — often only two-days — and have more players in them than before. Is this perhaps one of the reasons that home teams seem to have such a big advantage in Tests these days? In the first 12 years of the 21st century home teams won 266 Tests and visiting teams 175, a win/loss ratio of 1.52 to the home teams. But since 1 January 2013 that ratio has jumped to 2.88 (72 home wins to 25 away wins). I take the hour and a half drive down to Potchefstroom to watch some of the warm-up match between England and a South African Invitation XI (essentially a team of provincial rather than franchise players). It is a 13-a-side affair without first-class status. All told it is a very low intensity day as they would say in the modern parlance. While the vanguard of the English media was in attendance, not a single South African media person was there. Not that long ago these matches had first-class status and with it moderately decent crowds and were played as proper matches. Now they feel like nothing more than glorified net sessions. And not terribly 'glorified' at that. What was the score? I didn't take much notice and don't particularly care. I suspect nobody else did either. Matches without status are like that. Is it 'progress' or is it just 'change'?

December 17

Sports fans seem to prefer having winners and losers rather than drawn matches and thus limited overs games are designed to produce results. This hasn't quite been the case in Sri Lanka's domestic one-day competition this season, the AIA Premier Limited Overs tournament. The group stages finished yesterday and there have been no fewer than 23 'draws' in the 42 games played with 14 being abandoned without a ball bowled and nine 'no results' as rain has ravaged the event. A further 11 games were shortened by rain and only eight were full 50 overs affairs. Perhaps the tournament will have to be decided by a two-a-side affair on Noah's Ark.

It is Leo Carter's lucky day. The 21-year-old makes his maiden first-class century for Canterbury against Central Districts in Rangiora. On 99 he gloves one for two runs which are given as leg-byes by the umpire and then he is dismissed next ball. Frustration turns to elation a little while later when the umpires review video footage and change the score to give Carter his two runs and century. There are debates about whether the umpires should be reversing decisions in these circumstances or not and what kind of precedent it sets. But at least they got the final decision right and the man correctly got his 100.

December 18

It is Mrs S's birthday today, so we start the celebrations with brunch. Mrs S has an afternoon off from the kids as part of her birthday present as I take the kids off to The Wanderers where it is day two of the Sunfoil Series match between the Lions and the Dolphins. I manage to see the rarely spotted David-Miller-In-Whites as the T20 and ODI specialist makes an appearance in a first-class match. And much needed by the Dolphins he is too, as his 62 helps a bit of a recovery from 38-6 to 141 in reply to Lions' first innings 214. But there is nothing worth tweeting about.

Meanwhile the second Test between New Zealand and Sri Lanka has started in Hamilton. Sri Lanka are 264-7 at the close with Angelo Mathews 63*. He has done remarkably well since taking over the captaincy so I decide to check where his average ranks now. He is in his 25th Test as captain and after today's play he is now averaging exactly 63 as captain. This is near the top of the list of players in their first 25 Tests as captain, but there are three above him, albeit not by much: Mahela Jayawardene 67.17, Garry Sobers 64.82 (did he really captain West Indies that often?) and Michael Clarke 63.43.

December 19

It is party time for Mrs S, so I don't pay much attention to the cricket world. The excitement in Hamilton is mainly for Sri Lanka as promising quick bowler Dushmantha Chameera has taken his first (of what may be quite a few) five-for in Tests as Sri Lanka look likely to gain a first innings advantage.

December 20

The Oval in Pietermaritzburg is my old home ground. I grew up watching cricket there in the 1970s and the one three-day Currie Cup match we had each season was the highlight of the year although we also had some Natal B games played there occasionally. Having hosted its maiden first-class match there in 1895 it is the third oldest first-class ground in South Africa still being used today behind St George's Park in Port Elizabeth and Newlands in Cape Town, the two grounds that hosted South Africa's inaugural Test series in 1889. It is a pleasant old ground dominated by the old Victorian pavilion and so it is nice to see that England are playing South Africa A there. It is a good day for England as they dismiss South Africa A for just 136 and are 64-0 by the close. Stephen Cook carries his bat for the 'A' team, making 53*. He has carried his bat once before in a first-class match, so by my reckoning today's effort means that he and his dad Jimmy are the first pair of father and son to have both carried their bat twice in first-class cricket. Jimmy famously did it in both innings for Somerset against Nottinghamshire in 1989.

Earlier in the day I catch the end of play in Hamilton on the TV. Sri Lanka have let slip their advantage having been bowled out for 133 in their second innings and New Zealand are on course for victory in what had looked like a really close tussle before Sri Lanka's collapse. The hosts are 142-5 chasing 189 by the close.

December 21

Kane Williamson duly leads New Zealand home with 108* to finish the calendar year with 1 172 Test runs at 90.15. In the process he sneaks past Brendon McCullum's New Zealand record for a calendar year set way back in, er, 2014 (1 164). To go with the squillions of ODI runs he has made recently Williamson is clearly one of the premier batsmen in world cricket today and may well be on his way to proving to be New Zealand's best ever.

December 22

All good things come to an end and Brendon McCullum's captaincy of New

Zealand has undoubtedly been a Good Thing. Mildly surprisingly, he has announced that he will be retiring from international cricket after the home series against Australia in February. New Zealand have won 11 of his 29 Tests in charge which, at 37.93%, is the highest winning percentage for a Kiwi skipper. Add in the small matter of World Cup final appearances, triple centuries, double centuries, 100 sixes, etc. and his influence has been plain to see. He will be missed, although the Highlanders might see him more often now.

Growing up I used to read the Charlie Brown comics in the newspapers every day. Now, as with most things in America he has his own movie. So, it seems like a good idea to take the kids along to watch. Another thing I remember from my childhood was listening to the comedy slot during the morning current affairs program on SABC radio and one of these skits was particularly silly spoof on superheroes called *Chicken Man*. The only thing I actually remember was his catchphrase which was 'He's everywhere, he's everywhere'. I see Kumar has made the dash from the Bangladesh Premier League to the Big Bash in Australia. He's everywhere, he's everywhere. Don't go, Kumar. Don't go, Brendon.

December 23

Alastair Cook was born on Christmas Day in 1984 so will be celebrating his birthday in two days' time. While doing a bit of prep for the series it occurs to me that players born on 25 December will have made a significant runs contribution to England's Test cricket course over history, given that Marcus Trescothick (5 825 runs) was also born on Christmas Day. So, for a bit of fun I add the numbers up and discover that there is a day of the year, but only one, which has produced players who have scored more runs combined for England than Christmas Day. Players born on 24 November are responsible for 18 218 runs for England while the Christmas babies combine for 15 912. Herbert Sutcliffe, Ken Barrington, Ian Botham and Fred Titmus share that birthday and the bulk of those runs. I will keep that one up my sleeve in case things get a bit slow during the Durban Test starting on Boxing Day.

December 24

I have long thought that the Boxing Day Test in South Africa should be played in Johannesburg. The primary argument against it seems to be that most people from Johannesburg are away at the time. There may well be a lot of people who get out of town, but anyone who thinks Boxing Day Tests should not be played in Johannesburg should be forced to go shopping in the city on Christmas Eve. I spend 25 minutes in the queue to get to the cash registers. And that was just shopping for groceries. Seriously, you would get a big crowd into The Wanderers on Boxing Day. Really you would.

One of the never-ending projects in recording the history of the game is to get biographical details of those who played at first-class level. Earlier this year I received an email from a lady in Australia trying to find some details of her grandfather James Patrick McCarthy who apparently played in South Africa in the late 1890s. We didn't have any details of such a player, but there was a J McCarthy who played some first-class games for Transvaal in 1898. But we had no biographical details of him. Today I receive a parcel from Australia with various details about JP McCarthy and so, with a bit of help from a colleague in Bolton and expert in these things we can confirm full names and dates and places of birth and death. It is always good to be able to solve these kinds of mysteries.

December 25

It is a traditional Christmas day for me: Lunch with the family and then the flight to Durban for the Boxing Day Test. This has been the pattern for the past 24 years, apart from a few years when the flight has been to Port Elizabeth, a few in Melbourne and one year when Cricket South Africa bizarrely decided to play a Boxing Day T20. That year, I took the opportunity to move house instead.

Unusually there is actually international cricket taking place on Christmas Day as Afghanistan play Zimbabwe in an ODI in Sharjah. Afghanistan are bowled out for 131 but win quite easily by knocking Zimbabwe over for 82. I told you they never give up. Earlier this month Afghanistan's Under-19 team whitewashed their Zimbabwean counterparts 4-0 in a one-day series. The ICC's funding model which greatly favours Full Members creates an almost impregnable barrier to entry for everyone else. But it clearly mitigates against development and expansion of the game. If Afghanistan are better than Zimbabwe the playing and financial structures should reflect that.

December 26

It is an overcast day in Durban with a fair amount of rain about which no doubt puts a bit of a dampener on the crowd. About 12 000 attend which really isn't great for such a big occasion. It is a quiet day on the field as well with England finishing on 179-4 when bad light and rain bring a premature end to proceedings.

Australia have batted first in four of the five home Test matches they have played so far this season. Of those four times today is the worst first they have had. At 345-3 (with hundreds from Joe Burns and Usman Khawaja) however they are once again well on top.

December 27

Patrick Compton is the son of Denis and uncle of Nick. He has lived in Durban for many years and been cricket correspondent for the local *Daily Mercury* for much of that time. Nephew Nick is 63* overnight. So inevitably the question gets thrown at me: How often has a player had a close family relative in the press box when they scored a Test century? You may be a little surprised to learn that this is not something stored in my database. I wrack my brain for a bit and without being able to offer anything resembling a comprehensive list, I can at least offer the Benauds. John Benaud was not as good a player or as famous as elder brother Richie, but he did at least play three Tests. In one of those (v Pakistan at Melbourne in 1972/73) he made 142. Given that Richie spent most of his post playing career within the media as a writer and TV broadcaster I assume that he must have been there on that occasion. Sadly for Nick, uncle Patrick and indeed father Richard who is also here, he does not reach three figures, having to settle for a well-played 85.

Overall it is a fairly quiet day, both cricketing and statistically, as South Africa finish on 137-4 in reply to England's 303. It could be a close one. I certainly hope so.

Meanwhile there is no respite for West Indies in Melbourne. They are

91-6 at close in reply to 551-3 declared. Steve Smith and Adam Voges joined the century club in Australia's first innings with David Warner (23) being the only one of the five players who batted to miss out. It is just the third time that four of the top five in the order have made centuries in a Test innings. The other two were against Bangladesh (Pakistan at Multan in 2001 and India at Mirpur in 2007). Adam Voges passes 1 000 Test runs and now has 1 028 at 85.66 which is not bad for someone who only made his debut this year. He is, in fact, the third batsman to reach 1 000 Test runs in the calendar year of his debut, after Mark Taylor (1 219 in 1989) and Alastair Cook (1 013 in 2006). Against West Indies he is now averaging 542.00 having been dismissed only once in four innings against them.

December 28

There is a bit more for me to get into today as Dean Elgar carries his bat. It is the 50th occasion this has happened in Test cricket. He is the sixth player to do so for South Africa and the second since unity in 1991 after Gary Kirsten who did so against Pakistan at Faisalabad in 1997. On that occasion Kirsten made 100* thanks to an interesting incident. According to the scoreboard he reached his 100 shortly before the fall of the 10th wicket. Cue celebrations. However, the official scorers had him on 99 at the fall of the wicket. After some consultation a leg-bye mysteriously morphed into a run and Kirsten got his 100. Sadly this match doesn't look like being a close one any more as England cruise to 172-3 after knocking South Africa over for 214. Joe Root is in the runs yet again: 60*. He has just passed his captain Alastair Cook in the 'Test runs in 2015' table and needs a further 110 to break Michael Vaughan's England record for most runs in a calendar year of 1 481 set in 2002. The odds are that he will either get out or England will declare before he gets there. But, you never know.

The one-sided nature of the Australia v West Indies series means that interest levels in Melbourne are in rapid decline, although West Indies actually have a better day, recovering to 271 all out and then taking three wickets as Australia end 459 ahead.

December 29

A declaration at the start of play in Melbourne means that Steve Smith has ended the year on 1 474 runs at 73.70 so Joe Root has some work to do to pass that. West Indies manage a reasonable batting effort again, but 282 all out falls way short of the 460 run target. Since beating England at Birmingham in 2000 they have won one and lost 52 of the 70 Tests matches they have played away from home against opponents other than Bangladesh and Zimbabwe. It is a desperately sad state of affairs.

Root falls early for 73 so all the speculation as to his final figures for the year end. He has finished on 1 385 at 60.21 which at least nicks him second spot for England in a year having snuck past Dennis Amiss' 1974 tally of 1 379 shortly before getting out. His 13 scores over 50 for the year have equalled Virender Sehwag's 2010 record. And his frustration at another failure at converting a 50 into a century is evident in his 10 scores between 50 and 99 being the most by anyone in a calendar year.

Kingsmead has not been good to South African spinners since readmission, although visitors have had some success. In 21 Tests since 1992 before this one there had been only one three-for and one four-for by South African spinners at the ground. So it is good news for the twirlers that Dane Piedt (5-153) is the first home spinner to take a five-for at the ground since 1957 when Hugh Tayfield did it against England.

England don't bother to declare, preferring to be bowled out for 326, leaving a target of 416. So South Africa have to gear themselves up for another blockathon and they finish on 136-4. Only three teams in Test history have batted through the final day to save a Test having been four down overnight.

Dale Steyn who went off yesterday with a shoulder injury after bowling 3.2 overs makes a brave effort to try again today. He breaks down again after just three balls. Two other bowlers have had to complete those overs and with another bowler finishing the innings after one ball of an over the bowling figures look decidedly messy (certainly more messy than they usually look in my hand-writing) with four bowlers ending with incomplete overs. I write a quick query to check how often this has happened and find only two previous cases. This is the kind of real trivia that you need to save for when there is not much happening in either the cricket or the on-air conversation (Imagine, for example, if a bowler was on a hat-trick and I said, 'This is only the third time four bowlers have finished an innings with spare balls in their figures') and when such an opportunity arises I throw it in. This, of course, gives Aggers the opportunity to suggest that I should get out more and enables him to steer the conversation towards the kinds of activities I should be getting up to rather than slaving away at my laptop each night. All good fun.

Richard Compton, who has also lived in South Africa for most of his life makes an appearance at tea-time on Test Match Special and greets people with the good old Seffrican 'Howzit?' as he arrives in the box.

December 30

AB de Villiers is out to third ball of the morning and it is a bit of a procession after that. Temba Bavuma is stumped by Jonny Bairstow which is the first time an England wicket-keeper has affected a stumping in 38 Tests spread over three years since Matt Prior dismissed Cheteshwar Pujara this way off Graeme Swann at Mumbai in 2012. They have missed a few crucial ones since then as attentive readers of this diary might have noticed.

Night-watchman Dale Steyn gets out for a duck which puts a bit of a dent in one of my favourite stats. The great fast bowler's batting average in Boxing Day Test is now 'only' 34.72, compared to a career batting average of 14.11. He has made 377 runs in Boxing Day Tests including his five best scores.

December 31

I fly home from Durban in the morning — my 21st flight of the year. All told I have slept at home on 224 nights and away for 141. The 15 Tests that I was at had a total of 31 040 balls bowled including no balls and wides. In those games I scored 17 114 runs (that's more runs than Sachin Tendulkar scored in his entire Test career) and 518 wickets. And I have written a diary! I seem to have typed 'of course' no fewer than 46 times while writing it. It has been another long and busy year and I can look forward to more of the same in 2016.

Cape Town. It's the place to be at this time of the year. I fly there tomorrow for the New Years' Test against England. It will be my 200th.

Editor's note:
For a list of players mentioned in the diary, see
tslbooks.uk/authors/andrew-samson

Printed in Great Britain
by Amazon